I0819000

The Sane One

The Sane One

A MEMOIR

Anna Konkle

RANDOM HOUSE
NEW YORK, NY

Some names and identifying characteristics have been changed to protect the privacy of the individuals involved.

Random House
An imprint and division of Penguin Random House LLC
1745 Broadway, New York, NY 10019
randomhousebooks.com
penguinrandomhouse.com

Hardcover ISBN 9780593243992
Ebook ISBN 9780593244012

Printed in the United States of America

1st Printing

First Edition

BOOK TEAM: Production editor: Ted Allen • Managing editor: Rebecca Berlant • Production manager: Mark Maguire • Copy editor: Emily DeHuff • Proofreaders: Deb Bader, Graham Maby, Al Madocs

Book design by Caroline Cunningham
Title page and chapter ornament: Mirgunova/Adobe Stock

The authorized representative in the EU for product safety and compliance is Penguin Random House Ireland, Morrison Chambers, 32 Nassau Street, Dublin D02 YH68, Ireland. https://eu-contact.penguin.ie

"Can't you see how embarrassing this

is supposed to be for me?"

—Jerri Blank, *Strangers with Candy*

The Sane One

Chapter One

The doorbell rings again. I'd invited him here.

Alex, my partner of six years, comes out from the bedroom as though the bell has only just rung, and I guess it has, but it seems forever ago. I'm sitting in a brown leather chair, my chest stuttering, knocking at me to leave. Our dog noses the doorjamb and I peer over at my boyfriend like a child before the nurse comes back with a needle.

"I really need you," I mouth.

Alex squeezes some part of my body. Suddenly I'm up, pressing the lever of our front door with my thumb. I'm letting him in. *Because I invited him here,* I repeat to myself.

On the other side is a man who has my same hair, cheeks, and nose, and who I haven't seen for five years. He has loved me since I was only an idea of me. We'd stare at thunderstorms together, catch fish together, and when he ate a cookie, I'd watch him tap it against his teeth after each bite, dislodging every crumb so it landed on his tongue instead of the floor. I idolized him for the small things—for his nightly snack of cheese and apples before a bowl of ice cream, for the mousse he combed into his blond hair while he drove and half sarcastically said into the rearview, "Damn I'm good-looking." For our trips to the mall to buy me five-dollar shirts from that tacky store with the loud music, for the mornings he blasted Van Morrison while vacuuming our house, for the wood he turned into sloping lamps, and for the puppet he brought to life every night in my room to say "Sleep well," knowing that when he left, the dark would be nicer for me because our puppet would stay.

We stand inches apart, a wooden door and a screen between us.

Maybe if I freeze long enough, he'll have to turn around and board the plane back to Florida. Then everything stays the same, never having seen each other. That could be our reality if I want it to be. But to not open the door when someone knocks would not be normal. And I always keep track of normal. What would anyone do who is not me?

Do that.

Okay.

You sure?

No!

Alex looks at me like, *This is getting weird now, open the door?* Again, it rings. I adjust my turtleneck and baggy pants and take a final look around the house. *Do we look like we have too much money? Will he be angry for the simple fact that our apartment is bigger? Can he feel me standing inches away?*

I open it.

"Hi, Dad."

"Hi, Anna." He rarely said my name.

"It's been so long."

"Yeah."

"Come in," and he begins to but the door catches on the corner of my rug. "Whoops, sorry. The corner guy. Not the guy—the corner. Whatever."

He looks at me, worried but dressed nicer than I thought he would be, a crisp white shirt tucked into dark jeans. We hug but I'm not sure if I want to.

"Dad this is Alex. Alex, Dad. His real name's James but everyone calls him Peter."

"Or Mr. Konkle?" Alex asks.

"Nope, call me Peter." Dad's voice, already strikingly low, goes a few notes deeper on his own name. A male peacock showing hidden feathers.

Alex looks nervous. "I've heard a lot about you, Peter. Nice to meet you."

We all sit.

Dad's eyes go to the floor, to Alex, back to the floor, back to Alex. I can almost see him imagining the tales my boyfriend's heard about him and Dad looks scared. Right around the time we started dating, my relationship with my father disintegrated. Totally. I wonder if Dad thinks our distance could be Alex's influence, which it wasn't. Or maybe he's just upset I have a boyfriend at all. Somehow a betrayal. He hadn't liked any boyfriend in the past.

There's nothing for anyone to say for maybe twenty-five seconds but it feels like a full minute and a little man parades around the room with a mallet and drum, singsonging "You have nothing to talk a-bout! You have nothing to talk a-bout! You've already run out of things to talk a-bout!"

"The test," I say, finally. "That's tomorrow?"

"That's tomorrow, yup, yup," he answers.

"And you came for just like, one night for that? I mean—"

"Two nights, yeah."

"I meant two. I meant two. I misspoke."

He nods, chin bobbing like a professional. "Needed a day to see you, and one to take the test. Plus it's very early in the morning, so a single night wasn't an option. It worked out."

"Good flight?" Alex adds.

"Shitload of turbulence," and my dad inhales the last of his words, throwing his body onto the ground in the shape of a U, lungs all scrunched for a second, before sprawling flat onto his back next to our dog.

"Awschhhw good boy. Awschhhw good boy." Dad is repeating compliments in the tone of a Muppet. "Your breaf shtinks but you sure got a shweet shoul. Is it George?"

"Yeah, George," I say laughing.

On cue, he licks my father on the neck, eye, cheek, and back of the head.

Dad had always been crazy about cleanliness, with a sole exception for animal residue.

"We looked for the whole year before we found him at Pasadena Humane Society," Alex says, adding, "Do you have an animal, Peter?"

"Uh, no—not practical for me right now."

"Why. We always had cats growing up. You love them and you're retired now so why not." None of these are questions. Just go back to being the guy who had cats.

"No. I—uh, no. My volunteering at the animal shelter every week fills the cuddling quota, the, the pussy quota—"

Alex laughs, surprised.

I'm serious. "That's nice that you volunteer." My dad coughs. "And the scan— You said this is the only one in the country?"

"The, uh—?" He seems uncomfortable that I'm bringing it back up. Health talks with him were always hard. I try again, tactically cheerful this time, "The test, yeah!"

"Uh, that's what they said, seems hard to believe that it's the only one. But yeah. Three thousand bucks, this thing costs. Christ. If it saves my life, it's worth it." All of our eyeballs move a little. After a few seconds he goes on, "I really, really don't want to get claustrophobic. I do not like small spaces."

"I know, Dad. But the music they play in the machine helps," I say, assuming an old role.

He nods, comforted. Dad was always most at ease with the animals or the kids. At a party, he'd crack a joke to the grown-ups and then find us.

For a moment, I try seeing him that way once again. "Just imagine you're canoeing on a lake tomorrow, Dad."

"That's a great idea, sweetie. When I'm inside, picture being on water." And he chuckles, like it's a super clever thing to say.

Everything's nice for a second. Maybe Dad's best when he feels taken care of.

The restaurant's a nice spot, just five minutes from our apartment. I hate thinking about it though. I'm not sure why. Maybe because this feels like the eye of the storm: after the estrangement, before whatever comes next. From his vantage point, maybe I look fine, but I'm not. Maybe I look like I have my shit together. I don't. My life has largely been an exhausting pursuit of the opposite of what my parents put together. I have a long-term relationship. Pet. House. Financial freedom. A career I don't hate. Alex and I can afford ordering from a restaurant without looking at the price. And we round our tips up instead of down to the eighteen-percent penny on the back side of receipts.

This pulses through my brain while I browse the menu and work to push away my worry. It's made easier with the help of a new word I've become aware of through my therapist: *boundaries.*

Just because he may or may not be jealous doesn't mean I should feel guilty. I know that between his intelligence and talent, Dad believes he should have ended up a CEO, a millionaire, not an ex-hippie turned human resource manager for 7-Eleven. Yet for all his years there, he never even made it to regional manager, a real misstep by his boss, Steve. And we'd liked Steve! Dad always considered him more friend than superior, despite Steve's shortcomings. But the promotion never came. When I was ten years old, I'd asked how his friend-boss could let him down like that.

"Good fucking question. Steve, I supported Steve."

"When he didn't know what he was doing, you were there, Dad."

He liked when I spoke like an adult. The kids at school, less so. "You always offered Steve, um, guidance, right, Dad?"

"Yeah, he was in hot water one time. I figured it out for Steve. Made it seem like a promotion was around the corner. Idiot. Talks the talk, doesn't walk the walk."

"That's clear."

Whenever Dad was laid off, sometimes close to a five-year pattern, he'd stay jobless for maybe a year while Mom kept showing up for hers without much thanks. Financial struggles were sort of perpetual in that way. Dinners out were rare, vacations rarer. At Red Lobster for Mom's birthday one year, she started flicking crayons under other people's tables. Dad loved it. I even got a Shirley Temple. We were happy that night.

Tonight, the waiter takes our drink orders and I ask for a glass of orange wine. Alex tells Dad to get whatever he wants. It's on us. He nods, but won't look my boyfriend in the eyes.

"Yeah, Peter, I've heard how funny you are forever and I've just been looking forward to seeing that in person." Alex hesitates, then keeps going, "I know it's been uh, uh—a weird few years for you and Anna but family can go through stuff like this and it's just so nice we can all do this together. So welcome to LA, Peter, glad to finally get to know you." Dad's eyes shine and they make eye contact.

Like anyone who is alive, Alex can be an asshole, but most other times he is this. And if my dad thought that Alex heard the worst about him in my stories, he'd be right. So this acknowledgment, this intentional reassurance, allows my father to relax in my boyfriend's presence. I wonder if Alex really likes him or is just making an awkward situation more comfortable.

In any case, we eat Italian food. Starting with arugula in olive oil, lemon, scraped Parmesan, fatty sliced tomatoes in different hues of red, and mozzarella chunks that drip thick cream. Capellini cooked al dente in a butter sauce with rounded shreds of Romano, tons of pepper, and a little salt. We slurp. Next the lamb is passed around, and the broccoli with lemon shavings. And at the very end, like our waiter forgot, a pizza, with crusts dotted in roast spots and prosciutto laid like blankets, gets placed in the smack-dab middle and we grab at it and pull, chewing. Eating this, things seem normal again. For dessert there are bites of chocolate cake, and I realize how much I've been laughing.

Dad's really talking now. "Oh, the retirement community, I hate they call it that because it makes us sound like we're just jamming balls into Earth's assholes, our last hurrah before death—.

"Is that a golfing reference?" Dad laughs to himself, deeply, and keeps going, "Chaa. I prefer to be in the woodshop, swimming, drinking martinis, going for a bike ride. If I have to die, let it be in Florida. Fuckin' hate the politics. Love the taxes. Honey, I know you saw it last time you were there, the only time you were there—"

"Yeah."

"But you never got a chance to go in the pool. I'm telling you, sweetheart, the pool is like hoity-toity," he says, proud and giggling. "You should come down together, seriously." I nod along, knowing I will never go back. "There's a great bar too, great cocktails, beer on tap, Alex, all the people that work there are groovy. Twenty-year-olds but they actually know what they're doing—ya know? Good people."

I shift in my seat, picturing myself on the bench outside his cul-de-sac behind the community walls. Waiting hours for a taxi to pick me up, refusing to go back inside. He's still talking about the pool or the bar or something.

"Good, uh—Arnold Palmers too. I don't drink very much anymore. But yeah. I go with my bocce ball group every week. They love me."

"Bocce ball or the bartenders?" I ask.

"I was talking bocce, but actually both. Ha. But you know what's really neat?" He doesn't say "neat" like a mother from the fifties, but more like a brilliant gay man. "What's neat is that I'm going to Italy, honey. Finally. Really excited about that. If the food is anything like this, I will be a happy man."

"It'll be better." I'm annoyed with myself for sounding condescending. "I mean this meal is really good." And that's true. "But in Italy, you might have some meals there that are even better?" He wags his eyebrows playfully. I'd studied abroad my junior year of college and he'd barely been out of the country. It'd never felt fair.

He laughs again, happily overwhelmed. "Wow, amazing. Better? Really? Can't wait and, uh, and I know you sent me that check to contribute to the trip, and I'm gonna be honest—"

"Yeah, no, that's okay." Skip. Fast-forward.

"No, I have to tell ya. I felt offended at first. I didn't want to take it."

"Right."

"Your money, ya know, your check, and then Debby said—

Alex, you have to meet Deb, she's my best friend, anyway, and Deb said—"

I interrupt. "Was his girlfriend."

"No." He comes to a full stop before continuing, "No. I wouldn't say we ever were like that. Went on a couple dates maybe but we're just good friends. We, uh, hang out every day. She's my best friend. She's gorgeous."

"Gorgeous? So, you do want her to be your girlfriend?" I push him, thinking we'll all enjoy the banter.

"Anna. Life isn't that simple." His delivery is harsh. "Anyway, I was pissed about the check you sent."

"Got that," I say, rolling my eyes.

"But then Deb said I was being an asshole. So then I accepted it. Thank you."

"Well. It worked out. Thank Deb for me. Plus, I think about how, like, how much money you've given me over the years."

Historically, he'd been the one to point this out.

"NYU." He nods, earnest.

Even though I meant what I said, I want to take it back now. "Well, we all took out loans, you me and Mom, and none of us could afford it, don't forget that," I say, clipping at my own olive branch but adding, "I still appreciate you did that. Thanks."

"Mom and I, we could have said no to you."

"You tried. Oh, and I just paid them off. The loans. But you paid yours off a while ago, right?"

He nods like a commander in the military. "Lucky return from a stock investment a decade ago." And winks at Alex like they are in cahoots. "Anna, you paid yours when you got your fancy Fox show, right? *Rosewood*?" and he looks genuinely happy I ended up making more than minimum wage as an actor. At a certain point, maybe he'd believed that as long as I kept auditioning, I'd keep waiting tables. The idea wasn't unreasonable.

"Can't believe we let you go there. Gave you good connections. The rich kids of NYU. Alex, you were raised in Malibu?"

I pivot. "Yeah. Italy will be amazing."

Dad leaves the past, "Yeah, yeah, Italy is going to be something. Actually, Justine called and we were reconnecting and I said, 'Justine, I'm going abroad' and she said, 'I want to go too.' So long story short, she's coming."

"Justine, your ex-girlfriend Justine?"

"Yes."

I muster, "Wow that's . . . cool."

"It is!"

"So, are you back together?" Alex asks.

"No no no no." Dad answers like it's a strange question.

"K. So you're going with your ex-girlfriend to Italy. But you're not back together. You're not sharing a room, then."

"We are."

"But you're not together."

Dad's smiling, excited, "Two adults, traveling to Italy. You know (ha-ha) we are good friends. Just friends."

Even though I wasn't planning on saying this, I do anyway. "Does her daughter know she's going with you?"

"Ya know," Dad says, "I asked myself the same question. But Justine is an adult. She doesn't have to tell her kids everything."

"K. Which means she didn't."

"Anna, I'm not sure." There's my name again.

Unsure how to feel, I say nothing and peek at Alex, hoping the innocuous move of my eyeballs cues him to bookmark the moment for later, but he seems oblivious, thinking about something else.

"So this test . . . Peter, is it all right to ask about the test more?" Dad nods. "It's experimental, Anna said?"

"Yeah, yeah, over at UCLA. I guess it scans the whole body."

"And you said your PSA level is higher now?"

"Yeah, I get it checked every couple years but no biggie."

"PSA is an indicator of prostate cancer," I say to Alex, translating. "Sorry, is it okay to say that, Dad?" But before he responds, I continue, "Which we've had—he's had a couple times."

Dad corrects me, "Mildly."

"I mean—"

"Relatively mildly," he repeats.

"Okay. Well, they think that's back, then?"

"Good question. Uh. Or the doctor thinks my high number could indicate it's somewhere else."

"Where else? The cancer?"

He nods casually. "Because, you know, they removed my entire prostate, the whole fuckin' thing—"

"Picture that," I whisper to Alex. I am joking. It is reflexive and it does not land.

"—apparently the PSA level can still go up a little, but it shouldn't be able to go this high. If it's been removed. So that is why I'm here, doing a scan."

This doesn't sound good. "Could the number be higher for no reason, Dad, or they have to find the reason?"

"It, uh, does it . . . uh? Yeah, probably could be no reason, yeah."

"K. All right." I'm satisfied enough, though it looks as though he's floated to some other place. I have just a few more questions. Dad confirms that the test scans the whole body for cancer, but he's unsure of much else. I tell him I'm proud of him. When it comes to health, he used to hide under a rock, like his body was in trouble for doing something bad.

"Are you kidding, honey? I want to live a long life. I've got grandchildren to meet." And he winks again at Alex.

"Okay, slow down. Someday," I say, unsure if I'd allow that.

"You know Paul from Maine?" Dad has pivoted to a new subject. "Paul has lung cancer, you know that, and it's starting to affect his heart."

"No, I didn't."

"Yeah, the treatments are what's getting him, I mean. I think it's gonna be okay, though."

"Oh, no, that's sad," I say, genuinely. Paul is a longtime family friend I haven't seen in maybe a decade.

And now Dad is listing all the things he does to take care of himself, to show us he won't end up like Paul. "I bike every day, I have almond milk with my cereal. I take good care of myself. And I'm doing this test so we find it early. It's going to be good."

"Good, Dad. Better to face the issues head-on. Glad you're on top of it."

"Deb's been helping."

"Good. Good. Thank Deb for me."

Alex watches us like a round of table tennis.

"And so glad I get to see my daughter. And you, Alex. I'm so happy to meet you. Finally. You've been together how long?

"Six years."

"Hm." This sound comes from Dad's gut without trying.

I mirror back the same noise by accident.

"It's been too long, Peter, but I'm really glad I finally got to meet you. Crazy coincidence that the only test like this is in LA."

Dad nods. "Meant to be.— Oh. Anna. You see your mom recently?"

"Yeah. I mean, not super recent but maybe once a year. Why?" I ask, but I know why.

"Ope." He coughs, with eye contact. I hold his gaze, not allowing him to make me feel worse than I already do because in recent years I've seen her and not him. And I do feel bad about it. Later, when Alex and I talked about this moment, he'd say my dad seemed totally normal. Alex couldn't hear the vibration in Dad's voice sharpening consonants like I could.

"I'm sure you've seen her more than me." Dad doesn't laugh but sips wine.

I nod. Bring it.

But he seems to think better of going there right now. "Good. Yup. I hope, well, I mean— I hope your mother is doing . . . well."

Right now, Mom's probably sitting beside her on-again-off-again fiancé, Jack, also living in Florida, unbeknownst to Dad. A few years ago my parents moved from separate states in the Northeast to nearby Floridian towns. Still, neither knows they live thirty minutes from each other. And the weekend of their new home purchases, they both texted me the news. Despite running in different directions, Mom and Dad stayed connected, inadvertently stomping the same track. But I'd become tired of being the connection between two people who didn't like reminders of that connection. But after being married for twenty years, maybe there is no other track.

Dad, sarcastic, humor first. Mom, repulsed by self-deprecation. This simple dynamic was a major problem from as early as I can remember. And it remains one for me today. Because to be around my mom is to laugh. Often, *at* her. It's not uncommon for there to be something black stuck in her big, beautiful teeth, or sauce smeared in strange locations and she'll have no apparent interest in wiping it off. Between and during bites, she'll spew expertise on life, with meat specks and barbecue sauce somehow ending up on her ear, neck, and ankle. After eating nine pork ribs she'll say she can't believe she ate all of those because she's a vegetarian. During a recent weeklong visit, we'd had at least six meals together. One time she had fish, another a steak, another meatballs, one animal carcass after another. Then, grocery shopping later, I suggested we get some bacon, but she clutched her chest and said, "Oh, no. Vegetarian, remember?" And you aren't supposed to laugh at that? You can't, or else you've been rude. Insensitive. Hurtful. Another afternoon before leaving, Alex announced that our dog, George, had farted and that it was a bad one. Mom corrected him: "Actually, I farted. It was the ahchahee bowl this morning for breakfast."

"You mean acai?" I said.

"Whatever," she responded with the delivery of a sire and didn't crack a smile while I tried to bite back mine.

"Yes, yes. It was the ahchayahhee that gave me horrible gas—" and then she saw me. "What's so funny, Anna?"

Decades ago, when Dad and I got the chuckles, her eyes would move toward us, fast and surprised, before stopping to water like a girl whose pants fell down on the bus. In 0.2 seconds, she would pull them back up and belt them with a funny-looking rope that we're supposed to say looked great, and then her indignation would follow. This ping-ponging is my mother: hurt to pissed and back again. But there is such beauty in her couture clown suit and hand-embroidered balloon pants with golden thread at the hem, sewn deep into her skin. She can pull off whatever belt she chooses. She's a gorgeous comedic creature. But if I try to celebrate the clown, she'll insist there isn't one.

So maybe I played the clown instead. And sometimes I get my feelings hurt too. I should really understand more.

"It's getting late, babe," I say to Alex, accidentally interrupting them. "Oh, sorry—"

"That's okay!" Alex chirps, looking quite comfortable.

Then I ask Dad directly, "Think we should get the check? We want to get it."

"Yeah. Okay, thanks. Good idea on timing. I have to get up early!" and he doesn't fight me on who pays.

"Oh, right." He has to be up in five hours for his test. "Thanks, Dad, for coming all the way over to us." I feel sad it's ending, but mostly relieved.

Alex jumps in too. "This was nice, Peter."

"It was nice, sweetie, thank you for seeing me, sweetie." And I don't bristle at his pet name, said twice. "Very happy to meet you, Alex. You're a good guy." Dad nods extra-long. Alex does back.

In our respective cars, I watch until his taillights disappear, then breathe. I have no idea when we'll see him again.

"Well. I liked him."

"You did?"

"I really did," Alex adds, easy. "Not at all what I expected."

"Why, you thought he'd be like, a monster?" He laughs a little but doesn't say no.

"I mean. I thought he'd be weirder. And he is weird. Don't get me wrong." I laugh once and he continues, "But not like what I expected— And you never mentioned his lazy eye."

"Oh, his strabismus. You noticed . . ."

"Harrrd not to."

"That's mean! I guess I forget about it. I don't see it, really."

"I'm sorry, I don't intend it that way—it's not a bad thing, it's just prominent," Alex clarifies.

"One of my friends in high school pointed it out when I was fifteen. I'd never noticed it before. I dunno, I—I just thought my dad's eyes looked like everyone else's . . . dads' eyes. He'd always told me he'd had surgeries to fix it. I thought it was fixed."

We nod, thinking.

What if, for all these years, my own deficits had caused me to cut him out of my life for little reason? Or was I on track toward another impending disappointment from a man whose eyes I couldn't even see?

Our car in the summer feels like the air near a furnace when it's too hot to touch. I'm five and sweat sits on my top lip, the dippy part full, like a pool for my freckles. I lick it and pretend I'm a dog.

"Can't say it's not hot in Vermont," says Dad, and my chest drips like there's a broken pipe somewhere inside my body.

"Daddy, can you stop the car to make the window go down, Daddy? I'm hot. Can you stop." Even though I have a therapist for my tongue, I wonder if *stop* still sounds like a book hitting the ground rather than that red sign on a road.

"I'm the one driving, Anna. You should ask me," says my mom. "And what do you say?"

"Stop, Mommy, and, um, crank the window for me, p—?" Before I can get this whole thing out, Dad bends back his arm like a chicken wing and rolls down my window.

"Peter, I was saying—she needs to say please. Never mind."

"Please. Thank you!" I add, smiling because they aren't. "Mommy, does Daddy's car have air caritioning? Please?"

"No." They don't skip a beat, in unison now. Mom peeks over at him, pleased they are on the same page, and says, "If the parents are hot, it's okay for the kid to be hot."

"Do I have AC? Yes. Are we spending money on that?" Dad asks, turning toward me.

"No," I say like I already knew.

"But I'm hot!" Dad mimics me like a brat to be funny. "Wait, I have a burning question too, Janet. Can we change this fuckin' music. It's driving me insane. 'Please.'"

"That's—that's rude, Peter." And corrects him: "Native American chanting." Mom is Irish and five percent Iroquois. This may also be her reason for getting groups of women in circles under the moon and wearing bunches of turquoise jewelry.

"C'mon, Janet. We can't keep yelling over this shit for another hour."

"Yeah!" I add, laughing.

"WHAT ANNA? I CAN'T HEAR YOU," Dad is yelling. "PEOPLE ARE SCREAM-DYING OVER OUR SPEAKERS. BUT TURN IT LOUDER. I LOVE IT."

"Don't make fun, Peter. That's—that's rude. It's art. Ancient, ancient tradition. Ritual— It's—It's beautiful— exqui— takes me somewhere else. A moment I don't want to miss, with my— you guys, my family here and— Yeah. That's what I think." Mom often says a bunch of parts of words before she finds the ones she really wants. "The chanting completes the moment. So—"

"By 'moment,' you mean the odor of cow shit?"

"Peter—"

"It does smell really bad, Mommy," I say.

We are passing a dairy farm.

"Sorry, Janet, I can't fucking take the music, Janet." He's kind of laughing still.

"We are almost through the farm stretch and then we hit the big mountains and I want the music for that part, that moment," she explains.

Taking my dad's side, I giggle-out, "It smells like poo."

"It smells like shit."

"Peter. Stop it."

"Janet, lighten up."

"I'm light!"

She doesn't sound it.

"I like the music, actually." I try to help her now. "But also the Beatles are nice. Mom, you like that too. Dad does too."

"I hate when you say that. I'm light, Peter. I'm light—"

"YOU MISSED THE FUCKIN' TURNOFF!" and nothing is funny anymore. A green sign with a white exit number speeds by us, and my dad's head turns like there's a rope hooked to his right ear.

"I CAN TURN AROUND AND TAKE THE EXIT," Mom yells back.

Like a period to her sentence, Dad presses *Stop*, and a cassette tape pops out.

"BE CAREFUL WITH MY TAPE. I DIDN'T WANT IT OFF."

Silence.

Dad grinds his teeth, right to left, right to left.

And then she bangs the steering wheel with her hand, before cooing "Be careful with that," as though she hadn't just yelled. And pulls the tape out completely, looking for the case but settling for the glove box.

A horn blows.

"Jesus, Janet!" Dad grabs the wheel, bringing the car back into our lane. "What's wrong with you?"

"I WASN'T IN THE OTHER LANE."

"Right."

"I can't—I can't. You're scaring me, Peter. You're scaring me." She gets very quiet and says it again, "You're scaring me."

"Relax, Janet. You're so fucking sensitive."

"IT'S FROM A USED BOOKSTORE IN NEW HAMPSHIRE. THERE WAS—THEY ONLY HAD ONE. And you touched the wheel. That's not safe." She's crying.

Dad almost whispers, "I'd be heartbroken to not find another one, Janet. You almost hit that car. You're welcome." He's laughing again.

Should I laugh too?

"Okay, wow, thank you. Thank you." Tears fall and she doesn't even wipe them. What's the point? There are many more coming.

"Mommy, it's, it's—okay." I wait a sec to see if she'll look back before trying again. "Okay? It's okay, Mommy."

"No. It's not. Because we're on our way to camping with the other families and this always happens. Every year. Now your father is gonna ice me out for the whole week. And around our friends who actually love each other and hike together and spend time together and that are, are, nice to each other and GET ALONG." She's right but I hate that she's saying it. And crying so hard. "And that's the family I want and—"

"Mommy, we are, but the, uh, just to have other music for the car would be nice for us."

"Ohhh. Take your dad's side. Surprise."

From the passenger seat Dad looks back at me like *Don't let this get to you.* I shake mine back like, *I won't,* but check the rearview to make sure Mom didn't see me side with him. But she's just crying. I try once more. "I love you, Mom." After a while she says, "I love you too" and reaches around the seatback to hold my hand. We need each other. Dad looks out the window, somewhere else, unhappy and removed.

"Your turn, Peter," Mom pulls onto the shoulder of the highway and stops hard, like bumper cars.

"Christ."

"I have to pee. Anna?" but she's already feet away, walking. I know to follow.

Buried between big trees, pants around our ankles, we avoid our shoes and use leaves to wipe. Something she taught me before I can remember. And to make sure not to use poison ivy, so anything with three leaves is out. When it's time, we head back toward the car and Mom gasps.

"Mommy! You okay?" She's enthralled with long green stalks

and purple petals that tower on top of each other, so I know she's fine.

Because now she's smelling them like she does her incense when she's lost the label. "Lupine. Gorgeous." And rips one out of the ground and the dirt scatters on her wet toes.

Mom is back to happy. It just took a little something from the Earth.

Dad sits in the driver's seat now.

"No soil in my car. Hurry up. Let's go."

Maybe he's worried about traffic.

We arrive at the campgrounds flowerless, and my parents don't speak for the first couple hours. Dad builds tarps that hover above our tent, acting as secondary insurance against rain. Other families have similar setups but not as special as the roofing he makes and I know if it pours, they will all run to be under our blue ceilings.

Sitting in my own tent, I watch my parents speak far away through a crack. My attention jumps between playing cards by myself to observing how far or close they are and their movements. I'm worried that if this doesn't go well, they won't talk for the rest of vacation and I'll have to communicate for them, but they touch hands now. I can't be sure if it is a mistake or on purpose. My mom's face points down, moving fast like a bird's, and my dad lights his cigarette. She gets stiff and I know something happened she doesn't like. But he takes her hand, and it stays this way for longer than a mistake. They are walking to me now. I smile at them. My mom smiles back. Dad asks me who is winning at my game of solitaire, and I get the joke. They keep walking, and when I wish for them to kiss, they do.

The stillness of the early morning lake feels wrong, like we are taking it somewhere before it's ready. But when our canoe cuts through, I change my mind. We belong here. Dad teaches me how to put the sharp hook through the flipping worm and throw it in. We have to be quiet and stay so still that the water goes flat like glass. When the ripple comes, it's my fishing pole we are winding in, and at the end is a fish. I'm surprised, because before this moment, it was hard to believe any fish were actually here. Plus, if they like hiding so much, why would one come to us?

"Rainbow trout," he says.

"Rainbow?" Daddy holds the fish and turns it like something's supposed to happen, then looks up at the sky like it's broken.

"Move, clouds."

Surprised the sliminess is not a thing to him, I pretend it's not to me either and touch the fish quickly. He's still rocking it back and forth and an edge of sun peeks out. The scales move from gray to pink and shiny.

"See? Neat."

"I thought it was a gray fish, Daddy, but it's not."

"Gray like all the other ones, right? Yeah. Nope. You found a special one, Angel." He looks at me like he's so proud. "Like you. You're my rainbow trout, honey."

"You're my rainbow fish too, Daddy."

"Yeah?" He chuckles to himself, thinking of something else and looks back up to the sky. "Sweetie. Here's a question. When you can't see the fish, are they still there?"

I nod yes, remembering how I didn't really believe that earlier this morning.

"Even when you can't see them," he says nodding, "they are always there. Swimming. The same is true with me. Always there. Okay, sweetie?"

"Daddy, okay, Daddy. Okay, Daddy."

Chapter Two

Kathryn is a teenager with short red hair, a few silver hoops on one part of her ear and a choker I plan to steal whenever she babysits me. Except I would never really do it because that would be wrong.

"See, this is Professor Coldheart," I teach her with the TV, "and he loves 'The Land Without Feelings.'" I almost cry, trying to describe the plot of *Care Bears* to her, because a world without feelings is devastating to my brain. Even though I know Kathryn is sixteen and cool and probably not into cartoons, I figure she'll appreciate the concept, and I think she likes me well enough, but I can't be sure because she's being paid to be here.

Last time we were together, Kathryn gave me her school picture, which showed her in front of a pink background with striped lights, which is something you only give to boyfriends or best pals, she said, so I know we are pretty close even though I can sometimes not remember her last name because I've only met her three times.

I hear footsteps and creaky stairs. It's my parents.

They are dressed up, ready to see friends for a murder mystery party, and today, as far as I can tell, they are getting along. I'd even left them unsupervised while I watched shows, which usually made me nervous. But in the doorway now, Dad touches her lower back and scoops up her purse without saying anything too sarcastic, which makes her happy. Like me, Mom notices every single thing. She watches and watches and watches. Me too.

"Turn off the tube and spend one-on-one time with Kathryn," she tells me.

I play it cool, smiling at Kat and almost winking before reminding Mom how we only get the Disney channel free for a couple days and it could vanish again at any moment. Dad tells me the VHS player will continue recording my show with the TV off and he and I can watch the rest tomorrow. He makes the rules sound better than her. But I like anytime they are on the same team, even if it's against me.

They leave and Kat and I are finally alone to become best friends. We sit cross-legged on the dusty carpet and stare at each other.

"Do you know my brother," I ask, "from um um your school?"

"From U-32?"

"What?"

"From my high school in East Montpelier?"

I'm not sure, but I nod.

"I like, I don't know like, any Konkles I don't think."

"He's not Konkle—his dad is different. Yeah."

"Ohhh. What's his name?"

"Ken." And I make a face.

"Your brother's Ken?"

"No!" This makes me laugh because Ken is Jamie's dad. Not mine. "We have the same mom, not the same dad."

"Wait, what's his last name?"

"Jamie is my brother, and he is cool." I check her to see if she thinks that's neat and go on, "And he has dark hair and his nose is like this," but I don't know how to make my hands describe what it's like. "And his eyes are like this," I pinch fingers here and there, hoping she'll get the face that lives in my mind, but she looks confused. In my head I see his small, kind eyes, and same big forehead like me and Mom's but it's not *too* big, it's smart. His wide, reassuring smile and dimples that are not always there. He has dark waves of hair that go up and down at the same time, but mine is straight and almost white in summertime. So, we don't look alike at all. I'm like my dad and Jamie like my mom. I wish we looked more alike because maybe he'd remember me more. Even I forget he's my brother.

"His mouth is like this," I say, trying again and smiling big.

She's laughing. "He sounds familiar," she says, but I can tell she's lost. "What's his last name, though? Yours is Konkle." *I'm thinking.* "You like, know his, or—?"

"Um. Um."

"That's okay. That's okay."

She got me. "I can't remember." I feel stupid. Then— "Libertoff!" I yell, happy to not forget my own family. "Oh, and his girlfriend broke up with him this year. So he's single. Do you want to do that?"

"Be a girlfriend?"

"One of his."

She laughs. "I don't even know Jamie!"

I'm not sure why she looks so happy but I think it's good.

"I'm dating someone, but I'll like let you know if something changes, haha."

"Why are you laughing so hard? Jamie is real. He's a teenager too. But my dad doesn't like his dad."

She pauses for too long and then says, "Ohhh. Do you, like, see him a lot? Does he babysit?"

I frown.

"Oh, I'm sorry, sweetie. I didn't mean to ask a sad question."

Something about Kathryn saying "sad" makes the water in my eyes roll all the way out. Once I start crying, I can't tell if it's real or if I'm making it go on longer to feel it more.

I explain through heaves, "Jamie—lives with his dad—he doesn't come over all the time—but he only lives down the street and yeah, it's just—his house is bigger than mine but I'm not mad about it, it's just he has horses too and I don't even get to pet them but maybe when Ken goes on vacation—I'll be allowed. I bet my mom knows where the keys are, she used to live there too. But Ken got her crabs."

Kat side-hugs me but also looks like she might laugh. I hope she doesn't. "Ohhh. I'm sorry. Wait. Gave her crabs? Is that what you said?"

"I think—no, I mean lobsters."

"That's really different." She tries not to laugh again.

"Yeah. Um, after she took, um, Jamie to live in a cabin with no lights or electricity. And also, her car flipped over. Did you know that? But then she met my dad, and they really wanted me, so I was born. But yeah. He's never—here." I'm over the emotion now and it's just a fact.

"Oh. What happened when your mom's car flipped, like, do you know?"

"Oh, it went like this." Even though I don't know, but I flap my hand around like I do.

"Was everyone okay?"

"Jamie was stringed up like ham at the meat store."

"Oh, he was upside down? Gosh."

I nod, fast. "That's what my mom said. And so um then a neighbor came out to save them and put them over the right there with all the um, his strong and they drove home. Even though the windshield was lined up—had lines all on it."

"Cracked?"

I nod. "But Spirit helped. And Spirit's angels too."

Kat scrunches up her face. "I'm sorry he's like, not here a lot, Anna. I'm sure your brother loves you very much."

I nod small. "Yeah. He had a girlfriend with blond hair but then she was bald one day because she shaved it. It was not good but he still thought she was beautiful."

"People are like, beautiful in all different ways, huh?"

I nod, confused. "Are you a teenager?"

"Yup!"

"I know."

She laughs for some reason and asks, "Do you want to go visit like, another teenager? I'm friends with your neighbor."

My eyes light up. A day hanging out with more than one teen sounds groovy, but when I say that she laughs again. I look at my wrist like I have a watch and say, "Wait, what about dinner? Isn't that soon?"

She laughs again but like I'm too much. "We'll be quick, okay?"

Kat and I walk across our pale green carpet, past the out-of-tune piano that's shoved up against the wallpaper, and head out the front door. There's a hill next to my house and we go up the slippery grass holding hands. I'm smiling up at her the way I wish I could with Jamie.

I wonder what my parents are doing and picture them swinging by the hardware store after the murder mystery party. Mom could be poking fun at Dad while picking out incense by the cash register. Maybe they're holding hands right now. Maybe they're connecting over philosophy, my dad's college major, or religion, Mom's obsession, discussing who "God" really is, careening from joyful fights to poking fun at Catholicism together. Maybe their love is firing best when they're slightly agitated and alive.

The front door opens and my sixteen-year-old best friends and I hang out. One of them is smoking a cigarette, like my dad, and I tell her it's bad for her, but only once. She makes me promise not to tell my parents, twice. And it goes on like this and it's perfect until it's time to leave, back down the steep, grassy knoll.

Five minutes later I'm laid up on the couch, tears drying, trying to keep my leg bent, because if I bend it, I stop screaming. Kathryn is pacing, dialing all the phone numbers my parents left for her on a list in gray pencil. When they get home, I'm watching *Care Bears* again and instead of being mad at me, they hug and kiss me. My mom says, "I'm a nurse," like we don't know that, and changes the position of my leg and I scream again, wondering why I can't choose the way my own body goes. When Kat leaves I wonder if we will ever be friends again because it sounds like my dad isn't going to let her come back. I blew it.

On the way to the hospital, my parents speak in secrets. "No, I'm certain, Peter. Her leg is broken."

"Broken?? Nooo, Mommy, no."

Dad reminds her how I broke my wrist with Jamie when he babysat two years ago.

"No. No, Peter. He wasn't babysitting. Jamie was eleven and you were home, sitting in the living room."

"Jamie didn't put up the gate on the porch stairs, Janet, and that's why Anna drove down them," Dad answers, overlapping the ends of her sentences.

How could Jamie not know to put the gate up? Does he smoke too? But then I get mad at myself for thinking that way. Who drives their egg car down stairs? Dummies. Or maybe Dad should have put the gate up if he was so serious about it instead of just sitting on the couch.

"You okay, pumpkin?" Mom's talking to me. I sit in the back of the car taking up the whole bench with the seat belt stretched out far.

I nod. "It hurts."

"I'm sorry. You're so brave."

I love compliments. They make the sick feeling I have in my stomach go away. "How was your date with Daddy?" I ask.

"Good, until this." She goes on, "Kathryn told me she was holding you and dropped you walking down the hill."

"I wouldn't have dropped you," my dad adds.

"Neither would I, Peter."

They've been getting along so well tonight, I hope my leg doesn't change that. "You both wouldn't," I say, meaning it. She probably wouldn't. Dad definitely would not.

At the hospital, the doctor keeps straightening my leg, which I don't like, and neither does Dad, so he's asked to go in the other room. I don't know why Mom isn't in here, maybe it's too hard to see your little girl in agony. Maybe they love me too much.

My whole leg is in a cast from the bottom to the top. But it seems to mean less school, more parents. Dad's been working in Burlington City Hall, which looks like a princess's castle, so I like it here.

"You know I'm breaking the rules with Mister Fred, right?" Dad raises his brows and feeds a chipmunk on top of his old Burlington desk.

"Against the rules?"

"Well, there are actually no official rules about feeding chipmunks inside. No one thought to write that one." And the little guy eats another peanut from his hand. I'm a little nervous to do the same but I put a nut on the desk for Mister Fred to eat instead.

"A lot of important things happened in these offices, you know. Beyond the work I do with my associate here."

My eyes sparkle and he continues. Though I don't understand everything, I love when he talks to me like an adult. I watch his mouth and wonder how it got there.

"I used to share this office with Bob Jefferson and— Bernie had just decided to run for mayor of Burlington. He's in the U.S. House of Representatives now. Bernie Sanders."

"Wow." I don't know what this means.

He keeps going. "Bernie had no experience, okay? Did he have any business running for mayor of Burlington? No fucking business. And I'm working here, making, ya know, strides with the teachers' union, influencing the direction of their contracts. Bob is impressed by the progress. Bernie walks in elated because he just won. But he was a newbie, didn't know what he was doing, no experience, but he fuckin' won. He was the mayor of Burlington but he looked like he'd just robbed a bank."

"Did you give him advice?"

"I mean"—he laughs, perhaps wanting to say yes—"we kind of just talked and maybe that uh, that chat influenced him? Who's to say. But Bernie didn't know how to be mayor, what to do. He had just run as a man of the people. We were his sounding boards for that moment, and he made the decision to set up booths and ask every person in every neighborhood what they wanted. It was so simple. Just *What do you want?* Funny how simplicity can sometimes be the revolution."

Maybe he thinks I'm capable of being someone like Bernie one day. I smile big.

"Marry someone like that. And someone with money."

"Did Mom have money?"

"No." He laughs. "And I still fell in love with her. But if you can fall in love with someone with money, even better."

"What if *I* make it?"

He's tickled by this.

"I like that too. Ha. Pay for my retirement."

"Why don't you run for mayor, Dad?"

He thinks but looks disappointed in himself and changes the subject. "Well, this is the advice my mother gave me. You never met her. But she grew up wealthy but married my dad, who was poor—"

"You don't think she should have gotten a wedding to your Daddy?" I can't believe anyone would ever feel that way about their own parents.

"I didn't say that. But money and their backgrounds made things more complicated."

He tells me that my great-great-grandfather Wunderle founded a large candy company after coming to America. At first, he could only get work in construction and helped build the Brooklyn Bridge, but he sold homemade sweets on the side of the road to get by. That cart eventually grew into a factory, on par with Hershey's, Dad says, and they invented candy corn. This I'd heard before. "And Wunderle Candy Company accrued enough money for many generations to live in, ya know, mansions with drivers."

And cooks in white hats. My face gets serious and my eyes wild. To build all that for your family from one candy cart sounds amazing. It had almost been ours.

"And my mother, Doris, babysat for Grace Kelly, who became a princess."

"That can happen?!"

"But then Mom goes and marries a guy with no generational money. None. From Newark—shit place, especially then—but my pops did pull himself up by his bootstraps to become an All-American football player, expected to go pro, that's when Mom met him, but an injury put an end to all that. I bet that was a real disappointment. Moved to an Illinois suburb, had my sisters and me. Probably not the life she signed up for."

"So you weren't rich when you were little?"

"No. We were good. We were well off. Me and my sisters, all the cousins went on big family trips, and this is pretty cool, honey, we received barrels of sweets at Christmastime, but I remember in high school, the candies got way too sweet. Way too sweet. Stuck in your teeth and stayed there. Must have been too much wax or something. They ran that company into the ground and sold it for nothing. You'd think we would get a cut of every little candy corn some kid eats at Halloween, we get nothing. Don't know how my cousin managed that."

"Why didn't you do it?"

"Take over the company?" I nod, eyes wide, and he looks proud that I know he should have. "Well, I was too young. They weren't gonna give it to a teenager. Plus, I was becoming a hippie, so I probably wouldn't have taken it anyway."

"But maybe if you were a little older you would have taken over?" I say, trying again.

He seriously considers this. "Maybe, maybe. Yeah," and keeps nodding.

"We were almost like Hershey Kisses, if only you'd gotten to be the boss of it." I liked this reality.

"I did test at the genius level. Smarter than most people." And he winks.

"I know, Dad."

He reminds me how he got into Princeton, but not until after being waitlisted, and he'd already decided to go to Indiana's De-Pauw University instead. Closer to home, he'd say. I wondered what was so great about the Midwest that he wouldn't go to a school whose name he said like a trophy.

Hippiedom came at DePauw, where he grew his hair long and stopped wearing collared shirts and using mousse. He explained how he got good at his guitar and a bunch of songs by the Beatles and did acid and protested the Vietnam War and his friend even blew up a building at the school but I can never tell anyone that because the FBI could still be looking into it. When Dad tells stories, you listen, no matter how long they go on for.

One night, after jamming through a slurry of originals with his friend Jimmy, the guy announced he'd be leaving for LA in the morning and pursuing music professionally. Jimmy asked Dad if he wanted to leave with him. Go to LA. But Dad said no. And now every time "Mr. Bojangles" or "Pooh Corner" comes on the radio, Dad tells his story all over again—about how his buddy Jimmy Ibbotson, a member of the Nitty Gritty Dirt Band invited Dad to Hollywood, how he could be living in LA with money, but maybe a drinking problem too. And he wouldn't have me, so it wouldn't have been worth it at all. That's what he says.

But when Dad sings along, "Winnie the Pooh doesn't know what to do, got a honey jar stuck on his nose," it sounds nice, like he could have been on the track too.

When I ask Dad if Jimmy is rich, he says, "Chaa—"

"But you wouldn't of had Mom either," I add. "Daddy, how'd you and Mom meet, again?" Dad shrugs, lighting up a cigarette, balcony doors still open. Foosball is the answer, which they played while helping their friends Gary and Claudia move in together. She'd been divorced from Ken for many years by then and he tells me that when Mom and Ken split up, she didn't kick Ken out of their house. She left and wouldn't accept his money. Instead, she scoured for a cheap cabin in the woods and moved in with only a toddler and a cat in tow to reckon with the mice. Mom told me how she chopped wood and filled the lanterns with kerosene, raising Jamie as a single mom finishing nursing school, while Ken's girlfriend moved into their house just a week or two after Mom moved out with their son. I think it sounds really brave and I try to remember to be like that part of her. But Dad seems annoyed by it. "She didn't demand what she deserved. The guy has a doctorate from Harvard. He could afford more."

But I remind him of the good part of the story that he likes to tell. How eventually Mom met a man who got mistaken for Robert Redford except he had a different wandering eye. Peter was a carpenter, impressed with the lady in the cabin, with his own home in Plainfield, Vermont, a woodshop where the saws hummed, and he had his own symmetrical vegetable garden and cherry cabinets in the kitchen that he built to house the porcelain plates his mother left. My mom describes his old home like magic. Peter was a man quick to grab a guitar, and he'd play late at night before waxing his canoe in the morning sun and storing it high above the woodshop in the afternoon, safe from critters, atop strong beams. A thirty-five-year-old bachelor, kind, smart, one of those reliable hippies, if not also anal or controlling, Mom would point out. But potentially an excellent stepdad and mate. To my mom, meeting him seemed like being rescued, and the photographs of life before show Jamie and Peter and Janet as one family. Happier maybe when it was just three. I wonder how I changed everything. Ken isn't allowed near our house. When Jamie walks up the hill from his dad's car, Ken must stay at the bottom. When Ken drives away, my dad watches closely like he is moving him with his eyes.

"Ken's mother is loaded. She sued New York City when a public bus ran over her toe," he tells me. "She's got an apartment on Fifth Avenue now." He makes a judgmental face and looks jealous.

"Would you get your toe run over for a lot of money?" I ask.

"Just the toe? Yes."

By the time Dad's contract with Burlington City Hall ended, my leg was healed, but I still saw him more because he was jobless. Mom went to her nursing position every day, taking care of old people, visiting house to house while dying patients stayed in their beds. And sometimes I'd go with her. But lately, when we get home, Dad looks like he hasn't moved much and Mom won't talk to him. Plus, when sleep is near, I hear a lot about problems with money through my bedroom door.

This repeats through many days and many nights and my stomach spins.

One afternoon, Dad gets a call.

For a few days after, I understand he will drive a long distance for meetings, and before each of them he shows off a new suit that isn't corduroy and tops them with ties from Filene's, not Sears.

The final night Dad arrives home, he brings flowers.

"These should be for me but they are for you guys!"

"You got the job?" Mom says, teeth showing.

"We are, cough cough, moving to Massachusetts."

They hug and kiss and I don't really know what we are doing but I throw my arms around them too.

"Wait, can I still say 'Fuck the Man' if I am the man?" he laughs, and tells Mom how much he'll get paid. Her eyes go wide, but before she congratulates him, he smirks. "And I think I can negotiate for more."

"When do you start?"

"Next week."

"But my job. Anna has school, Peter."

"You guys can just come when it makes sense. Doesn't have to be right away."

And because Boston is a way bigger city than Burlington, Dad says maybe he can become a singer or radio personality on the side because his DJ voice is excellent. And it is. But for now, he officially is a human resource manager for 7-Eleven.

This sounds important. Like Harvard.

"Okay. Um. How long do you envision living apart, Peter?"

"Oh. A couple months, maybe. This is new. We'll have to talk about it."

Mom looks down.

Dad rolls his eyes.

I'm late for school with wet tights because I've fallen on black ice three times. The fourth time I don't get up, and I sing, "Nobody likes me, everybody hates me, why don't I just eat dirt?" Though I'm six, I am often mistaken for eight, but now my age is showing.

An hour earlier, Mom couldn't find her glasses, though I later found them on her head, and she also couldn't locate her purse, though I later found *that* next to the door, plus an earring fell out and she couldn't wear just one and promised me a prize if I found the other, which I did later, next to her crystals, but it turned out the prize was a hug so I kind of wish I never looked at all. Sweating in the jacket I'd put on too soon, I worried about my dress underneath, specially picked out for the school field trip. Finally she looked at her watch and said "Ready," but then kept staring at her wrist and then lamenting and moaning about how late for work she was and *was I really ready and did I really have everything ready to go and she didn't think she could drive me to school now and would I mind walking?* It wasn't too far. Walking sounded like being older, which was great. "I can do it by myself, yeah!"

But now I keep falling like a clumsy baby and I'm missing my field trip too. What was the point in getting up again just to be welcomed by an empty classroom?

"You okay?" From across the road, two nice-sounding women throw their voices at me.

With hair around my face and touching the icy sidewalk, I look up a little. But I wonder if they heard my song about hate and dirt. My cheeks get hot.

"Um, that's okay." But I'm also nodding and like magic, one is already here, helping me up.

"What's your name?"

"Um, Anna. What's yours?" But I don't listen, really. I can't.

"I'm just—"

And then I slip again. Hot tears pour. "Sorry," I say.

Each of them holds one hand and one arm until I'm totally on two feet.

"Are you alone, Anna?" they ask, walking me through dry spots.

Both of them are very nice but something about this makes me feel worse.

"Mhm, but I think something's wrong with my um my um boots maybe."

"Well. Maybe. But even the best boots can't see invisible ice."

I'm not sure why this makes me sob. "I missed my ice cream field trip."

One of them rubs my back and I lean into her with too much trust.

"Maybe your class is waiting for you. Let's get you to school, okay?"

I don't say much more except "Thank"—gasp—"you."

A yellow bus rounds the corner. "Could that be your field trip?"

"I don't know. Um."

But now they are waving down the bus.

I want to ask them to stop but that would be rude. Our class is "multi-age," made up of first, second, and third graders, and the older kids don't want anyone around who acts too young.

The bus slows, and sure enough it's my teacher, Mrs. Marsh, who comes out, concerned.

"Hi, Mrs. Marsh, um—my mom, sorry, she was just late for work and um I wanted to walk. Sorry." My teacher juts out her lower lip like she feels bad for me too.

Climbing the stairs of the bus, I pick the first empty seat and sit alone. Leaning my forehead against the cold window, I wave goodbye to my temporary mothers and they do it back and my brain wonders if they are friends or in love. They hold hands and I picture them locating lost items for each other every morning, with patience. Maybe me and Mom could join them. We were supposed to move in with Daddy but I'd been thinking lately how it could never happen.

Now the moms are small ants that learned to wave, and I wonder if a kidnapping with them would have been so bad. Looking around I realize the only other person sitting by themselves on the bus is Garret. Not to be mean but everyone knows Garret has problems, because he says things like "I won't let you get your stuff from the cubby unless you have sex with me." Garret walks around when it's sitting time and scratches himself until everyone looks away. He even stares at the wall during reading

When Garret said that thing about the cubbies, I was proud of myself because I said, "No, you can't do that," even though I only knew what he meant a little bit. I went past him and got my stuff from my cubby anyway, pretending I didn't feel scared at all. But now we are both without bus seat buddies, sitting in the front, seeming like the kind of kids who make you question their parents because of constant itching or strangers helping them to school. I try to stop thinking about this.

After touring the Ben & Jerry's factory, we get back on the bus and the only reason I get to sit next to Lindsey F is because her best friend, Abigail, can't have dairy and has to lie down on an entire bus bench. With Lindsey F's full attention, I reframe my late-to-school shenanigans and how all that wasn't typical for me or my family because I'm nothing like Garret, or even Grace, that third grader who had been assigned my reading partner, need I say more.

Grace had recently moved away, and in computer class, someone cracked open her files, newly accessible because she was gone. Opening her paint art, we all gathered around and laughed at the simple yellow stars she drew. Someone commented how she was "dumb," and someone else said "slow." I'd vowed then and there to never be talked about like this. And if someone ever opened my paint art they would say, "Wow, look how well she used the filler-in-y thing, y'know, the one that looks like a bucket. Very good!"

We get back from the field trip and I feel the need to prove to Lindsey F that I am not like Grace or Garret and that I'm not weird and not a child. So later in computer lab I click a red record button on the screen and speak into the hole of my computer next to the speakers, and do a joke, "I want to have sex with Benjamin . . . Not." During camping last year, my best friend, Janna, a whole year older, kind of told me what sex was, even though she never finished explaining. But I got how it was something gross and also funny. I know that because after, we couldn't stop laughing.

Lindsey F laughs now but also looks startled. Or maybe impressed, I can't tell.

"I'm kidding!" I yell.

My chest sweats. I'm not sure why I chose Benjamin, a random second grader who doesn't like people talking to him.

Once Lindsey F looks away, I click *Exit.*

Before the program closes, a computer prompt asks if I want to *Save.*

Save. Yes. Wait. No. Not save. Shoot. But I already clicked it.

The program shuts down and I'm back on the home screen.

I double-click "Paint," opening it.

My recording isn't popping up again. I can't find it anywhere. Good news. Yes. Good news. *Thank you, Spirit. God. Whoever.*

But just to make sure the recording is dead and gone, I click *Exit* one last time. The computer doesn't ask me if I want to *Save.* More good news. Deleted, for sure.

My dad would probably have known how to fix this. He's the real computer guy. But I don't need him. I figured it out myself.

At six o'clock, we're eating dinner and Daddy finally calls. He tells us how he befriended a stray cat. And says I'll get to meet the cat soon because in just a few weeks, we are all moving to Massachusetts. Someone finally bought our Vermont house. Mom squeals.

He tells us about the lobster boats and how they dot the harbor, about ocean waves and how they move differently from lakes. About the smell of salt water because it makes him feel awake, and how the public schools are better than my school in Vermont. Mom looks relieved. And so am I. In just a few weeks, my old school will be far away. *What happened today won't even matter.*

In bed later, Mom is more relaxed and pets my head, describing a town called Salem. This is where she was born. Her family had to relocate from Massachusetts to a golf course in Connecticut where Grampy was hired as a greenskeeper, how the position came with a small home, lent out near the greens, and if one wasn't careful, you could get tricked into thinking you were them, the houseowners, the clubgoers, like when Grammy won golf awards before Grampy decided her involvement was inappropriate.

Mom and her sisters were the daughters of the greenskeeper. Never to be confused with members. But now she'd have her own house in a town with a country club, bought, not borrowed. They would cut their own grass and tend to the garden on weekends, and wear polos because they wanted to, not because anyone demanded it.

She twirls my hair and keeps eye contact, breathing steady. And even though the kettle whistles in the other room, she can't think of anything else to do but stay here with me, thinking about our lives in Massachusetts.

Chapter Three

I WAS A FOOL to befriend the Amys.

Amy One spoke with stagnant air from the back of her throat. Most people said she didn't speak at all, but she did, her thoughts whispered to the other Amy who translated. Amy Two's situation was different but not better. Her hair was falling out and she hid it with expensive clips that I envied, yet she was mocked in school for trying too hard. But they were my neighbors, my age, and despite Mom's efforts, the other Massachusetts kids I'd met weren't banging down my door to hang out. That opportunity had come and gone like a quiet breeze or a small fart, over by the time you register it. My choice was now to sit alone on the bus or with the Amys. I'd chosen them, the girls gracious enough to have me.

Months earlier, at the very end of first grade, Mom and I waited in an empty classroom for my pre-summer introduction. I'd be starting second grade with these kids after the summer and would be with them until college. This was their first impression of me.

"Are you excited, Anna? How do you feel?" asked my mom.

I smoothed my dress and adjusted my hair like a twenty-four-year-old before a date. "Good, Mom. Yeah. I hope they like me."

"That would be great!" Like my optimism surprises her.

Without time to process the nature of her response, I peeked my head out the door and into the hallway.

"There she is!" I heard. "Oh my god! Is that her?"

A line of small people stood by the wall with their tall teacher, maybe twenty feet away. She shushed them as they spotted me.

"She's *still* there!" I heard one of them say and I looked behind to see if maybe they were talking about someone else. Nope.

A tall boy wearing white sneakers with black lines moved the brown hair folding over his forehead without effort. Even from afar, I knew I liked him. I couldn't help but smile before pulling my head back into the classroom to become hidden once again.

For a moment I felt like I was on a TV show.

And then the classroom was full and I was surrounded. A gaggle of soon-to-be second graders ready for summer, mostly shorter than myself, poked and prodded the teacher with questions about me until Ms. Rose invited them to sit down. My good feelings skyrocketed. I could barely speak without a laugh pushing through. *Cool it, Anna, cool it,* I thought. *Steady, now. Don't blow this.* Mom wanted to bring me to Massachusetts before the end of the school year so I could make real friends before summer. A considerate effort, one that I appreciated, especially because right now, I'd never felt better.

Everyone was in their seats, the teacher introduced me, and it was my turn to speak.

"Hi, everyone. Um. I'm Anna (hahaha), something interesting about myself is that I moved and I was um missing where um I was um, I was living in Vermont cuz Vermont's great but you guys are changing that, I think. Thank you."

Kids met one another's gaze and I was feeling a bit proud. *This is great.* I kept going. "Oh. We have two cats now. Not just one."

"I have a cat too!" someone else said. But I quickly thought not to stay on cat stuff because I didn't want to alienate the dog people.

"Cool! I do like dogs too though. Um. Um. My great-great-grandfather or great-great-great, not sure, um, um, invented candy corn."

Someone from the back piped up. "No. Native Americans invented that!"

"Do you mean corn, corn?" I said. "Mother Earth invented corn. Right, Mom?" She nodded. "But our family invented the candy? Right, Mom?"

"It's true," she said. "It is."

Some kids looked very impressed. Others had identified a mother-loving bragger.

"So are you rich?" asked a girl who said her name was Allison.

The teacher gave them a look and my mom quickly said no. Allison seemed disappointed. I was too.

"I need to um, um, make something more clear, please," I said.

The same kid that questioned our corn invention earlier called out, "Why do you use big words like that?" And I knew he meant *words*, but it sounded like *wads* because sometimes here people don't sound out their *r*'s. I couldn't tell if he was saying something nice or making fun of me. With Vermont kids, especially the ones in my church, I could usually tell when they were being mean. This place got me confused.

"Thanks. Um. So my house in Vermont was a mansion but we aren't rich. Right, Mom?"

She looked down at me surprised but didn't answer so I kept going, "Yeah. And so. I'm a Unitarian. Religiously."

The kid with the folded brown hair who I still have a crush on stared like he was looking at my ear. I said again, "It's a religion. Ya know? Where you don't have to believe in anything."

He clicked back in, "I believe in God?"

"I actually do too um but we um call them Spirit? You don't have to, if you want to be in our church I'm saying, you don't have to."

"I'm Catholic," my crush said to no one, looking at his desk.

Allison raised her hand again, "Yeah, Jordan is Catholic and I am too. We go to the same Mass and if you aren't Catholic, my uncle said you don't go to heaven."

"Hell," adds that kid, again to his desk.

Most of the students raised their hands to show how Catholic they were. Except for one in the back who was collecting boogers on the corner of his desk.

I was starting to give up. It's always worse when things begin too well. Then I watched as my crush, named Jordan, apparently, whispered to a girl who was beautiful even at age seven. She put her hair behind her ear and he laughed like she said something funny.

Immediately, it hit me: *I've said too much.* They smelled how bad I wanted this. Just a few minutes ago, I was the neat new girl. How quickly it could all fall apart.

The teacher attempted to wrap it up but I interrupted—

"Oh, my dad is working for 7-Eleven," I said. People looked surprised, but in a bad way.

"In the corporate part—in the offices," Mom added like she was helping.

I almost yelled, correcting myself, "In a corporate way! In a corporate way!" even though I didn't really know what that meant.

Someone nodded. *I'm getting them back.* I took a final swing, "Yeah, so I have coupons for free drinks—"

"Slurpees?"

"Yeah, I think they are called that maybe and the hot dogs with cheese inside also, I do."

Eyes lit up. "Can you, um, share some?" one yelled.

"I can! Yes. That's what I'm trying to say." Heads nodded. Others who were checked out were back again. The ball of acceptance inched toward the green but then there was silence and interest was waning, the wind blowing us back toward the sand trap.

"Um. Um. Um." I was panicking.

The teacher announced the buses were here.

One more try—"Raise your hand if you like candy corn!"—but no one could hear me. And most of the kids walked past without a glance. I put my palm out to high-five them, and only an Amy slapped it.

For the next few days, I held out hope that new friends would call. Nobody did. I decided we should move back to Vermont because that's where all my real friends were anyway. But later, we were sitting in the drive-through line for McDonald's and Mom told me how my old teacher from Vermont, Mrs. Marsh, called to tell her that my classmates played a recording from my file in computer class.

No.

"Your file." *No.*

I nodded along, pretending to be calm. Pretending I didn't know what was coming.

"And in the recording, you said, 'I want to have sex with Benjamin. Not.' Anna. Does that sound familiar?"

Mom handed me the Happy Meal with a toy I knew she'd never let me keep past thirty days and I sat in my own hot shame, getting gloomier, stinkier. I explained how I didn't mean it, reminding her I said "not" at the end. Because I didn't want to do that but thought it was funny to say. *Why did I think it was funny? What is wrong with me?* I wondered out loud if all the kids in Vermont think I'm disgusting and assume I have problems.

Like Garret.

"But all the kids didn't hear what I said, right? Just the person on computer headphones?"

"Well, it was played out loud, apparently," Mom responded. "And there were two classrooms in the lab that day."

I'll never go back. I closed my eyes and wished for erasure but I was still in the hot car and Mom was staring at me for more. There was no choice but to accept rankness. At least I knew Massachusetts now was home.

And so, the Amys.

We walk the winding streets of our neighborhood. The road we live on is maybe three miles from the main street where the high school, police station, four Catholic churches and, in my mind, the cool kids live. The Amys and I are five miles from the beach where the mansions are. We sit beneath thick woods at the base of an unending warped road. Most people who drive it for the first time find themselves way over the line at least three times within the first five minutes. So, when the Amys and I walk the neighborhood this hot summer before my first school year in Massachusetts going into second grade, we usually trot single file and I end up in back.

It's almost like walking alone.

A black animal darts across the street as a car whips by. This vehicle knew the roads well and took them fast, properly gripping the shoulder. But the cat is more familiar still, knowing when to become perfectly immobile or sprint. A cat with street smarts who doesn't fall victim to the panic that some squirrels, chipmunks, and dogs succumb to, throwing themselves into double yellow lines.

"Oh my god," Amy Two yells. "Did you see that?"

Amy One nods, small. I'm unsure how to properly communicate with Amy One because most things she says must go through Amy Two.

I'm on my knees, making kissing noises. "Moe. Mohammed Midnight Tweeweep Konkle. C'mere."

"What did you say?" says the Amy who speaks.

"I'm calling for my cat. He's so far from our house."

"Your cat? That's the black neighborhood cat. We feed him all the time."

"Oh, even like this month? He was a stray, I know that, but he lives with us now."

She doesn't answer me but asks, "Oh. Did you trap him with your family?"

"No. What do you mean? He's right there. My dad just has been feeding him for a while. And he started sleeping inside. Moe chose us, we didn't trap him."

"That's weird," says Amy Two.

Moe is circling my legs now and purring as I scratch his neck. I continue, "My dad loves animals and they are best friends now."

"You named him Moe?"

"Well, I wanted to name him Tweeweep . . . tweeweep, like the wet drops that are on the grass in the morning from the trees . . ."

"Never heard of it," says Amy Two, before getting another whisper in her ear from Amy One.

Amy Two speaks for her, "Amy says, 'You mean condensation?' " I knew Amy One was very smart. I knew it.

"Con-sation, tweeweep, it's the same. Anyway, everyone in our family got to name him a different name so it's um that's why it's such a long one. Mohammed is a god from I think Islam."

"What's that?"

"A religion."

"Ew. Do you like Islam?"

"I dunno. My mom likes to like things that other people don't know about. And 'Midnight' for his dark hair and then 'Konkle' is my last name—"

"We know," says Amy Two right as Amy One whispers in her ear, "Jinx." And I know that because Amy Two says "Jinx" out loud. And they giggle.

"Mohammed Midnight Tweeweep Konkle, but we call him Moe for short," I finish.

"He's sort of the neighborhood's cat, though, and you're stealing him."

Moe is lying on soil now, belly up and purring, but a sound in the tree brings him low to the ground, on his paws. Not wanting to lose the only friends I have, I explain gently, "Actually my dad called town hall and they said to put up missing signs in the neighborhood."

"Oh yeah, I saw those. It didn't make any sense because he was already a stray. So, no one is missing him." I catch my breath to respond, but she continues, "Chocolate was—"

"Okay, so you called him Chocolate, but now his name is Moe."

Now Amy One takes a swing, saying something, swallowing consonants as she goes—"A srayant beemitta."

"I'm sorry, but do you speak Polynesian, Amy?" I ask, trying to be funny and laughing and so does Amy Two, but we don't know why it's actually funny.

Amy One tries again—"A stray ant bee missing."

I get it now, "Ohhh . . . a stray can't be missing?"

"She said a stray *cannot* be missing," Amy Two corrects me, wanting to prove she's the only one to really understand Amy One. "They can't, because they don't belong to anyone."

My face gets red and my stomach turns, maybe because they have a point. "Well, I guess you're right, they can't be missing if no one had him to begin with, but—

Amy One nods.

"—but we paid for his shots and got him fixed and all that so Moe is our cat. And the reason we put up missing signs, is to know he's not. Missing."

A pause between girls. Then Amy Two:

"I bet he will still visit the other houses he used to go to."

"That's okay, you can enjoy him," I say.

We are all petting him again. In this span of explanation, he has already traversed a tree and come back.

"He's my dad's best friend," I say again, basically to myself.

Amy One whispers to Amy Two. Amy Two speaks it. "Do we want to go and dip in Amy's pool?"

I say I can't because I have to help my parents finish unpacking, which is true: the boxes and the bickering are never-ending. Plus, last time I was at Amy One's, her father sat in his recliner, telling her brother to get him beer, and I'm not sure if the place smelled sour or felt sour, but I left early.

So almost bowing, I say goodbye, hoping I won't have to call during my next moment of weakness. They point out how I'm walking the opposite direction of my house but I don't want to walk with them anymore. Instead I follow Moe away from them until their footsteps quiet and I hide in the trees, against the occasional sound of cars. This is different from my neighborhood in Vermont where you could always see a neighbor. I wonder if my brother is having fun at his dad's and chide myself for never asking if I could ride his horse while we still lived there.

I'm walking home, though this road doesn't feel like home. I hear echoes of "uch you—ca ooo-ooo" and round the bend.

"—top it Janet—et—et—t."

You'd think the homes being farther from each other than they were in Vermont would be more private, but our neighborhood has an echo. The louder my parents' voices get, the more I hurry. I pass Joe and Belle's and consider knocking on their door instead of going into mine.

A week earlier, I'd met this couple in their eighties and my potential new grandparents. My dad's parents died before I was born, and Grammy and Grampy, my mom's parents, loved me lukewarm at best. I tried not to take it personally and my dad didn't think much of them anyway. So I like going to Joe and Belle's, watching them play gin rummy while I eat tuna on Wonder Bread and that's when I asked if they'd be my fairy godparents. They laughed before saying yes. Touring their house, I noticed how their twin beds sat comfortably within the same room, with no insistence on marital extremes. They seemed like real friends. Maybe I could get my parents there too. If I could just help them really meet each other, see each other like I see each of them.

But I know if I don't come home, I'll be in trouble, so I'm at our front door and I'm hearing stuff slam. I've waited too long and shut the front door hard so they hear it. Their voices hush for a second and Mom unpacks plates while Dad leans against a doorway, watching. He swings his voice up, all happy.

"How was your walk, sweetie?"

"It was okay," I say. "But I could hear you guys all the way down the street."

Dad rolls his eyes, playfully, like he doesn't want to care.

"Oh, that's great, Peter. Wonderful," says Mom.

"Cut it out, Janet," Dad answers.

"So. Embarrassing." She throws out each word alone and closes every window, shooting paint chips off the sides.

A kitchen drawer is turned over on the floor, forks and knives spilling out. Mom's purse is unzipped in a heap on the ground, throwing up keys and tissues. Dad stands in one place, still just watching. I guess they'd been here awhile and I wish he'd just go in the other room and watch TV.

"Everyone knows." Mom is finding more windows to close and doing the thing where she seems like somebody else. Her eyes dart around like pinballs and repeats, "Everybody knows."

Now I'm also feeling hyper so I close the windows with her.

"Can you both— You're chipping the paint," Dad snaps. I stop but she doesn't.

Looking like he might physically stop her with his two hands, Dad sits instead. He always says he doesn't believe in violence and that's why he fled the draft. He also doesn't believe in spanking, though his dad smacked him around and it didn't bother him too much. But he doesn't do anything like that, even though to me it looks like sometimes he might. Instead, he sits in a dining chair and makes it a joke. "I guess I'll be fixing that Saturday. Thanks, Janet. Add it to your running list. I'm your servant boy, right?" He laughs more, looking at me funny. I laugh back.

Mom screams from what seems like nowhere, "GET AWAY FROM ME!"

Like responding to a gunshot at the start of a race, Dad flies off his chair, grabs cigarettes, and looks for his wallet.

She closes the last window, unsure where to go or what to do for a moment, but finds something to hold on to. "Oh good, Peter. You're—you're—you're going to smoke. Perfect—perfect timing. Thank you."

"Mom, Mom—do you want water?"

"You're fucking crazy, Janet," he says before walking out the front door.

"I'm crazy. I'm crazy. There goes that word again. Crazy." To me, she sounds like Iago, the bad parrot from *Aladdin*: "Crazy, I'm crazy."

Dad hasn't left yet but sits on the stoop, Mom pretends not to care and goes back to unpacking like nothing happened, so I help. Through the glass of the front door, I smell his lit Camels. I told him I was going to put my picture on the pack so every time he smokes he'd see my face and maybe he'd finally put them down for good—remembering his future grandkids and how they want to meet him, like how I'd wanted to meet his parents but they got cancer. For some reason we talk about his future grandkids a lot. But he always smokes again, careful after to collect the butts in the sand-filled coffee can so Mom can't yell at him about them, and then he follows up with Red Hot cinnamon gum.

Now it's Mom opening the front door. She can't decide what to do but I wish she would leave him alone.

"I have been unpacking most of this myself, Peter." She is pretending to be calm. "And I would really appreciate your help."

"What the fuck are you talking about Janet? I did the den."

"Only because—hah—only because—you—you—wanted to watch the match. Whatever serves Peter best."

"Ha. That's not what it's called."

I help, "The race."

"You watched it for hours. Peter. I kept"—her voice is escalating, so she slams it back low—"kept, I kept unpacking. And now I need to cook dinner for Anna, and the kitchen is empty."

"Is there ice cream? I'll just have that," I add.

"Whose fault is that?" he asks, quiet.

"Mine? Is it mine? It's MINE. IT'S MINE." She slams the

front door and I'm impressed the old windows don't break. She opens it again. "It's mine." But slams it closed like the end of a song and it still doesn't crack, which makes the moment almost funny, and then I think about how sometimes things that look fragile are actually strong.

"You're going to fucking break it," Dad yells, then buries his big voice inside himself and continues, "God, she's so fuckin' crazy."

I wish he wouldn't say that, but I can't disagree. And he walks back inside next to us and I hear him say stuff to himself like "Such a bitch."

"I can hear you, Peter. You're a—an asshole." It almost sounds like it's hard for her to swear sometimes. But he doesn't respond, searching for something. Car keys are in his hand and I don't know if I should ask him not to leave.

"A year away from us wasn't enough, Peter? Oh! Do what you always do. Leave. Leave, Peter. Leave."

But I don't want him to.

"If you love us, you'll stay," Mom adds.

I watch her face. Each side looks nothing like the other; mucus comes from just one nostril and it's far too thick and clear not to be leakage from her brain. She hurts so authentically it's overwhelming, like she needs a mother, but Dad doesn't see it or understand it or care, and instead she follows him down our front steps. He feels chased, I think. I don't know what to do so finally I go upstairs and close the door to my bedroom but the silence makes everything tight so I open my window and watch.

He's saying, "Give me my key-ee-ees. Be an adult and hand me my keys, dammit—give me my keys Janet-et-et-et-et." I can't make out the next part as Dad gets in his car but whatever he says makes Mom hand back what she took, and he finally backs down the driveway. I'm not sure if he'll sleep at the beach, if a Scituate cop will ask him again what he's doing in his car at four A.M. by the ocean. Or come back to the TV room couch.

My journal waits for me on the bed. "My mom is crazy. I will never be like her. No no no. I h8 her." Then I add, "I think." Amy's brother taught me to write it with an eight and maybe it's not as bad that way. It sounds like things are being thrown downstairs so I throw my journal too, and find the old cassette player with that microphone in a half-unpacked box. Without even caring what I'm recording over, I press the red circle and sing, "Mama I'm— Mama— I'm brokennnnn. When all the world is a booby trap and you don't know where you're at, think of me. Think of ME—" I'm scream-singing, maybe a different version of yelling but when it's in a song you can go as loud as you want like Mom's classical music on high or her Native American chanting. I feel better than I did a moment ago.

Boom, boom, boom. Footsteps up the stairs like a gorilla. I watch the door handle to my room turn.

"Hi," I say, pitching up high and sweet, but I can hear my own fear. I hope she hears it too.

"Is your room unpacked?" she asks, almost stoic-sounding but more like someone who contains nothing.

I tuck everything under my pillow. "No. Almost."

"Why—why—am I alone in this?" she says, suddenly full again, bursting at the seams.

"Sorry. I'm gonna help now. I just took out this tape recorder, look." And I put it on those plastic shelves. "See?"

"I'll do everything. It's fine." She's touching all my stuff and tossing it on the ground. "Am I asking for too much?" I wish she wouldn't touch my things.

She drops my Polly Pocket. "That's my favorite one—!"

"I'm so—so alone," she whispers to herself and keeps moving.

Now I'm getting annoyed and think to myself, *You're not alone. I'm right here. We're unpacking. Polly's alone.*

"Always. Always. Always," she chants.

"Huh."

"We—" she says, airy and intense.

"We are." I don't even know what I'm saying anymore.

"Take his side."

"Well, didn't Dad help a little? He should have."

She answers like I'm really out of line, "He only helped in—the—the the the, TV room because he wanted to *watch it.*" She exhales the way I do when I'm looking at my hot breath in cold air, and says, "You and Dad against me and Jamie. Always. And you know why your dad is against Jamie?"

"Why?" I don't want to know, but I also do.

She laughs and it feels mean so I try again and say, "Well. He—he doesn't like Jamie's dad."

"I KNOW that."

This makes me say, "Why are you so angry, Mommy?"

She answers, "Because, because I'm not happy. I was happier away in Vermont. From your dad. With just us."

"But I thought you um you think I'm against you too." When I realize what I'm saying, something about this is too much. I'm almost eight but I snap. "You never leave him alone. Leave him alone!" I'm screaming now.

She screams back, "I. DO. EVERYTHING. I'm tired. Can I be tired!?"

"MOM. Please stop."

Her body is folding in. "I was happier when he was far away."

"We just got here."

She's not really looking at me. "It's been"—she's almost gasping for air—"a very long time of me being un-"—she tries to catch her breath three times—"happy."

"You're happy?" My eyes are tired.

"Unhappy. Unhappy. Unhappy. Unhappy."

She crumples into a ball on the ground, on the golden, long-haired carpet.

"I hate my life. I hate my life." She can't stop the chant. "I hate my life. I hate my life. I hate my life." I'm kneeling next to her now and I see it coming from the deepest part of her body where the lobsters live and similar feeling runs through me like we are dying or something.

"I am your life, Mommy. I am. If you hate your life then you hate me."

Her eyes open and everything leaves, like the last drops of water evaporating from the bottom of a glass. Her voice goes high and innocent like a baby. "Oh, Anna, I don't hate you . . ."

But it's my turn now. To be the baby. I try to say something but stop, eating it.

"What?" she says, stroking my head. "It's okay, Anna. My little girl."

"You saaii—aadd you—you—hate me."

She looks big-eyed and confused. "I didn't say that."

"Your life, you said you hate it. But I am your life." In that moment, I know something is very wrong with me too.

"I—" Mom's voice is airy. She's totally different now, like a lost doe. "I—don't remember that. Saying that. I don't remember."

"Mommy. It just happened. Now. Just now." I'm confused and just as upset.

She's suddenly peaceful, with me on the ground next to her. "No. Oh, honey. I love you more than anything in this world, Anna."

We hold each other, finally.

Because she's back. I'm home.

But after some time, I wonder when she'll let go.

Chapter Four

Dad wears his business suit and I eat Burger King, flying down the highway toward the city. We've reached that part of the drive where the water tower sits, like a bubble on stilts decorated with pretend paint spills in blue, green, orange. Us kids love it, the parents say, because without having to ask, we know Boston's nearby. And if you stare long enough, sometimes you can make out the face of an old man in the blue spill.

"Dad, look! The man's face? With the beard, Daddy? Look. You see?"

"Asshole," Dad responds, focused out the rearview. "Stop tailing me, you fucker." Then he brakes, but just for a second.

"Dad! What if that car hits us?"

"Hit me! From the rear, it'll be his fault." And he continues jamming his foot on and off the brake, flicking the guy off, and then slams the gas.

Now we fly away like bandits.

"You shouldn't do that, Dad!"

"You shouldn't tell me what to do, you're a kid." He opens a new pack of Camels and presses *Fast Forward* on the cassette player several times until he reaches the track "Moondance." It's a new mood, and we sing along:

Can I just have one more Moondance with you, my love
Can I just make some more romance with a-you, my love

And we don't care who hears us through the open windows to winter. He lights up and blows smoke out cracked glass. I'm ten but my voice is finally becoming big enough to do some damage, but not like his. I'm hoping the chorus at school will help me grow.

"This baby has a rockin' sound system, right?" Our champagne station wagon vibrates.

"Oh yeah!" I yell back and he rolls down the window even more till my hair whips and I'm laughing a lot.

Compared to us, the people in the other cars seem seated next to someone they wish wasn't there, like paper dolls. I like who I'm sitting with. One teenager looks a little more alive, maybe. But not like this. Nothing like us.

When he finishes his cig, the song is over and Dad stops the music.

"Rehearsal time? Run lines? We got ten minutes, baby."

I forgot to eat my dinner, so I nod and shove the burger into my mouth.

"Wanna run it? Or *have it your way*?" He says the last part with a deep voice like in that burger commercial.

Putting all my energy into each line of this script is pure joy. Months earlier I'd done a local theater class in some Presbyterian church. By miracle of miracles, a casting director was hiding in the pews and asked my parents if they would consider bringing me in to Boston a few times a month to audition for commercials.

Dad's eyes lit up, Mom looked mixed, but I was one hundred percent ready to be a star. Eventually they agreed that if an audition came up, Dad would take me.

"You're not enunciating, honey. You don't want to swallow your words. Enunciation will set you apart from the other kids. Try again. Ta Ta. S S Ssss. Say the full word, right?"

I do *"Hi, Mommmm."*

"K, too much. Too much 'mm,' a little lighter touch: 'Mom,' 'mm,' 'Mom.' See, like that. Yeah. Mommy Makes Me Eat My M&Ms." And smacks his cinnamon gum after, like a seasoned coach.

For a sec, I forget what I'm supposed to say again so read off the page, *"Hi, Momm."*

"Hi, honey," Dad reads back, using his mom voice.

I put the script closer to him, realizing I'm on the side of his bad eye. *"Becky, you better not be doing dessert before dinner!"*

"Pleeease?" Oh, real me has a question. "Wait, and then it says I 'hold up an ice cream cup and eat it.' Do you think they brought us ice cream?"

"I don't think they'd waste product." He always knows the answer. "At least if it were my company, I wouldn't. Be ready to mime it, Angel." So I try. But he's got notes. "Angel, if you're gonna do that, really taste it." I do it again. "No, no, better ask for a real spoon. Here, I have one." And in his organized car, the opposite of Mom's, Dad takes out a baggie with three plastic utensils from the middle console.

"Shoot, never mind. I used it yesterday. Forgot to wash it." At times he's washed his car utensils for reuse, originally free from McDonald's. If he uses paper towels at home to dry his hands, he'll lay them back down damp to use later.

He sings, "Honey! We're here!" and pulls into a spot.

I know this is to the tune of something from *Leave It to Beaver* because he sings it a lot.

Walking to the building, I see so many fancy cars and ask him which one he would buy.

"None. Too much."

"No, if we had enough money!"

"Don't want 'em." I thought he loved money. "Nope. Showiness is tackiness and that's usually a new-money thing." He adds, "Not always but usually. Old money, half the time you don't even know they got any. They don't *need* you to know. Wealthiest guy I ever met dresses like he's homeless. Saleslady kicked him out of the GAP one time. He. Let. Them." And looks at me for a long time, nodding like he's teaching me a lesson but I can't figure out what it is. "Think about it, sweetie. How much could the rich guy have bought if they treated him right? The commission they would've gotten! Don't judge a book by its cover." This hits. Instead of the Audi, I pick the Saab. "Nice," he says, "but what about a Volvo? Solid vehicle. Not gaudy."

"No. A Saab, Dad."

"K. Maybe I'll do the same."

Inside it smells like the library. I'd always assumed that smell was from all the paper but turns out it's also the smell of glass and stone. The elevator dings, landing in front of us. When the doors open they are extra loud, like pressing a heavy metal stapler instead of plastic. When we get in, Dad makes silly faces at me, but if Mom were here, she'd make me hold her purse, or wear a dress she approved of instead of this funky sweater and denim skirt. I'd have to watch myself in public and make sure I wasn't like, embarrassing. But now I dance for the security camera and keep going until Dad belly laughs.

Inside, a bunch of actor kids wait on wood benches, studying their lines, and I'm amazed they've let us in again with all of them. They look experienced. But my dad signs my name like a prize and picks up a script, different from the one we studied in the car.

"New draft. Shoot."

"Anna Konkle. Come in, sweetie," says Maura. "How are you?" I scan the new words hoping I can wing it, straighten my skirt, and peek back at Dad, who looks full of hope.

Talking fast in the car afterward, my father is almost yelling, "She said you were amazing! Did you enunciate? Did you remember to enunciate? See?"

"I think I forgot?"

"Okay. Well. And how many people were in the room? The clients?"

"Yeah, five, five, five in the room," I answer, going faster.

"That tiny room, they squeezed in five? No."

"Five! Dad. You've never been in there. It's not that small." They had told me I'd done well and I'm the experienced one now. I'd teach him to enunciate.

He's thinking out loud now. "Next time we go in, I'm gonna tell Maura I am open to auditioning as well. For the right thing. Has to be the right thing!"

"You should! Do you have time, though?" Because it is more my thing. But I don't say the last part.

"Well, it would be hard with my schedule."

"That's a lot with . . . corporate. Corporate."

"Yeah. And you're the priority. But I have a great voice, people say. Gotta give them what they want."

"So you should give them you in a, um, like, a diaper commercial for adults—"

"An adult diaper commercial"—he's laughing—"that's right. Or a herpes medication, right—?"

We toss around the idea of me getting famous and him quitting his job to manage me. I grant him my permission. Mostly

I'm just proud he believes in me this much. I'd never even gotten a callback.

"What if you didn't know how to be a manager?" I ask five minutes later, having second thoughts.

"I'd figure it out. I was president of the teachers' union. I didn't know what I was doing then. AND I got the contract they wanted. I'm smart, sweetie."

"I know! No, I'd want your help. I'd need it."

He nods, thinking. "Ya know, Hollywood's probably like any other industry, just more . . . vapid."

"Vabid?"

"Puh, vapid. Without substance. The artists, I bet some of them are deep. But then there's everyone else. You need someone you can trust. Your pops."

This sounds right, and he is good at a lot of stuff.

He reminds himself of his own potential and goes on, "You know, I started writing my book last week."

"Yay! Wait, I thought you started it years ago."

"I have a job! I had the idea then. But—"

"You watch a lot of TV."

"Anna. 'Belfast thinks I'm deaf.' That's the first line."

"Oooh! What's Belfast?"

"Belfast is the boss to the servant who was in an explosion and became deaf but when he healed he regained his hearing—but he pretends he's *still* deaf." And then he quotes himself again: "Belfast thinks I'm deaf." I'm confused, but he goes on, "I'm telling you, honey, cuz there's a role for you—when it's made into a movie. Nicole Kidman would be so good as your mom. There's a sort of villain older woman character called Geraldine."

"You named her Geraldine? That's Grammy's name, you have to change that. Mom's going to be mad."

"If Gerry was nicer to me, then I wouldn't give her that name.

And then you are the little girl. She's eleven in it but we could make her thirteen. So, I've got a year to finish this because it'll take a couple years to get it there. But I would say, 'If you want my story for your movie, you have to put my daughter in it.'"

I'd never done that before. I'd love to do a movie. And I wouldn't be one of the vapid ones. And all the kids in school would flock. Not just the Amys.

Despite the Boston traffic, we are home before dessert, but Mom's not, working late at Reindeer Cove. Norman, one of her patients, stopped having bowel movements this week. Whenever I'm constipated, I think about how this is also an end-of-life symptom.

Mom's patients at the assisted living facilities are her other children, which I know because I'd seen her with them. Even in Vermont, I'd gone to the Gary Home to help, where Jamie had a job too, cooking in the kitchen, and I got to bring food on trays. She's told me about patients over the years, like the hermit in the woods, or the spouses so in love they die days apart, and the crazies, like the guy who stopped taking his meds, spreading white shoe polish on a bagel instead of cream cheese to poison his wife, and when the smell was too obvious they all laughed. When I get to go, certain elders stare at their laps but others want to chat, and for the most part, I enjoy it. *We'll all end up like them someday*, I'd think, so liking elders was the same as liking yourself. But being with so many at once could feel like a time travel machine where they are moving you forward by years at a time. Still, I like being there with all of them.

Reindeer Cove is mostly a Jewish community, her favorite of the religions. She really loves everything Jewish. Ken is, or was, and even though she doesn't love him like that anymore, she kind of talks about him like she does. Ken's mom said she didn't want him marrying a shiksa. But he did it anyway. I learn these things when I don't talk too much and let her go on and on, plus it's safer if I don't have an opinion.

Norman, her patient currently declining, invented a spot cleaner for rugs that was sold at Sears. Bottling cleanliness to get rich sounded like magic, and all this after surviving the Holocaust. "Norman showed me the numbers on his arm," she told me one day.

"Auschwitz." She explained, "The Jewish prisoners were given tattoos in the concentration camps as a way of uh, uh, uh—namelessly, namelessly identifying a person. Can you believe that? An atrocity. Like a bar code on books. Awful. Abhorrent. There's not a word strong enough for it. A number, an item number on a box of garbage bags. That's the equivalent." Mom always offers my brain the oddest images. "They tried to break them," she says, almost crying. "But the Jews are a very deep, beautiful people . . . and maybe, maybe because of this, they were targeted." Mom continues, "Like women. Women are magic. We grow living beings. We give birth. Pretty miraculous. Native Americans. Magic practitioners of the land. We are part Iroquois."

"I know."

But she's not listening. "Isn't that amazing? Black tribes in Africa. No modern medicine and some live the longest. Maybe the uh uh, humans or I hate thinking about it like this but maybe some of 'em have a bad chip, and must control whatever, whoever— in—in—in—timidates them. Who they are threatened by. Something like that. So sad."

I nod, almost getting it, and don't want her to stop, so I stay quiet.

"I, uh, I— What was I saying? Oh. Norman's will to survive. His *will to survive*, every atom of his humanity had been undermined, *taken* . . . but Norman, I swear, wears his tattoo like a badge of honor, as he should. As he chooses to. Some other survivors got them removed with a laser. *Ouch.* He said he wanted to see it every day. To witness his strength. To will gratitude. What an incredible human being." She's talking to someone who lives in the sky now because she has that look on her face when she meditates. "For what he survived. And then he comes to the states and invents Spot Erase."

"For the floor?"

"Rugs. Carpets. I hear it works incredibly well."

"What's in it?"

"Don't know."

"Woahhh."

"I know," Mom says proudly because it's she who takes care of his well-being now. "And he loves me." She kind of hums happily before her eyes go wide. "Hon. Have I told you that story?"

Her voice is activated, satisfied by this conversation, and there's another thing she wants to say. "Another one of my astounding patients . . . was at a rally for Hitler, can you believe that? Just before that evil fucker came into power."

"What?!" I say.

She keeps explaining. "So before the Nazis were really *the* Nazis, the dominating political force of Germany."

"I know, I'm not a kindergartner!"

"Don't be rude."

"I'm not!" But she's giving me a look back. "Sorry."

Satisfied, she goes on, "My patient listened to that evil man speak in front of a group of people in, in, in a square when he was doing speeches to garner, to, to find support and to find, you know, supporters—." She is getting excited and so her words jump around more. "Okay? Right. And so, oh, and my other patient is anti-violence. That's an interesting piece to it all. And so he was totally terri—horrified by what he heard from this wannabe uh, uh, brute and disturbed by what he heard, so my patient left."

"That must have been so scary for them, I mean did people know he was Jewish? In that crowd?"

"Of bigots?" she ends my sentence. "That's a—well, that's a good question." And she's really thinking about it. "Armbands weren't a thing yet. It sounded like he listened to a lot of the speech, so there was not an um, an immediate threat . . ."

"But he must have been scared," I say, feeling my belly flip.

She nods. "He's a brave man," adding with the deepest of reverence, "but he's human and I'm sure he was . . ."—she throws her voice deep, giving the last word gravity—"terrified."

"Wow."

"My patient was ten feet from Hitler. His biggest regret was not killing him."

"Woah! Did he have a gun?"

"No."

"Oh."

I consider this. "But we hate guns . . . and we hate the idea of shooting someone . . . but you think he should have murdered Hitler."

"If he had a gun?"

"Right."

"Yes."

I agree. "Yeah, he should have shot him. Someone should have." But I look at her to check if I'm right. I can tell Mom doesn't like that word "gun," but she's nodding slowly. "Mom, what do you think—?"

"I don't believe in violence, I wouldn't even let Jamie pretend all that with a stick, but this is an exception. But if he had done it, he would have been killed too."

"Your patient?" A twist.

"He could have murdered Hitler."

"I thought you meant your patient."

"Him too." She nods. "By security or supporters or someone . . ."

"But you still think he should have done it?" I say.

"Oh. I hate to think of a world where I never met him. Or where he didn't have his children. His whole life. But to save humanity from a massive atrocity. Maybe the ultimate sacrifice. A modern figure of atonement, right? But he couldn't tell the future, he couldn't have known."

"And like, Mom!" I say, realizing. "No one would even know he saved everyone because the Holocaust wouldn't have happened."

"True," she says. "We never really know, do we? We do our best. You can't fix everything. But you try. You do try."

I think of her staring down any roaring ambulance and blessing whoever is inside. Or meeting a new dog and warning me to be careful because of all the bites she'd seen in the ER. Mom couldn't stop Norman from dying, though he'd lived a long life. I picture Reindeer Cove stuffed with her old patients and all their tales but few friends left who can actually hear them.

It's cool that Mom listens to them. It's cool that Mom cares.

I make a mental note to visit soon.

"Is it hard to watch a patient . . . leave?" I ask.

She is direct and cold. "Yes."

"Where do you think they go when they die?"

"I believe in reincarnation." I'd like to poke holes in her visions of this and have her do the same with mine until we come up with a collective answer on death. This is something I do with Dad, not her, but I try until she gets tired and remembers I haven't washed the dishes and so here it ends.

I'll remember her patients' stories, just some of the millions dying out with the old.

Never assume the stakes are low.

Stop the bad thing from happening before it happens.

Never stop looking.

Sitting beside Dad now, we watch John Edwards on TV and wait for her to come home. The show is about a spiritual medium who communicates with the dead on behalf of the audience. I wonder how Norman is doing. Leaning back, I rest into my dad's stomach. At the commercial break I say how I think Spirit is probably a woman and that heaven isn't like clouds, but like Earth just brighter and there is no hell and people with the clearest souls are closest together in the sky and then I want to know what he thinks. Dad tells me that actually the whole universe is connected, like a spiral of light above us and all around us and there is a part of this light inside each of us and when one dies, how our light reconnects with the bigger spiral up there, the one that connects us all—Dad saw it one time, tripping. Before acid, he'd been agnostic.

"But you always need a trip leader, sweetie. Someone not on the drug to watch out."

At the next commercial I have questions about drugs but tell him there are issues with his spiral of light theory. He laughs.

And then the back door opens. When Mom closes it, she drops most of her things straight onto the floor. Pieces of her curly hair poke into her eyeballs and I can feel her frustration. Usually I'd help but I'm trying to figure out the afterlife with Dad on the couch right now. She says hello and we say hello back but then Mr. Edwards is about to say if he believes the little girl's death really was a freak accident or foul play.

I can feel Mom blinking, waiting for me. I'm just hoping she sits and watches with us without saying a word so I can still hear everything on TV, but I don't think that's ever happened before.

"What is this?" she asks.

"John Edwards, *Crossing Over*," I say, too fast to not sound rude.

"Is it appropriate for Anna?"

Dad makes long eye contact with her but says nothing.

So I do instead, "Mom, it's fine!"

And she stares back for a long time and then walks away.

My stomach flips and I feel like I should follow her. Maybe she needed a better greeting. But we've had a long day too. School, Boston, and back. So instead I'm lazy and lean again onto the couch cushion that we have put against my dad's belly as I sit between his legs. This way my back goes almost flat like I'm lying down and can use his legs as my armrests. It's comfortable and we can both stretch our legs, even though it's such a small couch. We'd perfected this position years ago.

The TV room door opens like she never left.

"Yes, Janet?" Dad says with a sigh.

"Peter."

He closes his eyes and shoots breath out his nose. "Yes, Janet?"

"Can you come—uh, come here and speak with me, please?"

"I'll speak to you after the show." And then he swallows. "If that's all right."

"Now."

He laughs before muttering "Fuck me," and gets up.

My backrest leaves. Grabbing the remote, I flip channels. Saved by the bell.

But when Dad reenters, he doesn't lie back down but sits upright, feet on the ground, flipping channels, as though I wasn't supposed to touch the remote. They probably got in a fight. I try to move his legs back where they were but he's not budging.

"We can't sit like that anymore."

"What?"

"Your mother doesn't want us sitting like that." I'm confused. "She thinks you're too old to sit with me like that. What happened to *Crossing Over*—?"

But something's rising in me, "Mom. MOMMM—."

Dad stares straight ahead, clicking the remote.

"MOM!!!" I can't help it, tears fall. I'm humiliated and mad. The feelings burn through my cheeks, baby fat incinerated.

She reappears and I'm already begging, "Why would you say that?"

"Oh, you told her, Peter. That's great," she throws.

"You said it, Janet."

"Mom, don't blame it on Dad. Why I can't—can't I sit with him like that?" My words won't work right and she doesn't answer either. "What's wrong with how I sit with my dad?" I say again, pleading.

This part seems hard for her to say: "You're just too old now, Anna. It's not appropriate."

"How, though?" But I'm catching on, picturing every frame.

Dad is lying down with his head on the armrest and takes one of the back cushions and puts it behind him to prop up his head but his legs stay straight down the couch like a cadaver propped up in a coffin. And then we take a second back cushion and I lay that against his stomach. And sit between his legs. They are supposed to be armrests.

"There's a pillow there, though. There's a pillow. There. Look how thick the pillow is. Mom. You're gross!"

"Anna—" She struggles, looking really sad. "Good job, Peter. That wasn't information for her to know. Why you would ever tell her, I'll—."

"You said it, Janet."

"That doesn't mean *she* needs to know."

"STOP YELLING AT HIM. WE DIDN'T DO ANYTHING WRONG!"

Mom drifts into the other room and I wonder if she's crying too. If she lost Norman today. But I can't comfort her. I'll just sit here next to Dad, with my feet touching the ground, refusing to stop being near him but knowing I'll never be comfortable against his stomach again.

I just didn't know it was wrong.

Chapter Five

There was Kim from Scituate who was the most popular girl in our fifth-grade class and came over my house one time but never returned after Mom tried to heal her sprained ankle with energy work. We probably could have recovered but when Dad drove her home later, he put on a high voice and said he was born a woman before the surgery changed him—

"—into . . ."—he threw his voice to his lowest baritone note—"Anna's dad."

"He's kidding, he's kidding," I stammered. "My dad didn't have surgery. He was born a boy. Right, Dad. Right!?"

"Yeah . . ." he responded, purposely sounding like a liar.

And even though Kim and I were strapped next to each other in the back seat of my station wagon, facing the drivers behind us, it was like she was miles away already, no longer my friend. And I knew I'd never get her back and it wasn't worth trying.

But in this extra hot Northeastern summer, untethered from my parents, I found another Kim. Kim from New Hampshire, whose father was allegedly doing time in prison for something horrible and his daughter is now my bottom bunkmate at Camp Heyoka.

Prison-Kim has unusually short bangs, spackled to her forehead with gel, which could be cool in twenty years. But to us they just look mad and wet. She suffers from a full body rash, clustering under her armpits, tummy folds, and upper legs, all of which she's taken to scratching with her glitter hairbrush. There's also Tina from New Hampshire who wears wolf shirts, and a dark pony, low at the nape, forever wet like Kim's bangs, and listens to *Joseph and the Amazing Technicolor Dreamcoat* on repeat. Conny has thick black hair on her head but none on her arms because she does laser hair removal and *it's expensive but worth it.* There's Alyssa with the perfect braids, Shandy who is quiet, and of course V who is funny and smart and lives in Burlington, a reminder of the exiled home I still think about. I hope she likes me. V is for Veronica. V is for Vermont.

The top bunk sways a bit and I realize I fell asleep during midday siesta but all I remember is asking Spirit to keep my parents together while I'm gone and being wide awake.

"Anna. Anna." Shandy, Alyssa, Veronica, Tina, and Conny are on Kim's bed below me. I do not see Kim.

"Anna. You are the only one not on Kim's kill list."

"Huh?"

"Shhh. You're the only one not on Kim's kill list," and they hold up her diary. Instinctively I cover my eyes. Someone has stolen Kim's journal and I think it's wrong, but V tells me I have to look anyway because there's a list of campers Kim wants dead. This is alarming, so for safety reasons, I read it.

"It *is* a list . . . ," I say, looking closer, "but it's 'The people I hate,' not 'The people I'll kill.' "

"Oh my god," Conny snaps. "Easy for you to say. You're the only person from our cabin not on it, Anna." And it's true. Everyone's name is listed here except mine.

"SHHH," says Shandy. And we look around expecting to see Kim standing in the corner, listening. Thankfully, she's not. "Sorry, thought I heard something."

"Guys," I say, jumping back in. "Think about it. Isn't this what a journal's for? To vent?"

"Yeah, but none of us have like, a *hate* list," V answers.

"Well, no," I say, agreeing. "I mean, not that I can remember." Sometimes I wrote *I h8t Mom* after a bad fight but that was different.

"See?" says V, and I notice Tina is extra quiet too, probably adding Kim to her own rolling list.

"Hi, Kim!" Tina screams, and we all move like we weren't doing anything wrong even though we are and Veronica shoves that small book under my butt. This time it *is* Kim, and she's back from a shower, using her glitter brush to scratch more splotches.

"Uh. What?" Kim says without smiling.

"Nothing-ing-ing," three of us girls respond at the same time and try not to laugh because saying "nothing" in unison is awkward. Now everyone is nervous-laughing, except for Kim. To undercut the moment, Tina belts out,

"Go go go go, Joseph, you'll make it someday!" but this just makes us laugh harder.

Conny joins, "Ja-Ja-Ja-Joseph, don't be afraid—"

"Go go go Joseph—" Tina sings back, stepping on my trunk as her stage.

"You guys, stop," I yell. "You're gonna dent my trunk!" But no one's listening. "GUYS!" I say, standing up—

Something next to me falls and hits the ground. I freeze.

Pretending to ignore what fell, I keep talking. "Sorry to be like, bossy, you guys, but if my trunk dents, my mom will be wicked pissed." And this is true. "She just bought it on the—the—credit cards." But people aren't even looking at me now. Instead, they stare at Kim and down at their feet, because Kim has picked up her diary from the floor.

"Where did you get this?" she says staring at me. "Anna."

"Whoddyahavewhat," I respond and shake my head.

"Did you steal my diary, Anna?"

"No. I didn't steal it. Nope. Not me." And it wasn't me. I didn't even want to look in the first place, but it was a safety thing. What could I do.

"Yeah right," says Kim. "Then why did it fall from your . . . fucking asshole when you got up?" She's willing herself to be extra mean. We had been friendly.

The other campers bite their lips or look at their nails. I'm alone. "Well. I've been constipated, so it couldn't of been me, Kim."

"Couldn't of been me," Kim mocks, "Ibeeconsapatedleetlycdnt-binmekeem."

Most of the girls laugh and offer Kim their contraband candy. All I can think to give is a French braid but she doesn't want it and stops looking at me in the eye like she used to.

In the middle of the night, I wake to the sound of scratching. I know it's just something in my dream, but after an hour, I realize it's coming from below. "Kim," I whisper.

The scratching stops. Eventually I drift off.

Screeeaaccckkktcch.

Throwing my body over my top bunk now, I'm able to make out a blob, blacker than night, doubled over the bottom. "What are you doing? Kim? What are you doing?" And again, the scratching stops. "Are you okay? Can you go to bed? Sorry, I'm—I'm just trying to sleep . . . cuz it's night." Everything is still, finally, and no one responds. When the extra dark part of the night moves back onto their bunk, I lie back too, but like a sailor in a crow's nest, I sway from the tossing and turning below till morning comes.

The bugle wakes us up as it does every morning. I'm extra groggy but excited to start wind surfing lessons today. Others are already throwing on their sweatpants and sweatshirts as they slink out of their sleeping bags and brave the cold air of New Hampshire mornings. Someone makes a joke and a few people laugh. The drama of yesterday's life-or-death concerns has dissipated somewhat. I climb down the wooden ladder and see my trunk. The top is covered in deep scratches, like it was keyed over and over, and the cardboard under the pleather shows through.

I'd thought it was real leather and it's not.

Regardless, it's ruined.

My parents will be very pissed.

Kim is still asleep below me. "Sleeping." I stare at her in a way that she should be able to feel, because she's probably pretending to sleep until I leave. And then she'll burn my trunk with contraband.

Outside the cabin, V and I hug, intense and scared.

"What do I do? Tell the counselor?"

"Tell on her? Are you sure? That like, seems dangerous. What's she capable of, ya know?"

Later, Tina grabs Kim's journal a second time and sees that I'd been added to the list of people she hates. After lunch V suggests we play a game of truth or dare.

This makes me nervous.

"Dare," Kim states, unafraid.

Conny inhales. "Take your shirt off and run around camp."

"No, that's—no. Truth. Truth."

Conny doesn't miss a beat. "Kim. Did your dad kill someone?"

Oh god.

It seems like forever before Kim responds. "He's in prison, but you guys already know that. I told Alyssa on like, day two and I'm sure she told everyone else." And Alyssa had.

Kim goes on, "Obviously. Why wouldn't you? You're all the same. So, I pick a different truth."

She has evaded a dare but offers a second truth telling. Impressive.

Wolf-girl takes over. "Okay." And steals tiny glances around her, gaining confidence, "But you have to answer, Kim, because you skipped a dare and that equals two truths." That's a new rule I've never heard.

"So, like, have you ever thought of killing someone? Be honest."

Pause.

"You have to answer," Conny adds, but Kim lets the silence hang in the air and my stomach crawls to my throat, landing only when Kim does.

"Yes."

Tina hides a swallow but doesn't stutter. "Anyone here?"

"No more questions," Kim says. "Anna, truth or dare." But my mouth won't close.

Tina responds like a lawyer, "Kim did do two truths but one we already knew, like you said. One more. Like, anyone here?"

"Yes, all of you," Kim says fast. Some of us are terrified. "Gawwwd." She adds, "Kidding." I watch her. Kim has the face of a kid who doesn't like us, sure, but doesn't look sinister either. Or maybe I'm telling myself this because we share a bedframe.

Conny jumps in, "Tina's question was a joke too. Her real truth is, did you scratch Anna's trunk? Or no? Whatever you say, we'll believe you."

"Uh? No?" I watch her again. Kim has more to say, "Nope, I was scratching something else. Is what the sound was." Kim bites her lip and bends her toes up and down.

If anything, her skin splotches look better, not worse. Guilty.

"It's rude to stare," Kim says only to me.

"Sorry," I say, and maybe this makes her look away, but she's only gathering her thoughts. "I know you think I did it, Anna, and I'm like, I *am* sorry your trunk is, um, messed up and that sucks but it must have been an animal or something. Because I didn't do it."

"An animal?" I hear myself saying.

"A raccoon or something," Kim adds, brave.

"Okay . . ." My eyebrows shoot together. "I kind of like, saw you, Kim. It's okay, but—"

"I swear to God I didn't! You saw me? That's not possible."

"Well, I saw a shadow lean over my trunk and then heard scratching and then the shadow went back onto your bunk after I said 'Kim.' "

"Ohhh," she says, remembering something far away.

"Yeah, you remember now?" and I try to sound soft. "It's okay, I just like want the truth."

"Yeah, I remembered I was scratching my rash. Which is private."

Now I'm pissed and talk quickly and low. "You mean my trunk? Which was supposed to be private, as in like, not for messing with?"

"No, I meant my rash."

"You swear?"

"On my dad's life." For a moment, the gravity of her promise knocks the wind out of me. But I spot the hole. “Isn’t he serving a life sentence, though?”

“Anna—” Conny warns, looking afraid.

“I don’t mean it like, mean, though.”

Kim snorts, “Right.” Her eyes are watering.

“No! Sorry.” I keep going, trying to tread lightly now. “It’s just if you are promising on someone’s life who already has had it taken away, maybe it’s better, or would be easier to believe if you did that on someone else’s life who is like, free? Who has one. Outside jail.”

“Prison.” Kim’s eyes well.

I crossed a line. What was I supposed to do, though? Not point out the obvious and let her be bitch-bag and ruin the stuff my parents got me when they were already tearing apart? I didn’t want to think about any of that, but this damaged trunk will cause an issue for sure. Except when I look at Kim, she seems very sad and I wish I could take it all back. “No, I believe you. I’m sorry, Kim. I’m sorry I said that.”

“K.” She whimpers and then swallows, talking to herself, “I thought it would be different here, than it is at like, school. I thought I could have like, friends at camp. But who cares.”

Eventually, Wolf-girl says people make fun of her at school too. Conny agrees. All of us do, except V. I knew she was popular.

“People call me a goody-two-shoes for telling people not to swear,” I admit.

“I’ve heard you swear like, twice at camp.”

“But I’m different here. I’m a dork at home.” They all nod, getting it. Feeling partially naked anyway, I go ahead and undress my soul, explaining how the mere *idea* of having a crush on me is used between guys at school as an insult, about my parents fighting and how it’s getting worse and that my trunk was bought on credit and Dad’s already mad because she spends all his money but still I know Kim definitely didn't scratch it and it was probably a raccoon or something. Plus, it's hard to sleep at night, no matter where I am.

At home, I'd stay up late, studying their old wedding albums to find out exactly who they were back when they weren't so hard on each other. Maybe I would eventually introduce them anew and they'd remember all the good. It would be my Hail Mary.

Tina says sorry but also reminds us that Kim's dad is in prison and how that's probably a lot harder than what I'm going through. And Tina's parents are already divorced so she's right. Of course she is right. But Alyssa helps me, pointing out that one person's pain doesn't cancel out the other's and tell us her mom only cares about her stepdad, and I wonder if that's how Jamie feels.

Finally, Kim wants to share. "To answer your question before . . . my dad didn't kill anyone. I lied. But he tried." Silence. "I don't like talking about it. And also, I don't really like, talk to him." And then she checks our eyes. So I do it with her. Most of us look scared. For some reason, this makes me teary. But Kim's crying has stopped, so Conny calls me a word I would hear, and hate, for the rest of my life.

"Anna, you're like, so sensitive."

Even though I want to be able to wall up and look strong, my emotional dam breaks and now I'm sobbing. *Great.*

Kim hugs me. "I'm sorry an animal did that to your trunk, Anna."

"It's fine, Kim. It's fine," I whimper. "I'm sorry I blamed you."

"Um, I'm the one who took your journal, Kim," Veronica suddenly admits. "And it was wrong. I was scared you hated me. Maybe because I'm popular at home so people not liking me, is like, not what I'm used to?"

"That's okay," Kim says. "Thanks for telling me," like she's maybe surprised or happy, not used to a popular person apologizing.

Conny asks, "Kim, do you think it's possible, like with the lists and stuff, that you are hard on people because your father was supposed to be there for the pure fact that he's your father but he isn't?"

I picture my dad, who is usually there. Unless he's sleeping somewhere in his car. Or at a casino. Or a work conference. But when he is there, he is so there. Conny keeps going, "So it's like, who can you trust if not your own dad?" She takes a deep breath. "It's like embarrassing, but after my laser treatments I see a therapist, and she said that's why I am hard on people, because I don't know my dad, like at all. And my stepdad is a dickwad." Someone laughs and Conny giggles at herself too. "He is. But maybe my real dad is great. Or maybe he's in jail too, who knows."

"Prison." Kim says again. "But yeah, maybe you're right. Why I'm hard on people. Maybe, who knows." And she shrugs.

Veronica offers to talk to her uncle who is a tax lawyer about getting Kim and Conny's fathers out of prison for good behavior. Alyssa mentions how her grandfather is a retired judge and says that he would help if he could, but he won't, because he recently passed. Shandy leads the condolences. But everyone's intention is just so nice, and I think how sharing brings people together. We finish our circle with a hug. And either I'll teach my parents this or live here forever, with the girls.

That evening, the mail arrives. I get a postcard with the Boston skyline and a single rooster stamp. Next to that is a little hand-drawn man with a huge nose and big feet, and a heart on his shirt. It's the cartoon guy Dad always draws. It reads:

Dear Pumpkin, we are at a hotel in Boston for the weekend! Can you believe it? Sorry it hasn't been the easiest at home but happy to tell you we feel in love again. Dad quit smoking. Proud of him! Not much room to write but haiku4u: Camp is there for play / Let woods take stress away but / home will always stay. love, Mom & Dad PS Keep your eyes peeled for Nasturtiums and Marigolds—it's July so they are in bloom.

Even though it's Mom's barely legible handwriting, they each sign "Mom" and "Dad" respectively, like a promise. I wonder how they got their act together. And then it hits me: I'm not there. I'm the problem. Probably, scientifically.

On the final day of camp, Kim and I are the last ones to be picked up. We spot cars coming straight for us so I tell her that even if she hated me for a moment, I can relate to that feeling and if it means she hated my trunk for a sec too, that's okay. Kim hugs me. I say, "You're awesome and I'm sorry your dad's not around enough. He's missing out." Now we are squeezing each other tight. "I still love him," she says.

"That's okay. I would probably still love my dad too." I pet her French braid and think about how strong Kim has to be and how I really am so sensitive.

"Thank you, Anna," Kim says, and then adds, like she feels really bad, "And I hope you can fix your parents."

"I'll try."

But when I get home, for the first time in my life, there's not much I have to do to make things good, except stay out of the way.

Chapter Six

Poke.

Mom waves the long, lit candlestick toward Dad's eye like a mistake.

"Watch out for my good eye, Janet."

She moves it back and forth, teasing him with a flaming baton.

"Janet!" he says again, sounding in love.

"Peter. It's like nine feet away. How is this even bothering you?" She giggles.

"Not nine. The table's six feet total, Janet." He says her name a lot lately, but differently, like he likes it.

"Okay, six feet away, whatever," she barks, laughing again.

"Well," Dad adds, "doesn't matter how far away when you're threatening me with . . . fire! Of course I'm going to flinch!" He's yelling, and both eyes, even the blind one, sparkle.

"Why are you blind, again, Dad?" I'm twelve, he's told me a million times. But he says it like he hasn't: "Born with severe strabismus. I think my dad was afraid he got a retard, not a football player—"

"PETER!"

"—and I got a bunch of surgeries to correct it. The last one worked when I was maybe eleven in that I looked more normal but took my vision. Who needs two eyes. One is enough. Two, overkill."

Mom puts blankness in her face like their game of poker is long over but stabs at him again with a flourish and a pigeon-like laugh. He ducks, yelping "Not my good eye!" and finishes with a sadistic chuckle, too.

Got him. Nice.

My turn. "Dad, try not to move. See if you can be a statue. Seriously! Don't look scared. My turn," and I hold the candle for a moment, fascinated by the experiment and move it toward him, inch by inch. I'm about to brand his pupil. He twitches hard. I burst out laughing.

Usually I would do this again, but I try to talk a little less these days when I remember to. So they have more space to keep getting along.

"Janet, do it again and I won't flinch this time." And with his calloused fingers, Dad holds open his eyes like an owl. "Go."

"Mom, go."

"No, you go, Anna." But this is a trick. At the same time, she moves the candle toward him and he involuntarily shuts both eyes so hard they could kill flies.

We all burst out laughing.

"Oh, this is Rachmaninoff, the final piece in his opus, um, thirty-fourth collection, no?" —she's talking to herself, discussing the music coming from the wooden speakers. I want to keep playing but Dad listens and responds.

"How do you know so many composers, Janet?" he asks, appreciating her. She smiles.

Moe slinks around our legs and jumps onto his lap, settling.

On the ground by our feet is what looks like a pile of ground meat.

I jump up, breathless. "What? What?!" Dad looks. "Mouse intestines."

"EWWW."

Oddly, Mom looks relaxed, inspecting it. "Too large. Maybe rabbit."

"That's disgusting," I say. "So sad."

Dad explains that actually it's an act of love.

"It means he loves us. We love you too, buddy." Mom agrees but suggests closing up the cat door to the backyard so he doesn't bring in dead animals.

"Love you," I say quietly to Moe, grossed out.

Drips of wax scatter the tablecloth. Napkins used to goad flames are slumped all over the floor. I take in our fun.

Mom says she'll put a bell on the cat's collar as a warning for the critters. "Give 'em a fighting chance, at least." A sad idea that animals would die by Moe's claws, but it wasn't him being mean. It was him being.

"Yup. That's life," Mom says, reading the questions in my mind. Dad nods too.

At the end of dinner, my parents kiss, and for the next nine months, the bell doesn't slow Moe down. He leaves gift after gift.

Seventh grade is starting and I kind of have boobs. I've been dancing naked in my full-length mirror on occasion. I'm on all fours, arching my back like a cat, and then I go in the other direction, letting my stomach hang low like a pregnant teen, then sucking it in deep and hard so every rib shows, and suddenly I'm less cat, more woman. Sometimes I can't tell which is realer.

Mom yells up to tell me that the bus will be here in five minutes but I hear it more like "Come out with your hands up, freak," and throw on my pale yellow hoodie and knockoff Adidas snap pants like I was never naked, not even when I was born, and head to seventh grade.

With my parents getting along, I've had more time to think about me. And since my absence seemingly made them grow closer, I have tried to become more absent. Which is fine, I'm focused on friends. Since camp, I've had a better idea of what outcasts do to remain outcasts and I'd vowed to avoid all that this year. I'm learning how to quiet the unaware girl in me, the weirdo inside. I stopped raising my hand all the time in class. I stopped telling people they weren't supposed to swear. I want to be popular, or at least not a target. I spent all my babysitting money on one Limited Too pink boatneck shirt. And the Rave has cheap acrylic fabrics in Abercrombie cuts, which provides enough variety in my wardrobe that no one suspects we live paycheck to paycheck. I still play the French horn in band, but now I know to make fun of myself for it, especially when it catches the back of a bus bench and throws me to the floor. When that happens, I do a fake trip again, like I'm an idiot. The people who used to laugh at my expense laugh with me and suddenly everything's better than elementary school.

My parents seem to like each other.

There's less to worry about.

One could even say I was liked.

But not by Charlie.

Never by Charlie.

Charles was one of the three Whitman brothers. Three white boys, always in polos, bright blond hair, extra thick from the extra salty air that blew into their bedroom windows from the brackish marsh behind their house. Perfect smiles. Charlie was mine, though he didn't know that. If I could get just a little more popular, maybe it would be official. In the low moments of our relationship that he didn't know he was in, I wondered if I liked him just because of his family's country club prestige, or his father's cranberry bogs, or because he made fun of me a lot.

Burn me with a candle.

I like when he wears his faded black Nike hat with frayed edges that look unintentional, even though I watched him scrape it on a sidewalk to get it to look that way. And how he always works the edges of the brim, like he's sculpting the perfect bill for a daddy duck. How he adjusts it in every class to make sure it's just so, as though it's moved, terribly. The way he says my name when he passes me in the hall like it means something bad. How he has trouble reading, and if we actually had a chance together, I could be patient and give him a leg up in English. I love him because instead of just ignoring me entirely he's a little mean. That's how they do it in the movies too.

I'd tried kissing once, but the feeling of two tongues looping around each other doesn't work for me. The thing itself was too salty, too warm, too sweet. And wet. Like a dog. I couldn't believe it was supposed to go inside nailing my uvula like an addict at a slot machine. I cried afterward. It had been several months since then, and I would never kiss another boy.

Unless it was Charlie.

If Charlie pushed me in the hall, I'd walk by him extra times. He couldn't fully deny there was something between us. But he would try. After all, he asked me to dance at the dance that one time. Our sweaty clothes touching. His hand on my lower back. He cupped both of my butt cheeks for a full moment while we swayed to Boyz II Men. And I rested my face-cheek on his shoulder and he never moved it away. After that, I'd started wearing his black hat around school for an entire four days because I stole it off his head and he didn't ask for it back ever. Only until he needed it for golf club. But he let me wear his sweatshirt in science always. Only until he needed it back for the summer. Which would have been understandable except summers are hot.

Now it's English and Charlie isn't here but he's on my mind again. He always is. So much so, even though it's the dead of winter, my armpits sweat through my acrylic top. Unable to concentrate, I sign out to the bathroom but meander the tiled floor of the brick middle school, taking the long way.

Charlie is walking toward me.

I look down. Fate.

"Anna?" He says with less disgust than usual. I don't know if that's good or bad though.

My eyeballs dart up like fish on hooks.

"Charlie?" using the same intonation he used on my name. This is me mocking him and it's hot, wicked hot.

"What are you doing?" He stops next to me. I stop walking too. I don't know where to put my hands. I land one slightly behind my right hip so my boob is pointed his direction and with my free hand I pinch his arm, but not too hard.

"Ow. What the f—"

"Oops. Sorry. It slipped. I'm going to, like, the bathroom," I say. "Not right now, but, ha."

I think maybe he looked down at my triple A breasts? I hide the sweat rings edging my shoulders and I don't stop talking. "Where are you going? Up my butt and around the corner?" This is funny.

"Ew, what?"

"It's a joke people say. Like, don't be gross. Where are you going, seriously?" Ending the sentence high and dumb.

He makes a weird joke back, "Not there. I'm not into that?"

I'm loving this, laughing. We are talking about my butt. "Ew, what?"

"Ha-ha. I'm going to the bathroom too," he says. He laughed, finally. Got him.

"Oh, cool. That's like, weird. Twins!" I go for a high five while crossing my eyes and do a lisp on the word "twins."

"You're so weird," he says, not high-fiving me back and I know I've gone too far so I laugh pretty and small, like Allison or Kim. I put my hair behind my ear and remind myself to rein it in.

"Can I have my hat back now?" he says.

"No," I say, worried but still trying to sound confident. "Do you want your hat for real or not for real?"

"What?"

I can't tell if he's flirting. "Oh, look. It's your best friend," he says, looking her way.

I turn around and, "Oh my GOD!" It's my new, effortless best friend, Courtney McGowan.

"COURT!" I hug her like we haven't seen each other in years instead of science class forty minutes ago.

She gives me eyes like, *Oh my god, you're walking with Charlie.*

I give her eyes back like, *Oh my god, you're walking with Graham* and wag my eyebrows, to be funny. Court pushes me playfully. Graham winks back at me like I got it right. Court's boyfriend is one year older than us but is repeating seventh grade. He is almost six feet already with a forced mustache. In my mind I call the hairs his trophies.

"'Sup Grah?" I say, extra girlie sounding.

In one upward motion of his chin, he nods, and it means "Hello" back.

"Hi, Court," Charlie says in a high voice to sound like a girl.

"You're so weird," says Court, laughing, and then kindly adds, "Hi, Charles."

She's so perfect at finding the balance between really nice and smart. And sweet but not desperate. It's impressive every time.

I trip on my fake Adidas shell-toes.

"Woah, skills," Charlie says in a voice more like Santa Claus than his own. Graham claps twice. So I punch Charlie in the arm.

"That didn't hurt," he says fast. So I do it harder, giggling too much.

And then Charlie says to Graham, "You know Court and I were together?"

"In fifth grade!" Courtney adds, rolling her eyes.

Charlie pokes her with his finger, "You broke up with *me*. I was heartbroken, Courtney."

I'd never—I've never—seen him speak so openly. My mouth falls despite myself.

Graham adds, "Couldn't get it up? Poor little Charlie-boy."

"EW—" Court laughs, pushing Graham, still laughing and adds, "You're nasty. Fifth grade!? Hello???"

"Oh my god!" I yell, feeling totally forgotten about. I roll my eyes and giggle, playing along, but I'm thinking about how Charlie looks at Courtney. How every guy looks at her that way. Somehow she doesn't take advantage of it.

Kindly, Court moves the spotlight. "I bet Charlie can get it up when Anna's around."

"Court!" I try to say, chiding, as if I'm not thrilled.

"Yeah!" Charlie says, intentionally sounding like a different person and gives me a thumbs-up but proceeds to shoot it down toward the ground, like a fallen rocket, simultaneously blowing a raspberry and punctuating it all with a Jim Carreyesque "Not!"

It's harsh. No one can say that it's not. Graham says as much: "Harsh."

Charlie shrugs.

"Good," I manage. "I don't get it up for you too."

"Oh shiz!" Charlie yells. "I knew you had a dick!" And with this final expression of grossed-outness, he walks off.

I watch my guy leave, trying to turn off my love for him, but when he looks back with something just below a smile, my brain tells my belly and my chest not to give up. Maybe it could still be me.

I walk on arm in arm with Court. She senses my shift and whispers if I'm okay. It's so nice not being alone after something shitty happens. Before I can answer, Court intuitively asks something else.

"How are your parents? Any better?" I'd called her after a big fight the other night. They'd been ramping up again for some reason.

"Not really," I say, "but in a couple weeks I'm sure they'll bounce out of it again. That's their thing."

"Ohhh hon," she says, and hugs me. I take it. And then Graham asks if we can have a threesome. Court and I emphatically say no and I make faces like *Gross* and *You're so crazy.* But I'm happy to be thought of. I drop them off at their make-out area and head back to English.

Like a whip of wind, I'm hit with a weird-sounding "Anna." An older girl looks at me and I act like we are best friends because she seems mad at me.

"Trina! What's up?" I make small talk: "How's, um, your bus driver doing?"

"Fine. I have to ask you, like, a question."

"Shoot . . . of course. What's up?" I already said that. My stomach flips over and I know I've done something wrong.

"I heard you put an ice cube in your, you know."

What?

"No, I didn't. Wait. An ice cube? In my . . ."

"Pussy."

"Why would I do that?"

"I don't know. You tell me." It was the Vermont computer lab all over again. "Did you or did you not masturbate with an ice cube, because that's what I heard."

"No. I definitely didn't. Who said that?"

"I can't say, but I know you did. They wouldn't lie about that."

The bell rings, which means I've been gone from English for at least twenty-two minutes. I'll tell the nurse my period got all over my underwear, even though I haven't gotten it yet, but she'll write a note to Mrs. Bell, explaining.

On the way, it feels like each of my peers is looking at me longer than usual. I tell myself it's all in my head. On my hand I see the remnants of pen marks, a tally of how many guys looked at my chest when they passed by me this morning. I lick my thumb and rub until skin and ink mix together to look like a birthmark rather than the scorecard of a pervert.

I round the corner and Charlie, Sean, Tommy, and Harris are all standing together, looking at me.

"What?" I ask. They didn't usually look at me all at once. This was reserved for Kim Lake or Katie Winsome with C boobs and big lips and who both talk like they're seventeen.

"Icebox," Harris says without reacting.

Charlie bites the inside of his lip so as not to laugh.

"Your box being your pussy and ice cuz you masturbate with it."

"That is a lie and that never happened," I say, too quickly, too passionately, like an admission.

"So why are you so angry?" Sean says with all the power and nothing to prove.

Without thinking I answer, "Because I'm not a slut."

"Slut," one of them says anyway and they all laugh and it hurts. Some of them look at me like they think I'm hotter than I was this morning. Before, I'd wanted these looks. Now I wish I didn't care about boys at all.

Green, yellow, purple, blue.

Green, yellow, purple, blue.

All the colors I could find in the seventies tile of the bathroom floors. If I keep repeating it, I won't cry until the toilet flushes again.

It had been a dumb thing and it was supposed to be funny. When I'd eventually weaned off the Amys, I'd discovered that just beyond, in a clearing in the woods, was a big-ass house with two sets of triplets and one older sister who led them around, named Theresa. I'd escape to this house of fun on most afternoons and Theresa, who was a year older, became my best friend for a year or two. She had been in fourth grade when we met, and I was in third. It was a loopy household where someone was always running around naked, or screaming at each other after playing Mortal Kombat for twelve hours or coming home from Catholic mass to gummy bears and wrestling. But when Theresa hit puberty, she looked more like my babysitter than my friend. Once, in a bind, my mom hired her to babysit and Theresa actually told me to go to bed. That's when I knew we were over, but fortunately I found footing in a friendship with her younger sister, Jess. It was then, in a session of fifth grade truth or dare, where I was either too desperate or too comfortable, that I allowed myself to dare the oddest of the triplets to put an ice cube in her underpants. And when she said, "Absolutely not," like I was the biggest weirdo she ever met, to prove *It's not a big deal,* I went to the bathroom and put the cube in my own pants.

It wasn't sexual! It was funny! Wasn't it? Or I was deeply messed up.

Either way, another sexual embarrassment racked up even though I don't even like a tongue in my mouth, but the world believes I'm masturbating, and like doing it cold. Instead of authentic indignance at the accusation, I feel like a liar, like I have a shameful secret and unfortunately someone has come up with a catchy name for it.

"Icebox. 'Bye!"

And my nickname is too brilliant to ever go away.

The bus makes a big deflating sound and drops me off at the bottom of our driveway, which is also the bus turnaround. After I get off, the huge thing twirls, big and yellow, and I prepare myself for it to topple, even though it hasn't yet.

Because it's after school on Wednesday, Dad should be at work, but his car is in the driveway. Since Mom started her own business out of the converted garage doing reiki as a second income, I must be extra quiet. She's usually done by the time Dad gets home, so I hope he didn't clomp all over the house and disturb her. Quietly closing the front door, I peek my head around the corner of each downstairs room and whisper "Dad," knowing how sound travels in our 1900s cape.

A woman's voice responds from upstairs, "Anna."

"Shhh," I say.

"It's Mom. We're upstairs. You don't have to whisper."

"Where's Dad?"

"Hi, sweetie! Come on up." Home from work early.

"You comin'?" Mom sings. They both sound chipper. Unnaturally so.

Everything slows. Tiny golden balls of carpet sit beneath the hundred-year-old dining table that belonged to the great-great-grandparents on my father's side, and the teacups, rarely used, from my mother's nana are in the glass cabinet. Lines of real gold shine too humbly from inside. To me, the different sets from various lineage match perfectly, like they belong together.

Taking my shoes off, I walk up the stairs.

Their bedroom door is closed, so I knock.

There's a delay before Dad says, "Come on in!" like I'm a neighbor.

I push it open.

Afternoon light shines against peeling window frames, bringing in different hues of yellow, not matching anything else in the house. They sit on the edge of their queen bed, facing me like they've been waiting here forever. And their faces glow like the stained glass in our church. It is unusually angelic, or maybe I'm just never in here when it's beautiful.

"What's up?" I say with a smile and wag my eyebrows just to make someone laugh.

"We want to talk to you, sweetie."

Dad looks down, with a little smile. "We need to talk to you."

Memories move toward us like synchronized swimmers and I'm not sure why but the ghosts have been called in. They sit, summoned but invisible, waiting to be recalled or redacted. I'm sitting on the carpet. Waiting. My mom nods, small. Her lips part by one tenth of an inch but quickly close and she nods like she might speak, but just her tongue moves against the inside of her lips. Breath whistles out one nostril. She'd had a cold yesterday. Dad keeps smiling but looks up and down, touching his hands, studying each finger, knuckles large and strong—hands I know better than my own with his otherworldly calluses from woodwork and gardening and rebuilding our deck. He brushes his gold wedding ring and touches his nail.

Mom parts her lips again, and I ask her to stop doing that, so that she'll say something instead.

"I know, you know, it's been hard . . . in our home. And Dad and I fight a lot."

"Yeah. But it was better—" but I stop myself, shaking my head for her to go on, knowing their happy time ended over a year ago, "Never mind."

She ignores whatever that was and looks for Dad's complicity. "We've had good times but a lot more hard, it's been hard, right, Anna? Peter?"

He gives it to her, nodding back emotionless. I force Dad to make eye contact with me and he quickly smiles but looks down again, only down.

"And so. Yeah!" She builds herself up. "Daddy and I are going to. I'm so sorry—" she gets caught in her words or her throat or maybe I'm already crying and she's comforting me.

"I'm sorry. You know what I'm going to say? Your father and I are not working together." She keeps at it but speaks quicker, like she's afraid stopping means she'll never finish and I imagine a different ending that goes this way, like, "Daddy and I are going to—have another baby like you always wanted us to" or "sell the house and get a smaller one that's not as stressful" or "start a new system for the grocery list because that's what we started fighting over again."

"We are getting divorced," she finishes, but I already knew what was coming. "It's time we separate."

"Mhm," I say, nodding. "It was probably only a matter of time. Because—yeah—there was like, so much that you like, don't see eye to eye on. And you aren't um, like, bringing out the best in each other so much? Ya know?"

Mom looks at me like my brain is melting.

"What?" I say, defensive. "What!"

"No, I'm just listening to you, Anna."

"Sorry, I'm gathering my thoughts." My cheeks feel red but I want to respond here, finally, to the thing that's just arrived, the thing that's been threatening to come since before I could remember. "Like, um, you said a divorce and a separation. So you could live apart and then get back together like the Donahues?" They were the closest I knew to divorced people, and after a year apart, they'd gotten back together.

Dad looks up, fast, nodding his chin once. "Yeah—"

"No," my mom cuts through, certain.

My father's face moves, responding to an invisible flick from her, straight to his cheek.

"It's a divorce," she finishes.

Dad looks down, pretending never to have started answering the other way. For the rest of the conversation, he goes to sleep with his eyes open. Part of me worries what if he never wakes up.

By the end of the conversation, I can't help it, I imagine us all dead.

It's not the first time I've done this. In my mind they are in their midforties and I'm eight instead of thirteen. Amid white light, we hold hands and wisps of something or other move around us energetically. We look out over the light that holds us, out to something else, and it's indescribably easy to feel peaceful and deeply, maturely happy. Like we were all born together and are dying together. Like we are one thing, not three. Like we have passed through intact, bruised and almost broken, but intact.

This is how it should be.

Chapter Seven

"Fifteen minutes, Angel," he calls up the stairs that he hasn't walked in months.

I yell back "Okay, Dad!" but I'm basically packed anyway.

The only vacations we'd gone on before this were camping in Vermont and swimming in the free communal pool among the old people in Grammy and Grampy's retirement home. I slept on the sunporch on their blow-up mattress, roasting like a pig in Florida heat. Peeling myself off rubber, we'd head to the pool with all the wrinkle-people, Grampy already up and out for hours, his skin red like raspberry fruit leather, his tall nose shining in the sun, and he'd smile big when he saw I was up. In those moments I thought maybe he loved me more than lukewarm. Everything with him was simple. I can't think of many other blood relatives I'd ever felt this way about.

So last week, when I received his letter, I felt special. Six months had passed since the divorce announcement. By that point, everyone knew and it felt good to not have to keep it a secret anymore. But it also meant anyone could talk to me about it now. Or write a letter. Grammy died when I was in third grade, and Grampy took over sending the birthday cards from their local mart that said things like "Happy Birthday, Pal" or "Let's Seal-ebrate!" with a cartoon seal balancing a ball on its nose, signed only "Grampy." This year's card had a big 14 on the front and he didn't sign it at all, but it was more than enough.

Months later, I received a letter-sized envelope in the mail and relished in the idea of not just a card, but full pages of cursive from him to me.

"Dear Annam."

He added an *m*. Okay, fine. It continued, "Your mother shared with me the thoughtful (though I imagine difficult) decision from your parents to divorce."

So, he knew. And he figured it would be hard for me. Thank you. It is.

"I do believe it is for the best."

Not sure where he's going with this.

"The way your father spoke to your mother always upset me. Their relationship was never the right kind of relationship, which I'm afraid you learned was love. As you may imagine, that is not what I envisioned for Janet or any of my daughters. I was married to your grandmother for 35 beautiful years and we were in real love. You may have noticed how I never took off our wedding ring, even after her passing, and that's because I shared a promise with your grandmother when we married. For me, being with someone else after her wasn't ever in question. What I saw between your parents didn't fit the bill."

Well, he's a bitch, I'd thought as soon as I had read it.

I'd thought he was my favorite relative, but I didn't actually know most of my relatives. After eyeing his inky cursive flowing down to the end, I noted how authoritative it appeared and logged it as poison. *You don't even know my dad, Grampy. Not like I do. Step off.*

"ANNA. Time to go, sweetie." It's Dad. Oh god. Just thinking about Grampy's letter makes me feel guilty.

"DAD! Coming!"

I open my bedroom door at the exact time my mom opens hers directly across from mine, and we make a motion with our heads like we are banging them together, two of the Three Stooges midgag. But it's not a performance. We're just in our own worlds. Her eyes go to the duffel I'm holding.

"Hi, Mom!" I say, pitched up.

She manages a smile. "Hi. You ready?" I nod back but look at my duffel too.

"Angel!" he yells again from downstairs.

"I'm coming, Dad!" and throw a tone like *You're being too much, stop!* Mostly because Dad is calling me Angel, which feels like a slap in the face to my mom, who is already being stoic about our daddy-daughter trip. By the back door, snow piled up to the windows, my dad stands next to a rolling suitcase and holds a little backpack. Convenient for him that the back door is right next to his new living quarters.

For the first six months, we pretended that literally splitting the house in half was normal. And in some ways, it felt like a more honest, normal arrangement. Instead of hiding sheets in the living room closet (for any given night or week or month that he could end up there), Dad's bedding is permanently on a mattress in a downstairs bedroom and it never comes off, except to be washed, which no one argues about anymore because we all know to wash our own stuff.

In the beginning, Dad slept upstairs in Mom's room sometimes, which was thrilling, dizzying, a little gross. But those nights gave me hope. Though eventually it stopped and they quietly feigned normalcy, pretending the other wasn't there while filling dinner pots from the same faucet for separate meals.

Mom and I have the upstairs bedrooms and bathroom and Dad never visits anymore. Moe traverses the whole expanse of the house but mostly sleeps with Dad. The living room and dining room, holding most of their ancestors' prized possessions like porcelain plates and antique chests, are in spaces that are technically shared but rarely used.

"K, Janet, we're going to head out."

"Mom. We're going to miss you."

I'm impressed that she's not crying. "I'll miss you, but you're going to have a great time. Caribbean cruise!" Her new antidepressants, working.

My stomach drops, knowing how fundamentally off this feels.

Then she says it, finally: "Our vacations were camping or Grammy and Grampy's." There it is. And she finishes, "But I'm still happy for you guys."

He doesn't say anything, so I do. "I know, right? Mattress on the sunporch," and I chuckle. She chuckles back. "Well, you'll get a little time for yourself, Mom. Without your annoying daughter," and I squish my face like an ugly baby.

"Enjoy it, you two."

His eyes light up for a second, maybe because he's included in her affectionate tone.

"Thanks, Janet." He hugs her. It lasts longer than she would like. I hug them too, as a joke.

"I kid, I kid."

And then, alone, I give her a long hug. It's bizarre she won't be with us, but at the same time, I can't imagine Mom lying on a recliner beside the pool, drinking rum punches and gambling with Dad at the casino. Instead she might announce her repulsion at the bass of the music, finding the only circular window with a calm atmosphere (our cabin), spotting a whale, tears flowing over its magnificence, before learning it's a reef.

No, a Carnival cruise wasn't her vibe. No one could say otherwise.

Still, it didn't feel right leaving her for the Bahamas in the middle of winter.

Moe finds us walking down the brick steps outside and slinks between our legs, almost tripping Dad.

"Dammit! Okay, buddy," as he picks up Moe and kisses him. And then I nuzzle Moe goodbye too. We climb into the new-used car, the Sebring convertible, black exterior, tan-real-leather interior, and we keep the top down because it's not actively snowing but blast the heat. He reverses from the house and my mom's thirteen-year-old Corolla moves out of my line of sight.

"Dad." My stomach flips. "How come, like, you can afford a new car and now this vacation? Because Mom never got that." The smallest muscles in his cheek harden so I try a different way. "Not in a like, bad sense of it. I know you have like, a good reason. Just wondering."

There's some silence and then, "I got a bonus this year. Not every year do I get one."

"Oh, can I ask how much?"

"Twenty K." His working eye shimmers and he continues, "I share money information with you, Anna, to help you in the future, but that's not for anyone else to know. Including your mother. We are no longer together, remember? We just live in the same house." This makes sense to me. "And I believe I made a responsible decision. The majority of my bonus will go into savings—but I'm using some for us to have fun."

"Got it."

"Good. So." And that's supposed to be the end of it.

"But Dad, it just seems unfair that we're going away and she's not. And her car sucks. It's like the oldest one when she picks me up at school."

"You just said that. You wanna talk unfair, Anna? Ha." But he doesn't finish the thought and goes back to the car. "Japanese vehicles last forever. She has reaped many a financial benefit from being married to me, Anna. And sharing finances."

"Right. Like you have from her."

"Ha."

"What?"

"I had a house that I owned when I met her. She didn't."

"Oh, right. How'd you buy that, again?"

"Savings and inheritance."

Blurred wood-shingled houses, red doors on Cape Cods, and white and green evergreens whip across my vision. Staring at the racing oblong shapes and trying to see them clearly is like a soft rub of my back before sleep. Van Morrison shouts from the powerful speakers, way more powerful than the ones in his old Ford station wagon. This is a bit of a midlife crisis move. I figure I'll just say it. I'm not a kid anymore, I can say these things.

"Your car, though I like it, does resemble like, a midlife crisis."

"You asked me to get this one!"

"I thought a convertible would be cool! But you brought it up. I hope Mom's going to be okay while we are gone."

Silence.

"Can we stop talking about your mother?"

"Fine. I just feel bad."

Silence.

"She wanted this. I didn't." He doesn't say this in a vindictive way but almost like he's working through the idea himself. And I feel guilty because I love the new car and the vacation. As a family we barely went out to eat, so driving to the airport in a convertible to then fly to Florida and get on a big-ass boat that takes us to different places where we'll eat meals that we don't have to make is somewhat inconceivable. And very wonderful. Plus, when I go back to school, I'll be hot because I'll have a little tan, whereas others will be as unhealthy-looking as when I left. The trip has the potential to give me a real step up.

"When do you hear back from the judge?" I hear myself say, knowing if I sound like an adult, he'll answer like one.

"Could be a year—or we could arrive home to a letter from the judge next week."

"REALLY? A like, a year? What do most people do? I haven't heard of people who are divorcing splitting the house like we are."

"Neither your mom nor I are willing to move out. Gives the other the upper hand in the court of law. Could look like one of us abandoned you. We both want custody." This hits funny.

"But I want to determine who I'm with, when."

"No one is going to keep you if you don't want to go that way, but we both believe we should have custody."

"Well, that seems dumb to fight about if, like, logistically or whatever, it's not going to matter and in the meantime keeps us trapped in one house."

"As your mother likes to say, we are still a family. So think of us all together in that way instead." He looks in the rearview at himself. "Damn, I'm good-looking." And laughs to change the subject, but he also means it.

"What are you going to do if the judge gives Mom the house?"

His lips in a tiny circle let out air, as though the moment I started my sentence he knew how it was going to end so held his breath to prepare.

"I, uh—" He takes another deep breath. I appreciate that at least I can get answers from Dad. Mom won't talk about any of this stuff with me, which I understand, but sometimes I need to know. How could I explain a split house to friends when they were over, even? That kind of thing.

"If the female judge, who, statistically speaking, favors other females—actually the whole state of Massachusetts legally favors mothers, which is fucking sexist—"

"Dad," I say warning him, seeing his jaw race together a second time.

"No, hear me out, you don't know where I'm going with this." And he turns up the music, even though we're already yelling against the wind. "If the judge decides your mom gets the house, even if that makes me homeless, and it could, I'd be happy if you two are happy."

Don't be a baby, Anna. He's not afraid. "I won't let that happen, Dad. But promise you won't be mad no matter what the judge decides? Even if Mom wins?"

He's nodding. "Okay," he says. "All right. I promise."

"Really? Promise?" He's really thinking now.

"I said I promise. I would never lie to you. Ever. Right?"

"Ever."

I can feel the sun trying to cook me and I wonder what temperature I'd start to roast like chuck.

"Three SPF, Anna?"

My oil has only 3 SPF because I'm trying to get a tan.

"Dad! I really think that's all I need. More is overkill. It's why I'm like, always so pale even after the beach."

"Your mother would kill me if she knew you're only wearing oil in Jamaica. Jesus." This makes me giggle. Him too. But he goes back to his seat, way on the other side of the beach, so I can be cool and keep layering the oil on by myself. Mom would have been sitting right next to me slathering on zinc oxide until I was a matte white plank in a red bikini, fingerprints all over the fabric. Then she'd badger me to play Scrabble and it'd be on the big standard-sized board from her forty-year-old L.L.Bean backpack.

Instead, my six-hour beach day is lying here all shiny, jumping in the waves and scrunching my hair to give it body, like Court's. I can feel myself getting tanner. I can't wait to walk back into school like a golden goddess. I am making the move from raw, blue-veined chicken skin to a perfectly roasted game hen. At hour three, I actually hold enough water in my body to pee.

I go to the bathroom and see myself in the mirror. Tan. A babe, even. I dip the bottoms of my swimsuit down and there it is. A real tan line proving I used to be paler. I do a small raise-the-roof dance while wiggling my hips all wobbly in the mirror. Janet Ryan and her sunscreen had been holding me back this whole time.

As I walk the beach solo, my waves and sun-kissed cheeks garner the attention of pervy older men and two cute teenage boys. Maybe they didn't talk to me, but at least they looked and I knew I'd been missing out on being hot for all this time.

Mom was fine by herself in snowy Scituate.

And I was fine here. In all senses.

On the way back onto the ship, my dad walks ahead and I'm approached by not one but two guys. *Better scoop me up fast before anyone else sees.* They ask if I want to meet in the teen club that night.

"Eight o'clock. After dinner."

I got this. "Oh, tonight? Like, yeah, that like, sounds like, really, like fun, probably."

"Tight."

I also need a word, even a sentence, to describe the potential I see for our night. "That'd be the shit."

"Haha. 'Bye, Anna."

The hottest one said my motherfucking name, bitch fuck mother twat, fucking gold, fuck yeah.

"We can pick you up."

"Okay." What does that mean?

"What's your room?"

Oh. "Nine one nine," I say.

"I thought you'd say nine one one."

"Oh my god! HAHA. Nine nineteen."

The two guys laugh a little too, so I put my hair behind my ear to complete the exchange.

Land it. Now. "Like, 'bye," I say, and walk off.

Both guys nod their chin upward as though actual words would destroy all the sexual tension we've just built. Maybe I'll get my second kiss tonight, and I still have a few hours to decide who I'd prefer.

At dinner I try the escargot, and my boyfriends, whose names I am realizing I forgot to ask for, sit a couple tables away with their large family who laugh and mess with each other.

Even their parents seem great, this could really work.

But I'm careful not to look over more than four times because appearing desperate could ruin our weddings. But could I do long distance? Certainly. Why not? Anyway, eventually one of us could move.

What if we fought all the time?

I'd break up with them.

You can't marry someone you don't get along with.

They have to be perfect.

I'd learned the hard way, through my parents.

But what if you loved them so much you got married even though you fought a lot and were unwise but couldn't help it?

I won't be because I'll have a mantra to not fuck up and be with someone bad for me. I'll know.

Wait.

I'm waiting?

If Charlie breaks up with Natasha, I'll reassess.

Of course.

"What the hell are you thinking about, sweetie? You're making crazy faces," Dad asks.

"Oh. Nothing."

"Did you like the snails?"

They weren't awful, but all of a sudden I'm feeling funny so figure a lie-down is in order because I've got a big night ahead.

Waking and unsure how long I've slept, I toss and turn, alone in the small room of our cruise ship, and wonder if I caught the flu. Or perhaps I'm seasick, but my body feels cold and made of paper. I tiptoe into the tiny bathroom, it's like an airline bathroom but with a small shower stall and a full-length on the door, and staring back is Quasimodo. My undereyes are puffed out and full, like lifeguard rescue rings sewn beneath my skin. My whole face is swollen and blisters have already begun forming on my chest. Under the fluorescent light, my skin's red like a highlighter. Something underneath it pulses. Organs? Are my organs burnt?

The doorbell rings. I freeze, thinking maybe they'll go away, but double back, not wanting the hot cousins to think I stood them up. That's not the kind of girl I am at all. I tiptoe out of the bathroom to find my sunglasses and the doorbell rings again. This makes me jump and I knock all of Dad's toiletries to the ground.

"Sorry, one second."

Long pause as I search and one of them finally calls out, "Coo."

I shove tight jean shorts on, add black sunglasses, and throw a hand through my hair, but because of my attempts at making it wavy earlier, my fingers can't get through and, maybe because the curls aren't authentic, it just looks slept on. I pull my tank top over my bright red poochy belly and open the door.

"Ah, the sun!" This is my attempt at making fun of myself for wearing sunglasses. Their faces fall.

"JK. Um, I'm sick. I'm so bummed."

"Shnickeys. Really? Okay."

Just like that, they leave.

"'Bye!" I watch them walk, trying to think of something else to say to keep them hooked. "Have fun at the teen club. Don't be strangers!" *Why do I always sound thirty-five?* "Hope it's da shit!"

I lie back down and the pain crescendoes, nausea hitting like deep barrel drums. BOOM. I wonder if it's the snails but no, I know it's the sunburn. And whenever my dad gets back, I'll tell him I poisoned myself with the sun. Where is he? Is he trying to find a date or something?

The handle turns, the door opens. My eyes go to Dad's hand—gold ring still on. Just like Grampy had said in his dumb letter. So it was real love between my parents too. Check.

"I thought you were going out to da club," he says.

"I'm sick. I feel awful. I think I have sun poisoning."

"Oh, sweetie. I told you to put on sunscreen."

"I know. You only told me once though."

"You're fifteen, Anna. I'll go get you aloe from the gift shop."

"But it's like, gonna be a gazillion dollars—"

"I just won a gazillion at the casino."

"Seriously?"

"Fifty."

"K thanks." I pull down my sunglasses. "I look like Quasimodo."

He jumps back. "Oh Jesus." He laughs really hard, realizing what I called myself, and repeats it, appreciating the reference I guess. "Quasimodo—you don't, but holy shit, you really fuckin' burned yourself, sweetie. Your eyes are almost swollen shut. Gazillion-dollar aloe coming right up. Do you need anything else?"

"I don't know."

Absolutely covered in goo and gobbling Advil—both of us try to remember what Mom would advise in this situation. I take four pills and hope I don't die. We watch *Matchstick Men* twice in a row because there are only three channels on the ship.

"Thanks for taking care of me, Dad."

"I feel bad I wasn't more insistent you wear the fuckin' sunscreen. Like your mom would have been."

"It's okay. I wouldn't have listened."

"You would have if your mom said it."

"Yeah, but she's scary. Um. Are you dating?"

"Nope. Not until I move out of the house. Or until she does." We speak at the same speed.

"You're still wearing your ring."

"I know."

We both watch TV in silence. Always that to go back to.

But I think of something else. "Are you going to take it off?"

"My ring? Maybe. I still feel married right now, though." My mom had already taken hers off and I wanted to tell Grampy about my dad. That he's not who Grampy said he is.

"Can I tell you something, Anna?"

"Yeah."

"I've been thinking about your questions—who gets what, etcetera." I think for a second about how most people don't say the word "etcetera," that they mostly just write it. He goes on, "Whatever the judge decides, I'll support. At the end of the day, I want you and Mom to be safe and happy. Even if it means I'm homeless, living on the street, ya know? Even if I'm living on the street"—he repeats himself, emphasizing the extreme consideration with fervor—"I don't mind."

"Okaaay," I say slowly because part of me doesn't actually believe him. Some days he speaks of my mom with such massive resentment. On others, like right now, he's loving.

"I hope you don't mean literally."

"Listen, financially, it's a fact in this life, you never know what will happen. Right? I truly don't mean—uh—'homeless' in a bad way, Angel. I lived in a van for years, remember? This room is almost as big as a van."

"Wow. You'd just drive around? That'd be okay with you?"

"Just because you live in a van doesn't mean you're always driving it, though of course that's an option. Yup. I'd love it." He's landing these sentences like he meditated while gambling and arrived utterly evolved.

"How would you pay for gas?"

"My savings. I have savings."

"If you lived in a van, when would I see you? I wouldn't have a room or anything. An apartment would be better, so you'd be around."

"This room isn't bad. Think of it like this, and we are having so much fun here."

"You say to your daughter as she's in horrible pain, her eye sockets the size of mini-donuts."

"HAH! You're narrating us? Okay. I could live in a one-bedroom apartment," he says.

"I need a bedroom too."

"Really? Okay. But if your mom keeps the house, then you'll be there."

"Uh, I'll still live with you as well. Right?"

"Right." But he doesn't seem like he means it somehow. "Anyway, probably won't be very nice, wherever I'm at. That's why I'd rather live in a vehicle. It would feel like a lifestyle choice rather than a reminder of a life I was kicked out of. Stuck in a static box, some apartment where the crime rate is higher."

"Dad. I bet I can find you a good place, like a cool apartment complex with a pool! Even though—" I'm catching myself. "But you'll probably get the house." Or— Then I think of my mom not being there and it's just me and Dad. I don't know if I can handle this kind of burn again. "Or I'll find Mom a good place. Whoever has to go."

He laughs, appreciating me. "You can try."

"I'm not going to see one of you every day."

"Do you really want to, you teenager? You sat on the other side of the beach from me today. I couldn't tell if it was you or a lobster."

"Ha. Ha." I speak like it's not funny. "I wasn't red that early on."

"I'm just saying you were so far away. Am I that embarrassing?"

"No," I answer, meaning it. And then we watch TV on opposite sides of one very small room. I think of not seeing him a lot. What would the dumb female judge rule? She can't take him away from me. I think of the bad nights that happen all the time now. Whenever he isn't there and how she yells and screams and follows me and throws things. Not at me, but it's still hard. I always seem to piss her off at night. If he goes, that will probably get worse.

"I don't want you to go," I say, watching Nicolas Cage hug his teen daughter on screen.

I picture my dad biting a cookie and knocking it against his teeth to catch all the crumbs before taking another bite.

"You know I don't want to either. And I have to tell you, sweetie"—the credits roll—"I'll never love anyone more than I love your mother. I know that. I never felt that kind of love before. I want *you* to know that." This brings me extreme comfort and also confusion. He finishes explaining so I can understand: "But I also hate her."

This makes more sense.

Because he didn't talk to her like he loved her. So, he loved her more than anything and also hated her. How difficult to be a human, I think, quietly. And make a note to never allow this to happen to me. I would only find someone who I didn't hate. And who didn't hate me. I'd be very careful to make sure that that part wasn't there, no matter how much I loved them. Suss out that part because it will ruin everything and rip your family to bits.

"I'll always have you, Angel. I love you more than myself. You're everything."

"Same, Dad."

"I don't care about material possessions. You are my biggest accomplishment. This, this, is all that matters." He's going overboard.

"I get it, Dad." With a tone intentionally built to laugh at ourselves, so we do, and his eyes fill in a way that's not so bad.

"And, Anna?"

"Yeah, Dad?"

"Can you put *Matchstick Men* on again?"

"Seriously?"

"NO!"

"What were you gonna say?"

"Oh." He sounds like he's crying a little but it's dark so I'm not sure. "I don't want you to blame your mother."

This makes me secretly cry hard. I wish my Grampy could hear this too. My dad's not bad. He's not the wrong one. There is no wrong one. Maybe he'd never take his ring off either.

"Even though it's her fault." He bursts out laughing. I'm kind of laugh-crying, unsure where to land. But he cuts in again. "No, I'm serious. I made mistakes too."

I nod vigorously in the dark. "I know." It's too sad, though, so I add, "Dad."

"Yeah, honey?"

"My back, it fuckin' hurts."

He bursts out laughing. "Am I bad father?"

"Not at all. Am I bad daughter?"

"Not even a little."

The room holds us like perfectly temperate bathwater.

"Don't tell your mother about the suntan lotion."

I'll take this to my grave.

I'll never tell a soul.

We go to sleep laughing. Me and Dad.

Chapter Eight

"Moe!"

"Moe?"

Mom and I call out into the dark woods and make kissy sounds until our lips go limp.

"Moe. C'mere, boy. Where are you, Moe?" I listen for the *ting*.

Years ago, as Mom promised, she'd clipped a tiny spherical bell to Moe's collar, serving as a warning to prey, but he'd taught himself to press his chin to his chest and blunt the rattle. He's smart. He'd show back up.

Mom moves out of the shadows and into the moonlight. She's crying. When Moe wasn't inside with us, purring, flirting for a belly rub, or held like a baby, he was outside in his neighborhood, but it wasn't like him not to come home when we called.

"I knew Dad should have kept him," I say.

Moving day had been only a few months ago.

Cardboard boxes littered the house beside balls of newspaper, and they argued over precious items.

"No, Peter. No. Your sister gave us—that uh—what is it, a butter dish? Um—gave it to us as an anniversary present. It's ours together. It's not just yours." And she inhaled with a ton more to say but Dad was talking already, rolling the item in paper, placing it in his box.

"Janet, this porcelain plate that we *use* for butter, or rather, that *you* use for butter without consulting me, is the bottom piece to a *teacup*, a porcelain *set*, that was passed down *to me*, from my mother, who probably hand painted it, and once belonged to *my mother's* grandmother and could very likely be worth a great deal of money. You will not be using it as a butter dish in your home. It will be going to my apartment and back to its original set. Thanks."

The bottom and top of her lips moved like strangers. "Fine, Peter. Fine. Our divorce doesn't have to be so—contentious! So fucking contentious."

"Your divorce! You mean the divorce *you* wanted."

She closed her eyes like that went straight to the gut, then silently built herself back up before responding, "You divorced me a long time ago, Peter. Just didn't involve a courtroom or papers. And that's a really shitty thing to say. I don't want Anna thinking it was my fault."

Calling out from the TV room, I yelled, "I don't!" But I probably still do.

"She's always listening, see. Even when it seems like she's watching TV."

"No, I'm not!" I yelled.

And from separate rooms, me and Dad chuckled. Mom didn't get it.

Dad never would have left her. He would remind us of that often. If this whole thing hadn't happened, if they got along better like other parents, if my mother could have been more normal—we probably wouldn't be walking around the edge of these thick woods, wondering why our cat who is always home for dinner, or at least breakfast, hasn't showed for days.

Years earlier, when Dad still lived in the house and Mom was working late, Moe had disappeared then too. Dad burned cardboard outside and we called out for Moe like a song, but after a bit, Dad said to wait because he was certain Moe heard us, already on his way home.

I wasn't so sure, but twenty-five minutes later, the ting of a bell and our black beast emerged, running from the woods' edge.

Now, years later, I'm waiting for Mom to deliver the *already on his way* line. But she's looking toward her nose, where her honesty lives.

"Is Moe like, okay? He is, right?"

"Oh, Anna, I—I don't think so. I didn't want to say it but the cat sitter told me he disa— disappeared two nights before we came home." She and I had gone camping with the rest of the Dunmore crew, friends Mom won in the divorce. "So, Moe disappeared five nights ago, not three. And the coyotes. Or if he, uh—wandered too far from home. Or—so many changes in our home. Maybe he missed your dad. He could have run away looking for your dad. Think about it."

"That's okay."

But she doesn't stop. "And the roads are so twisting. The cars go go go fast."

The day Dad moved out, I thought he'd change his mind and take Moe with him. But with both elbows resting on the window and our cat at my side, we watched his convertible get smaller in reverse, packed with all his stuff except us.

Moe missed Dad, got lost trying to smell for him, to find him, and was hit by a car. This idea breaks my heart.

—

Mom pokes her head into my room even though Dad has just barely picked up the phone.

"You tell him?"

I wave her away like she's Yogi Bear trying to steal our picnic basket. "Sorry. Mom came in but she's gone now." The way I say "Mom" is with an eye roll so he can see whose team I'm on. I'd called to tell him that Moe never came home, has been gone for over a week, but he has something to tell me first. "Go on, sorry."

"You didn't hear any of that, Anna?" Dad repeats himself. "There's a growth under my fingernail. They biopsied it, it's abnormal."

"Oh."

He sounds annoyed. "They had to take my fingernail off to do that by the way. And my doctor, uh, my doctor is worried it could maybe have traveled to the bone. Actually, it did, but it maybe traveled more"—I'm holding my breath—"but they have to do more tests, just my fuckin' luck. So at the very least they will remove one finger to the second knuckle. At worst, the growth has gone into all my bones, in which case, it could, uh"—he laughs out air—"it could kill me. Sorry to tell you. I don't think it's the latter, in my gut." And pitches his voice high before coming down again: "But I have to tell you, right?"

What the fuck do I say to that? "When will you, uh, when will you find out the results?" I sputter. "If you're going to, um, like . . ."

"If it traveled?"

"Yeah." My heart.

"A couple weeks. Don't tell anyone though. Health is private."

"What about Mom. Can I please tell Mom?"

"Nope." This wakes him up. "Especially not Mom."

I want to argue but it won't help. He responds as though I protested anyway. Lately he's been doing this a lot, as though we are in an argument when I meant to only ask a question.

"When your mother divorced me, she lost rights to my personal information, okay, Anna?" And even though he doesn't say anything else, I wonder if I can hear the smallest smile across the phone. She had taken something from him and he would hold on to something in return. The growth under his fingernail that could kill him.

I contemplate hanging up. This news was enough for anyone in one day. But then again, to wait to share my bad news for a couple weeks, after he learned he was going to, say, die, seemed worse. After trying to be there with him, I say, "It's sort of a sad thing but I can't imagine hanging up and not telling you, Dad, so—" *Everything is shit anyway, just say it, Anna.* "It's not certain but we are, like, afraid Moe ran away. Or was like, eaten? Not eaten but like— Ya know, coyotes . . . got him. I'm butchering this. Not butchering. Moe's been gone for eight days."

"Moe." He responds just with his name. I can't tell how upset he is or isn't. "Over a week. Moe? What, uh—what happened, sweetie?"

And I tell him how Moe disappeared.

Huh is all he says.

The day Dad moved out, before his car backed down the driveway, he hugged me for quite a long time, and afterward my shoulder was wet. He did the same thing with Moe, and when he handed Moe back to me, there was wet spot on him, too. But now I don't hear one.

"I bet he'll show up. It is the longest he's been away, though. Very sad if he's gone." Dad sounds professional but empty, like a Republican senator on CNN. Maybe when he moved out, he'd let more die than just his marriage. Together, we remember how Moe played fetch and was fat and ate everything like a dog and mostly wanted to snuggle. I cry and that gets to him, I can hear him almost choking up, which actually brings me comfort because he sounds like him again, the version before moving.

"Oh," he says, remembering, "I didn't even tell you the craziest thing, sweetheart. The bone thing." He snorts back a laugh.

"I don't think it's funny, Dad."

"No, no, you'll appreciate this. Because it's about how weird life is. What finger do I have to get removed?"

Before I can guess, he announces, "My ring finger. My fucking ring finger. The one our wedding ring is on."

I hold on to the part I can grasp: "You're still wearing it."

"I mean, not for long." He laughs. "Feels like a fucking sign, right? It's time."

I want to argue it but I can't.

"Can you fucking believe that, sweetie?"

"No, I can't. I really really can't."

When one is hosting a house party, a presentable abode is top importance no matter the occasion, even if that occasion is a high school rager. I am seventeen years old, chopping synthetic throw pillows that won't hold an indent and dusting framed photos, hiding ones where I look too unhinged, especially from fourth grade when I gained weight. After skimming for other poor representation, I leave just one childhood photo. I'm four in a cowboy hat, wearing makeup.

My phone buzzes. I slip it out of my back jean pocket; it's the size of an extra-long pack of cigarettes and it wears a matte gold case and the screen is sort of green and black.

Tom: Yo.
Me: hi hon
Tom: Sup?
Me: n2m

Tom: Coo. I'm at tedeschiis.

Tom: Rasberry Smirnoff right? How many handles?

Me: Yes! Thnx babe. Perfect.

Tom: K. How many.

Me: U da best uhhh two!??!

Tom: U r. K.

Me: LOL

An hour later, I'm almost ready. Tight white jeans so thick they almost don't reveal the navy thong I'm wearing underneath and my nude tube top with orange flowers is choice, despite it being winter. I've nailed the balance of black mascara and white eyeliner. The doorbell rings and it's my best friends. I rush to finish straightening my hair in the dining room.

"Hello!? We are walking in, is that fine?" We are at the level of knock and announce yourself, never wait for someone to open it.

"COME IN," I say, half muffled. "PARTY HARD," I yell, trying to be funny.

My naturally straight hair lies on top of an ironing board. They walk in to see me kneeling in front of it, my hair steaming.

Before they can say anything, I start, "I know but I like, like how the frizz goes away with a real iron."

"Anna! You can't do that. You'll get a horrible burn, are you kidding!?"

Nora is folded in, half laughing, and Court insists on doing the ironing for me but wants to know why I even do this if my hair is already straight. Fair. Court is still Court, wonderful, kind, and funny, and Nora is another best friend, a gymnast with straight A's and a very sharp sense of humor. She'll grow up to do literally anything she sets her mind to. A real catch in every sense.

"But you guys, like, my mom said she ironed her hair in high school and I finally tried it last week, now I can never go back to a straightener. It's wicked good. Too good. Seriously."

"Your mom has curly hair, though; it makes more sense." Court's right.

"And didn't she do that in like the fifties or something, right?" Nora adds. "They didn't make straighteners then."

"Yeah. Yeah." They are both right. But when Court's done, my long blond hair feels like silk. I flip it, hotter now, ready for the night.

Alyse, the tall model of my public school who is too smart, assertive, and athletic for most idiot Scituate guys, who seem to be more interested in flirtatious ineptness, enters with Emily, another babe of a friend, petite, blond, a painter, and also somewhat overlooked. Not tonight, hons. This is our night.

Bulbous octagons of soil scatter on the floor and I realize Alyse still has on her cleats from lacrosse practice. She asks to use the shower and I sweep the dirt wads off our hardwood floor. Me and my friends are about to do something wrong, but I've earned it, I waited to rebel. Now I'm going to host an illegal party at my house, but I'll be surrounded by girls I trust and who I'm sure will be lifelong friends. I decide to have one drink because it's only six-thirty and I'm the designated driver but my role won't begin until eleven-thirty because I think that's Nora's curfew and we are sleeping at her house after.

"Nora, where does your mom think we are, again?" I ask.

"T.K.'s," the Irish pub.

"Wait, where are your parents, again?" she asks back.

"Mom has a silent retreat. Dad is at his high school reunion, I think."

An apparent benefit of divorced parents is sometimes slipping through their cracks and evading being properly monitored for at least twenty-five percent of my life. Say they end up being out of town the same weekend, then I might do whatever I want or throw a party.

Alyse is back, hair wet. She moves quickly in the kitchen, locating the 1980s Cuisinart to make alcohol slushies like she lives here.

"Speedbag," Em calls out, and we all laugh.

Adjusting our sound system that mainly plays oldies and classical, I pop in a mix CD Alyse burned, and music from The Roots blares out.

I put my stick in her bush for laaayfe. I'm gonna push because I'm doing it right.

A group of cuties from the town over enters.

I've gotten to know these guys while dating their friend who dumped me during a trip to help rebuild homes in the Appalachian Mountains. Sometimes I go over the breakup in my head still, mostly because it's the only real relationship I've had.

His name is Darius, and six months ago Darius said we were breaking up because I was "too perfect."

Our butts sat behind an abandoned elementary school in Virginia and despite the smaller outfits I'd been donning, I'd slowly watched his flirtation move away from me toward "just friends" Ashley. Ashley who had a mansion in Cohasset because her mother was a scientist and invented the scent peach. That's right. She invented the scent peach. The mansion is on the ocean. Despite being absolutely loaded, they've instilled enough work ethic that Ashley had an hourly job at the same sandwich shop where I worked. And she went on missions to volunteer too. And now, Ashley with both money and a job had to be here in Appalachia with her shorter-than-me shorts, flirting with my man, and she was about to win.

But maybe it wasn't too late. Maybe I could still keep him.

"Wait, sorry, Darius. Wait, wait. So like, you're saying I'm too perfect?" I put my hair behind my ear and smiled a little like this is a joke and maybe he's actually about to propose.

"Too perfect," he said again, but with a smelling-poop-style expression. I was so far from perfect. He didn't even know. Or actually, he did a little, because of that one time in the woods when I tried to give him a handy next to his car. It had been my first time touching anyone's dick, ever, and it had ended both abruptly and softly. Which was unexpected.

Darius continued, "It sounds weird to say, but it's just like—yeah, I dunno, I can't explain it but perfect, not in a good way." K. "You're so great, though, Anna. You really are. Hot and funny." I flip my hair to the side and giggle, hoping to remind him I still match that description. "But also," he goes on, "I dunno. You're always . . . happy."

"Thanks?"

"No like. That's the thing. But—yeah, I don't know how to explain it. But it's not working."

Unbeknownst to Darius, his timing was awful. The night before, I'd been on my cot, sitting next to my friend from church, and I told her how I was finally falling in love and I'd been waiting for this very moment to lose my virginity and how it would be with Darius and the next day I would tell him.

But the next day ended up being this one.

Two days into the breakup, I did my best flirting, hoping to win him back, but on day three, the breakup was still intact and Ashley was sitting on Darius's lower back, giving him a massage.

Months later, I was still waiting for the upside of the disappointment to reveal itself. But "perfect" being a bad thing played on my mind ever since. I'd worked so hard to seem like everyone else.

But I was a try-hard. I was fake. He could see it.

Who else could?

Another hot kid from Darius's town walks in. This is the upside.

"Mark, Tommy, Noah, Justin from Cohasset, meet Court, Nora, Alyse, and Emily from Scituate." They size each other up and about six minutes later, I swear, most of us have found a perfect match.

Nora takes a turn blending more frozen vodka drinks until they are gone and our lips are extra pink. And more people stream in while a kid from bio sits on a side table thinking it's a stool before snapping it in half. A story for Monday.

Then I attempt to remind everyone about a DD. "YOU GUYS. DORK ANNOUNCEMENT NUMBER ONE. This is the West End of Scituate, okay? The roads are like, crazy. Like, uncharacteristically so. Have a designated driver. Seriously." From the corner of my eye, Nora downs more vodka and doesn't need a chaser. More people come in including Conor Curt, best friend of Darius. Conor immediately tries to make out with me and I reciprocate but it's too slimy and gives me a feeling of doom down there, so I tell him that I have to fix the broken table. But in the other room I bump into Justin who holds up the picture of when I was four in a cowboy hat.

"Awww," he says. "Of course you grew up to be a cutie."

"Awww," I say back and flip my hair to the other side and smile, trying to match, pleased that my curation of family photographs had been effective.

Justin and I are in my yellow bedroom and my bra is coming off but before he tries to go lower, I stop him. I'm not sure why but I tell him I must check on a friend. To be helpful, he finds my shirt and we walk back down the stairs. I am confronted with a feeling I would encounter many more times, a quick spiral of guilt at the thought of giving a guy blue balls while also listening to a quiet, knowing voice inside me that says *No, stopping there.* It speaks up at certain moments and not at others; when and why is still a mystery to me. If I had more to drink, it might quiet down.

"A little help," comes a male voice from the blue and green bathroom that was my dad's when he was living here and still reeks of mildew.

I yell back, "What's up, you good?"

"She could use some help, your friend." When I peek in, Nora is in the mini bathtub, trying to stand up by pulling down the shower curtain.

"Nora, Nora." I take her arm. "You good?" She smushes her lips together like she's ready for a kiss but also like they could be holding something inside her mouth.

When I try to lead her out of the bathtub, our hands touch in a way that usually lifts people up, but right now, it does nothing.

We take all her weight into the kitchen and get her big glasses of water. She tells us she's fine, but she's somewhere else. In Scituate, the end of a high school party is usually marked by sirens but occasionally a person who's gotten too drunk. I wish it wasn't my best friend.

Everyone leaves and we help her into my car.

"Okay," I say, driving the clutch and gears at the same time, booking it because we are late. Nora sits in the middle seat in the back, held upright by Alyse, who is entertained more than worried. "Nora, what the fuck did you drink, psycho?" Nora laughs a response and Court asks me to slow down.

"Okay. Sorry. We're like, late though? We gotta be at your house at what time Nor? Was it like, eleven-thirty, or twelve o'clock?" I steal a glance at the digital clock and it says 12:18." She's not answering. "Nora."

"That's wrong," Court says. "You guys, is the car clock wrong? Shit. Either way we're late." Court takes out her phone.

Alyse says what we are all thinking: "And Pamela's scary."

She's talking about Nora's mom. And it's true, you really don't want to disappoint Pamela.

"It's actually twelve-twenty."

I hit the gas. "Fuckk. Noraa. I love you. Your mom's gonna kill us. I'm sorry you are so drunk." Realizing I'm at that point in the crazy road, I twist the wheel hard to take the bend.

"Anna!" Court yells, "Chill!"

Nor swings from one side of the back seat to the other, her head knocking into the car window.

"Jesus!"

"Oh my god."

"Are you okay?"

"Nora!"

"Alyse! You're supposed to be holding her."

"Oh my god. Oh my god. She swung all the way over my lap into the glass!"

"Is she okay?"

"Iamohky," Nor says, and we laugh.

Alyse is dying, yanking Nora back up and holding her there. "You okay? Sorry, sorry."

"Olayvan tirty."

"Oliven's dirty?"

Alyse translates, "Eleven-thirty. Her curfew."

"Oh god. Do we like call Pamela and just say we are like, sleeping at your house, Court? And then sleep at my house after we drop off Alyse?"

"And have Nora talk to her mom on the phone?" We go through a bunch of scenarios to not take Nora home and have to face Pamela. When no other options illuminate and the curfew keeps getting farther away, we decide to face the music and roll into her gravel driveway.

Except Pamela's asleep on the couch.

After sneaking past and holing up in Nora's room, the vomiting begins. We empty a shoebox for her to chuck into because the family toilet would bring too much attention. We try to make her comfortable in her bed but realize Nor has stopped moving when she feels like throwing up, so every time she goes to vomit, we sit her upright.

"Is she safe though?" Court asks.

"This is friggen crazy. I've never seen someone like this before." And I've seen really drunk Catholic guys at our school. But this is weird because Nora's talking sometimes and not totally passed out but also like, so fucked up.

"I don't know. I don't know. Tyler, what should we do?" Court's on the phone with her boyfriend and I wish I had a boyfriend to ask too.

"Maybe we should go get Pamela?" I ask. "Is it weird if I call Darius, my ex?" Knowing it would be, we'd broken up such a long time ago.

A sound like wood cracking and I realize Nora's bedroom door is being opened.

"You're home, girls?" It's *Mom.* Pamela's head jerks back, eyes violated by Nora's light.

"Uh-huh. Yeah," I say, extra young.

"Courtney here too?" I nod yes again and look to Court for corroboration, but her body is slumped into the bed. *Awake but pretending to be asleep. Brilliant. I wish I'd thought of it.*

Pamela's eyes squint as if in pain, but makes a visor with her hand, wandering toward us, a dragon pulled out of its lair by said intruder.

"Nora, are you reading a book?" I assume she's referring to the shoebox. *Oh God.*

As her eyes adjust, so does her line of vision:

The pink teddy bear wallpaper.

Nora's cellphone.

Her purse strewn on the floor.

Shoes on in bed.

Her daughter's lap.

"Are you sick, Norine?"

"Mhm. I think so," I squeak.

She puts her palm against her forehead. "I don't feel a fever."

Court breathes heavy, leaning into "asleep."

"Huh" is all I muster.

"Norine. Norine. Are you sick?" And then it comes.

"FAWK OOO MAWM." Oh no.

"Are you drunk, Norine?"

"Fawick oo."

Because I can't stomach what the next moment could look like, I speak to change it. I lie. I'm so scared. "Um. Norine. Norine had a few sips of alcohol, I think. We were at T.K.'s of course, where she said we were going. Got the nachos. No meat. And then um um we walked to the beach. Peggody. And at the end of the night, it was late, so late—these freshmen, uh, children had vodka. And they couldn't take it home because they didn't want to get in trouble and they were really drunk so we didn't want them drinking more. Not safe. And we took it for them. And then Nora just had a few sips. We all did. Not just her. But she is really drunk it seems. Which is weird."

I feel like a snake. I'm protecting Nora, all of us and our reputations, yes, but if I'm being really honest with myself, I'm protecting my parents, my party, myself.

Pamela calls the hospital from the other room. She loves her daughter dearly. This is never in question. Court wakes up for a moment and looks me in the eye and I stare back at her terrified and Nora has to throw up again, as Pamela walks back in talking on the cordless. Court dives back into slumber, Nora's mom never the wiser.

"I spoke to the hospital. A few sips is never a cause for concern." And then she stares at Norine who becomes totally conscious and clear for just a moment.

"Fuck you, Mom," before almost falling into our shoebox of vomit, but I catch her by the hair and hold her shoulders.

And then Pamela looks right at me. "Anna."

"Yes, Pamela."

"How could you let this happen?" And given the whole beach story, this feels really unfair, because we were protecting the freshman kids. But she doesn't know how right she is. I'd even purchased the vodka.

"I'm sorry."

For the rest of the night, I do not sleep and wake up Nora every five minutes to make sure she is still alive, feed her water and to tell her the cover story so the beach cements into her dreams.

By six A.M., she comes to, more or less herself but remembering very little. I fill in the pieces like a CIA agent.

By ten A.M., Nora is grounded for a month. But with exception. We're still allowed over. If Pam only knew.

I feel guilty for not being a better friend, but beyond grateful Norine is okay. When my mom asks how the table was broken, I say, "What table?" She's got to know I had a party, and I brace for punishment but it never comes. Maybe it's her antidepressants. Maybe it was the silent retreat. Maybe she's happier.

In any case, I appreciate it, but the peace does not last.

Chapter Nine

I'M SEVENTEEN AND I'M still here. In this house. With her.

"DON'T COME IN!"

I've already been in a bunch of different rooms trying to get away but she's followed me, yelling, knowing she's my mother and this is her house and she can go where she wants. And now she's inside my room.

"Fuck you." I fold into the ground like a paper crane, which finally stops her. I should have done this hours earlier, but there have been so many nights like this one—it takes a lot for me to fold. She cocks her head, looking at me like a squashed tarantula, suddenly seeing a pet, not a pest. Mom tries to give me a hug, but that's the last thing I want.

"You've been yelling at me for hours. And I try to take it and then I leave, I need space, but you like, trail me and you find everything I've done wrong and then you break me. You do it like, all the time. What makes me so bad?"

"Oh." The flames in her peter out, smoke drifting from the top of her skull like a chimney. "I'm sorry, Anna."

"I'm not a bad kid. What do you want from me? What can I do better?" Now I'm yelling and she's not.

"Can I hug you?" she asks, like a totally different person. Gentle.

"I don't want one." I wish I did. I used to.

"Well, I'd take a hug," she says as though it's an offer, "if you'd give me one?" And then she gets sort of small-sounding, like a baby. "A nice hug, Anna? Okay?"

The repetitive fighting has done something to me.

"Stop making me take care of you," I say.

Half the nights of my week are taken. Mornings, too. When I see her lately, my skin crawls and I wish I could hide. I love her, but I find old methods of cowering to avoid her temper, my placating, shrinking, and being extra nice, to now be pathetic. My newfound power is in protecting myself fiercely by projecting back whatever she does to me. I don't like this part of myself but I haven't been able to find a different answer.

I wish she'd see she's pushed me too far tonight and just sit here. Beside me. Without needing anything. Not touching for as long as I want.

"Stop making me take care of you," I say again, and my outburst restarts the fight even though I'm still on the ground but Mom's slamming my bedroom door, screaming like a lion, finding more things to slam behind her as the yells fall into cries.

I hope to leave for a just little. So I imagine jars used for jams and pickles from country stores and throwing them, breaking them, taking thick shards to cut my wrists. In real life, I'm on the carpet, bloodless, hoping my chest will stop shaking, waiting for the physical pain to subside, but it doesn't, so I scan the room and consider cutting myself in real life. The needles in my sewing kit would do, but if I wasted those on me, I'd have to spend gas money on a second ride to Michael's to finish that throw pillow for the couch, so I don't move. After a long while, the feeling passes. I'm not sure if the decision to refrain is for an image I have of myself, or if I'm authentically not a cutter. I wonder if this is why Mom throws things, like in her mind, it's herself she slams against walls. But when Mom tries to open my door again because she forgot to say something important and wants to see my face while she says it, I hold it closed.

"Don't come in."

"Open the door, Anna."

"No."

"Open it."

"No."

She shoves it.

I shove back.

This goes on.

After a long while, I'm suspended from using my own car.

Driving the winding streets of our neighborhood, I'm certain she can't take away a car I bought with my own money, my own gas, my own insurance. Winter rolls through the open cracks of my windows and my tears freeze maybe knowing she can no longer control me. Sometimes I'd go to Dad's apartment, but better lately is Court's, so I park in front of a gray-pink colonial home and my fake Uggs crunch snow toward a wreath on the front door where nice smells of dinner mingle with pine.

I note the glow from every window.

Our house is usually dark—Mom working late. The glow of our TV draws me like a moth. I rarely remember to put on the outside lights, so when Mom pulls up, it's probably sad for her too.

Best of all, inside Court's is Court. My best friend. She offers me a box of tissues, the kind so soft they leave white residue.

Rosemary puts together a fourth table setting as though it had been there all night. This is Court's magical mother.

"Thank you, Rose," I say, appreciating the simplicity of interactions here.

Her husband, Paul, asks me how my day was, in a reassuring way, like if I didn't answer, it'd be fine.

Around their dinner table, surrounded by arching windows, there are no arguments. I eat pasta and meatballs like I've never tasted, slurp noodles and wish I too was Italian.

Paul applauds me for taking seconds. "You sure can eat, Anna, I love that about you."

Sometimes I say stuff like "Ilovaduhpastaandmeatyaballsa" like I'm an immigrant from Rome and Court says it back—we laugh and so do her parents and I wish I lived here. Sometimes they call me their second daughter. I'm lucky. Especially because I got jealous as a child when my mom held another kid's hand but Court never seems to mind how I've snuck into her family, even offering me the title of *sister*. I feel the same way about her. They let me eat their frozen Milanos, even though each one probably costs a dollar fifty. We watch *Fawlty Towers* and fall asleep in the same twin bed.

Rose knocks quietly on the door and Court is allowed to have an attitude, as long as it's not major. I want to do this with my mom too.

"Mom, we're sleeping!"

Rose chuckles through sentences, more like a song, "Oh, someone is grumpy in the morning, I see," and then whispers really quietly, "Would anyone prefer bagels or an egg sandwich? Once you're ready to get up."

Trying to be extra perfect because here I know I'm extra, I say, "Morning, Rose, how'd you sleep? Egg sandwich, pleasethankyou."

And then we turn on *Dawson's Creek* and lie in bed more until we get a call from Court's boyfriend, Tyler, and talk to him for a while, sharing the receiver, before eating warm breakfast sandwiches downstairs. Once we're ready.

I wish my hair would grow long and dark, like theirs.

It's Thanksgiving and Dad and I are in Maine.

Dad does midmeal stand-up.

". . . Janet takes the house, takes all the money, then I have to get my ring finger removed? Chopped off? Should I hand my penis in too?!"

People laugh midbite, spewing mashed potatoes and flecks of cranberry.

"Dad—"

"What, honey? Oh, you're right, I'll need my penis. Take the balls! Please! Those are useless now, take those instead!" he says, pleading.

Everyone is dying. Dad shifts up.

"Please, Janet, no. Don't revoke the shaft too. I'm using *that.*"

Um, ew.

Mom used to sit here too but now she's back in Massachusetts at another friend's house who I don't even know. And we are in Maine with my dad's college friends, talking about her.

Frank, maybe Dad's top-tier best friend, manages to push out a complete sentence. "Not true, Peedoo"—Dad's old nickname from college—"you could find a younger woman."

Mary juts her elbow into Frank's stomach. "Anna doesn't want to hear any of this, do you, Anna?" but laughs, still able to appreciate his set. I roll my eyes like I'm a forty-five-year-old, used to his shenanigans, and manage a smile.

"Oh. And!" He's still going, "And! I lost my pussy."

Everyone is loud and snorting, in a way that makes the whole thing more raucous, and Kurt, the college senior at the table, laughs big without trying to stifle it even a little.

"Dad."

"Oh, I'm sorry, Anna," and adds, "*Our* pussy."

"DAD."

"What? Moe missed me. The cat. Can you blame 'im?" my father says, flashing his partially chipped teeth and batting his eyelashes like Minnie Mouse.

"Wait, Moe? No, I loved Moe!" shouts Kurt. This sobers people up enough.

"Sorry if I'm behind on this." Kurt's sister, Monica, jumps in. She's twenty-six and has always called my dad Uncle Pete.

"Huh? Speak up, Monica."

"No, like, sorry, Uncle Pete," and puts her hair behind her ear. "I was just going to ask some more details on your—where, or why I mean, sorry, why did they cut off your finger?"

"It was the judge's terms for the divorce." I roll my eyes.

He brushes his single full hand through his golden hair while holding the other one up in the air. His left finger, the one his wedding ring sat on, is now half the size, no nail, no top.

"You know, I figured at some point I'd lose one, but to a handsaw." The other woodworkers appreciate the reference. "Instead, my wife divorced me."

Overkill. "It was cancer, unfortunately," I explain.

"Oh, wow," and Monica's eyes go sad. "That must have been scary."

"Yeah, it was," I say. Dad peeks at me. "We didn't know for a couple weeks if he was going to die. Thankfully it like, didn't um like, travel far to get really bad—but the waiting was hard, right?" Dad's eyes go to his fork and he takes a bite of food.

"Oh, Anna," Mary says, like *That must've been hard.* "Well,

Peedoo, we don't know what we would do without you, that's for sure. So, thank god you are okay."

The group floods him with more "Thank gods," and they reminisce over their college days.

On the side, someone asks what I'm thinking about for school.

"I applied to NYU. Yeah," I say, nervous.

Dad plugs his ears with his fingers. "La-la-la-la-state-school-state-school-la-la-la-la."

"Have your own conversation, Dad!" But because everyone's listening now, I have to explain, "He wants me to go to UMass but they don't have a theater program."

"La-la-la-la-better-hope-NYU-gives-you-a-scholarship."

"La-la-la-la-wish-you'd-saved-for-my-college-like-other-parents."

"Your-mother-took-all-my-money, la-la-la."

People spew again. Dysfunction is funny on him. It is.

But I hope he's joking about NYU. I'd already auditioned, traveled to and from the city twice, and gone through the lengthy application process with a fee. If I don't get in, my plan is, for some reason, to move to Canada.

"That's why I was thrilled to find these Velcro sneaks for two dollars and thirty-five cents from Walmart last week."

"Uncle Pete—are those really Velcro?" asks Kurt.

"Yup. Money saver, plus I can tie 'em when I'm drunk." He's already done this joke on a guy I went to the movies with last week. Dad's going through something. Or maybe he was always going through something and I'm just noticing.

"Oh!" says Mary. "How was your high school reunion?"

"Good. Very good." And he gets serious now. "I was, uh, I was actually nervous. But I re-met the prom queen from our high school. Said she remembered me"—he throws his voice lower like a newscaster, "High school vice president," then back to his regular one—"and I was able to make her laugh—"

"Is that what you call it?" says Kurt back at Dad.

"Ew."

"HA! Not like that," Dad says, but then makes an aside to just Kurt, with four over-the-top winks, "All night." And goes back to someone you can take seriously. "No, really, though. So the good news is we decided to keep in touch and been talking every day since, actually. I said on the phone this morning, 'What are you, my girlfriend?' And she said 'Oh. Sure.' So, yeah, I guess my girlfriend is the prom queen?"

I don't like him naming her this, like he lives in the past. And if I'm being really honest, I still don't like that it's not Mom.

Others jump in. "Congrats Pee-doo! That's so exciting!"

"If we get married, we'd be high school sweethearts."

I change the subject to Thanksgiving traditions. "Dad, you gonna play the guitar now? And then, some charades?"

But he flicks the stub of his finger, no ring. "Fuck. See how that hurt? No more guitar playing."

"When you heal."

"You think it's gonna grow back?" We skip charades too.

During the car ride home from Maine, he's more passive. "Sorry, sweetie, I promise to keep you more updated." His hand sits on my thigh.

"You didn't tell me you have a girlfriend. Weird finding out in front of a group."

"It just happened a few hours earlier, sweetie." He giggles. "But all right. I hear you."

This should be enough, maybe, but it's not. "Ya know, she is my mom."

"So? You want me to lie about what she's done?"

"Not lie. But you don't have to talk badly about her. In front of them." I correct myself, "Or in front of me. Please."

He's unimpressed by my request. I scoot my leg away.

I go on. "You just talk about her so much. So many jokes. You don't have to be like, so like, explicit or talk about her at all. You're happy, right? You have a girlfriend. Move on. Maybe."

"Your mother"—he finally moves his hand off by his own volition and slams his jaws together—"ruined my life."

"I know you are going through a hard time, but—"

"Me? No, I'm not. Everyone's saying I'm doing very well."

"You are handling everything well, sure. But I'm saying, I'm tired of you talking shit on Mom all the time. Okay? It hurts. And when you told me about your finger and that you might die and I couldn't tell anyone, it's just . . . you know those weeks were hard for me too, right?"

He's silent, and when he finds words, his jaw is stitched together. "I can't believe you are making all this about you." He hits a pothole. "Fuck."

I didn't want to fight with either of them and for some reason that's all I've been doing.

I bounce out of my seat. He doesn't slow down. "How do you expect me to have felt?" he says. For some reason this makes me cry. Maybe he doesn't think of me as his to take care of anymore. Maybe he's right.

"Really terrible. It must have been awful and I hate everything you're going through and I try to be there for you. But it's not just all about you, either, though. Like, do you think about me?"

"Constantly."

"But do you think about how things you go through are also hard for me? If you are suffering, I'm worrying. My *dad* is having a hard time and that's scary for me, as your daughter."

"I'm not having a hard time."

"Okay! You're not!" And I say under my breath, "What the fuck."

Now he's pissed. "It wasn't *your* fucking finger! *You* didn't have to move out of the house. You got to stay there, Anna. You have two homes. One at each house. Or place, rather. I got you a bedroom. You have two. I have one, minus many other rooms. That I *used* to own. Minus a wife that I loved. I'll never love anyone more than I loved your mother. That's painful. I had to leave because I was told to. I had to leave my daughter. Your brother won't call me back." He's hitting a new register. "I had no choice. I had my fucking finger chopped off. No choice. I have no money because your mother took it all, no choice, and I live in a small fucking apartment after I've earned and owned three houses that I, I, *I* paid for and now I'm in a fucking shitty apartment that I rent. No choice. I didn't want this. Your mother did."

I should learn when to shut up but instead I adjust my tone to nurturing. "Mom contributed to most of your home purchases too? Right? Think about that. And also, like, I didn't have a choice in any of this either. You act like I did. It happened to me too." And in the moment, I realize it happened to me *more* than him but I can't say it. Staying calm gets harder.

Dad's somewhere else. "You are about to leave for college. You want to be selfish and go to NYU no matter the cost. And I'm supposed to be thinking about how hard it is for you. Sorry, life doesn't work that way, *gurl*."

I don't know why the fuck he said "girl" like that, but cool. "Cool. I'm selfish. Okay, I'm selfish. Nice. Cool, *guy*."

"Ha," he says, like it's not funny. "Act like your mother, you'll turn into your mother."

Maine in winter keeps whipping by. I wipe my face.

After a few minutes of what feels like mutual processing, he says, "You're supposed to sleep over in your room at my apartment tonight. I got those sheets you wanted." He bought them at TJ Maxx just for me. But I know where he's going with this, so instead of being the little victim, I finish his sentence.

"But you don't think I should."

"Right. I'll drop you at your mother's."

"And I bet are you done playing music forever too. You lose your finger, no more guitar."

Of course I'll pick up the guitar again, sweetie, I've changed, we all do, but I'm not dead.

"No. Anna. Keep up. It's not gonna grow back. I can't reach the fuckin' string. Guitar's done."

I suggest a prosthetic, and he acts like this is the dumbest thing he's ever heard.

Two months go by without speaking, until I call and apologize. He apologizes too but I keep wondering how long it would've taken for him to call me first.

Chapter Ten

I'M A STUDENT STUDYING musical theater at NYU at CAP21.

Scholarships helped but one hundred and fifty thousand dollars of loans helped more.

It's my first day at the studio and I'm midreaudition, singing.

"The sidewalks shine like silverrrr."

In front of all the other freshmen in the musical theater program.

"All the lights are distant in the river."

Usually I do this with CD accompaniment, never to a real piano.

"In the darkness, the trees are full of starlight!"

The piano is harder. My peers are staring.

"And all I see is him and me forever and forever."

Octave change, UP. Blow 'em away!

"And I knowww, it's only in my miiind. That I'm talking to myself and not to him."

Keep going.

"And althoooughhh . . ."

Fucking punch it, Anna.

"I KNOW THAT HE IS—"

YES.

"BLYAGHHHIINNNND,"

Fuck, fuck. Everyone cracks, right? Fuck.

"Still I sayyyyyyy, there's a way for us."

Nothing matters. It's all over. I keep cracking.

"I LOVE HIM BUT WHEN THE NIGHT IS OVER."

Fuck.

Even though this group of students had already been accepted into the musical theater program, we were reauditioning so teachers could place us into proper sections.

Now I'm certain my cheeks are red.

I'd only met these kids four hours earlier during the dance auditions.

It was the first high-end dance studio I had ever been in. I'd worn my snapaway trackpants with a tight T-shirt. The same outfit I used to wear for soccer practice—and I fumbled with my new ballet shoes, watching the others strap, clip, and tie theirs like well-worn prosthetics.

My dance audition of course went poorly. I'd known humiliation was imminent, but the singing portion was supposed to go differently. This was how I'd gotten into college, after all, and now I'd cracked all the top notes. Not some of the top notes. All of the top notes. And I want to blame something. The adrenaline. The new faces. Yellow Cabs, polluting the New York City air.

Standing in front of the students, I laugh and try to make a face like *That never happens.* Jan, my new voice teacher, speaks first.

"Okay, thank you. It's never easy up there."

Oh god.

"I um, yeah. Ha. I've only done it to accompaniment on a CD. Doing it with a piano is different . . . than my CD."

"Okay," she responds, still serious. "Have you been assessed for vocal nodules?"

I accidentally look to students for help but their eyes are scarier than hers.

"I, uh—I don't know what that is. I haven't had voice lessons really?" She looks pleased with herself, informed, like a doctor.

"I'm not an ENT, but I do have a doctorate in voice," she says, and adjusts her glasses. "But essentially vocal nodules are when your cords have calloused because of incorrect singing technique. Straining. And so on."

I try to work out when the cracking started. It had always been there on occasion, but waitressing at a very loud Mexican restaurant this summer, run by white people and unironically named "Salsa's," had made it progressively worse. I'd saved up three thousand bucks to avoid a job during school, but my voice had not been the same since.

Walking the hallways of CAP21 after class, I look at my shoes.

"Hannah." Hearing a man's voice, I look up, and during that *between* moment, I wish for it to be one of the three straight guys who had fallen in love with me while I faltered and that they meant "Anna." I lick my lips so they'll shine, and then look up.

We make eye contact.

This person is not in love with me but I love his orange scarf. Maybe a cashmere-wool blend. I adjust my synthetic sweater and try to appear unbothered from class.

"Me? I'm Anna Konkle."

"I'm Thomas."

"Hi."

"That was intense. Did you sing that song to get in, too?"

"Yeah, it was better when I auditioned. Ha."

"That's a like, cliché musical theater song."

"Oh. Is it?" I find myself imagining his orange scarf getting tighter, a lot tighter, around his neck.

"'On My Own' from *Les Mis*? Yeah." I don't know what to say, so he goes on, "Actually, kind of impressive you got in with that." I know it's mostly an insult, but I hang on to the last part and look for something funny to do.

"Yup!" I say in a proud tone. "Don't know much about musical theater! Pretty cool being here." He smiles a bit.

"Where are you from?" he asks.

"Outside Boston. You?"

"Oh. Me too."

"Really, where?

"Acton."

I point to myself. "Scituate. Cool scarf. Ha."

"Marc Jacobs."

"I thought it was Thomas."

"I'm Thomas Gibbons, my scarf is Marc Jacobs."

"Love. Him."

"The designer?"

"Right."

And we both laugh for different reasons.

This is the Barneys Warehouse Sale. I hear it's annual.

Holding four-inch wooden heels with Kermit-green leather straps, I'm careful not to fingerprint the big-ass D&G that doubles as a big-ass golden buckle. I toss my hair back like Carrie Bradshaw would. I'm spending my babysitting and waitressing money meant for textbooks and food on the highest heels I've ever worn, but given the circumstances, I can't deny alternate paths to status. No matter how base. Also, I am trying on a series of identities, finding out who I am and who I am not. For the first time in my entire life, I am unburdened, alone, adult, and away.

"It's okay to smile," a security officer inside the sample sale tells me. But I've seen supermodels in person now and the thing is, they grimace. I'm five foot eight with a thin frame and a strong nose and I wouldn't mind being mistaken for one. I'd done runway for Filene's Basement in Boston, but the local agency said I'd have to pay five thousand dollars to do it again.

Some lady holding a real Gucci bag compliments the shoes I hold in my fingers.

"I know, right? Can't believe I snagged the Dolces, in my size. Dolce and Gabbanas," unsure she heard me the first time and hoping I'm saying it right. "Such a steal."

She nods, not needing to give me much back. "How much?"

"Oh, these? Just over two—two hundred and three, I think. Oh four. Yeah." Three textbooks.

"For Dolce?" I hadn't said it right. *That's fine, I have forever left to buy more and nail the pronunciation.*

"I know."

"That's good!" *Ohhh. That's good!*

"I knowww. *Dolce!* They are—"

"—perfect for the pool," she says finishing a different sentence.

"For the pool? The pool? Yeah, perfect for the pool." It's fall in New York. I did not think people here had pools. Where did they hover? "You're talking about these, right? The wood heels." She nods again. "A pool. Yup. A little . . . bathing suit bikini top . . . and bottom . . . cuz I'm not going naked, ha-ha, at my friends' pools." Before she sniffs out that I have no idea what I'm talking about, I switch her attention to my college bestie. "Oh, look my friend snagged a Jacobs—Mac Jacobs."

"Marc Jacobs."

"His name is Thomas, actually. My best friend at NYU." And I call for him. "Thomas!"

The shirt he came in wearing is on the ground now, because everyone tries on things in front of each other at the Barneys Warehouse Sale and even gets naked and stuff. Because *who cares, it's New York, look at my nipples.*

Just forty minutes ago, Thomas came in wearing a salmon Lacoste polo with a popped collar and I'm in my tank from TJ Maxx that's double-layer silk and was a steal, overlooked in the sale section. I'd also asked my dad to buy a two-hundred-dollar Versace gown from there for my first red carpet. He bit. I'd have to make that purchase worth it for him someday. But today it's Citizens of Humanity jeans with Asics sneakers that are simply practical—we'd walked forty blocks to get here. But the sneakers need to go, nobody who lives in New York City would wear these, only tourists. Still, Thomas doesn't tease me about them.

Despite our meet-cute being a musical-theater-themed roast, he had pivoted to being the most accepting person I'd met at school. On the walk here we summarized our pasts, how Thomas's parents divorced when he was young, how he felt his stepmother never wanted him, and how he came out when he was a sophomore and felt somewhat accepted, but then again, his uncle was gay, so it was less "coming out" and more like another possibility of what one could grow into.

Our pasts feel kindred, and I realize I've never met anyone or loved anyone with a dysfunctional-type family like mine. And I let him in on my parents' divorce, how they told me in seventh grade but lived in the same house for two more years, both refusing to move out. How my dad had his finger partially removed and how I'm still a virgin because I'd wanted to be in love when I did it but now that it was college, I was ready to get it over with. And the incident after acting class a week earlier when this kid

John, who I barely knew by the way, had a question for me in the hall.

"You're Anna, right? Are you a virgin?"

"Uh—"

"I knew it."

"Wait, what? None of your business." I'd flipped my hair into its side part, smiling, trying to make this a flirtation.

"Doth must not protest too much. You can always tell," John said, before walking away.

Cool.

Thomas defends me now. "That kid probably had sex once with like, his family friend who is almost a younger cousin except they technically weren't related but it's still unacceptable. And now he has to live with that so he has become intent on figuring out who has had sex. And with who. To process his own shame." I like to think Thomas means every word of this. I'm filled with warmth, knowing I get to do the city with this guy.

Now he tries on a furry sweater. To me it's too hairy, so I yell out, "Meow."

"It's Gucci, Anna. I might get it," his voice rings over all the roll-in racks. The way Thomas says "Anna" is like he's known me for a decade. I love all of him.

To the lady in line, I add, "It's Gucci. Thomas might get it," but I realize I'm talking to nothing. She's already up at the register and it says $2,421.63. I bite my lip and finger my fraying Gucci purse from Canal Street. Weeks ago, I'd taken it to the real Gucci store on Fifth Avenue, hoping the elderly couple on Canal had accidentally sold me a real one for twenty dollars. The sales associate looked so sad for me, like I might die at any moment.

"Hon, see how the silver hardware is plastic on yours? Like if you tap it. Look. That silver paint's peeling a little too, right? Those are your first clues. Authentic Gucci hardware, *our* hardware, is usually brass, plated in 24-karat gold or sterling silver. It's physically impossible to peel. You bought it, what, ten days ago? Our bags fray at the bottom corners just a skosh shy of maybe a decade."

"Got it, got it, got it, got it," is how I responded and promptly left.

Now I pay for the shoes at Barneys and note the buckles are gold-colored. Probably a brass base. I tap one with my silver ring and it clinks like a bell. "Definitely not a fake," I say to the teenagers behind, but they don't respond.

One of my cards declines but the other one works, and like a real New Yorker, I throw Thomas kisses goodbye and realize I'm late.

Nicole is my old manager from Salsa's. She's come into the city and has invited me to join her and Jason, her old high school friend, at a restaurant he's partial owner of called Pure Food and Wine. I'm unsure why she passed this cool invite to me but I figure maybe this is just what happens when you move to *the city.*

Despite arriving ten minutes after our dinner reservation, I'm the first one here. My toes are covered in blisters from walking twenty-five blocks in my new pool shoes. I wait to speak to a host and am behind two behemoth people. When I realize it's Tom Brady and Gisele Bündchen, I grimace harder, hoping that the only feeling that slips out is annoyance over the wait. The two celebs are scurried away and joy pulses through me. I knew I was meant to be here. Why else would Spirit, or whatever invisible force above, put me next to two of the biggest celebs in the world for a second? It was to say *You're in the right place, Anna, you can have a different life than the one at home.*

"Victoria's Secret Angels are frequent patrons, cause it's

vegan." Nicole has arrived. I turn around for a hug before remembering it's the city, so we kiss on the cheek.

"How's New York treating you, babe?"

"Good! How's Salsa's?"

She rolls her eyes. "I have to leave soon, but they'll be lost without me. Dave's opening a bunch more in Boston so I'll probably help him out and then bounce." She talks like money is no object and her handbags communicate the same. Then she swears to God that the ice cream sundae here is literally the best I will ever eat.

We are seated on the wooden back deck, surrounded by the most beautiful trees I've seen in the city. My heels stick between the wooden deck planks and I trip, catching myself on the back of someone's chair.

"Sorry. Sorry," I say, bent over, trying to dislodge myself. Behind me, Jason Cantor and Nicole Harris greet each other and I realize my ass crack is hanging out of my jeans. I pull them up by the belt loop, which partially rips, but I manage to unstick myself, get up and turn around to hug or kiss cheeks or shake hands with Jason. Whatever someone like him wants to do.

When I see he is hot for a thirty-eight-year-old I get nervous. He smiles as I imagine him as a boy who called me "Icebox" in high school but who regrets it now. The chef comes over and she and Jason greet each other like old lovers, which it turns out they are. His ex's name is Sarma Melngailis, a bleach blonde and sexy as hell, a real woman. I'm told that she and Jason dated in high school for years when she was in her Goth period and Jason was a skateboarder. Sarma says hi to me too and I'm self-conscious that maybe I'm too young to be here. Last week a bouncer called the fake ID I'd purchased on St. Marks the worst he'd seen in his twenty-year career. But here they don't ask for identification and serve me loads of wine. And the ice cream sundae, made with nuts and, I guess, vegetables, is truly the best sundae I've ever had. At the end, nobody pays. We just leave. But it's not illegal.

Standing in the elevator of my dorm in real time I'm realizing how much older my dates look and how maybe one could think Jason and Nicole are my two young parents. Why they were interested in checking out my dinky crib, I'll never know. But I'll wonder. When we enter the dorm room, I make fun of how small it is and am acutely aware it's reminding them that I'm only eighteen, not actually their peer. I'd always wanted to be older. Nicole suggests we see each other again when she's back in New York, but that it won't be for a few months, and I hear Jason say, "Yes, that'd be cool, but that's not for a while—if you're up for it, Anna, we could hang out before that, too."

Am I being asked out by a thirty-eight-year-old restaurant owner? What would my parents think? I brush that thought away. He was probably just looking for a friend. Plus, I'd come here to stop trying to fix them and make my own life great. If I married Jason, he'd leave the adult frat house he resides in with his motocross-riding twin and other bros from high school and buy us a nice place here. We'd drink the blue algae Sarma gives him to live longer and we'd both stay looking young forever. And when he's eighty, looking sixty, still riding his motocross bike at our country house while I'm forty looking thirty and on Broadway, still playing Maureen in *Rent*, with five children poking around backstage, no one will think it's a weird union anymore, they'll just wish it was theirs. Especially because we won't fight.

We will never fight.

An unlikely couple, they'd say. *Meant to be. Soulmates.* And maybe

Jason's twin would date Court or Thomas or something. This swims through my head in the first fifteen seconds of the elevator ride, but I'm thrust out of my thoughts by a fart.

It's loud. And it's long. And it's mine. I try to stop it but can't. After, the elevator is pin-drop quiet.

Mother fucking goddammit. All that fucking cashew cheese.

I face the front of the elevator like a statue. *If only I was a real statue, with no intestinal tract.* Nicole and Jason are behind me, facing my asshole and the doors. I don't move one muscle and try to stop my heart from beating so loud.

No one moves.

No one says anything about how horrible it smells.

Ding.

Then I let out a small burst of laughter. My cheeks must be beet red. Nicole laughs a little bit too but Jason is hard to read. I stop laughing and say nothing.

Chapter Eleven

"College is great, Mom. No, I love it. It is more like *The city is your campus*, less *cheering for the Violets*—the mascot here, haha—I'm a New Yorker, I guess. Like, trying to be." I wonder how this will land and she's already interrupting the end of my sentence, excited.

"That's what they said it would be like when I took you on the tour there! Isn't it?"

"Yeah, you're right. They did."

"Oh, I'm so happy to hear that, Anna! It's what you wanted!" Mom sings. Even though it's a big sacrifice, she never complains about the cost.

"And I think I might like, go on a date next week. Wait, are you dating, Mom?"

"No. No," she says, still buried. "But I— Maybe when I'm settled, maybe then I'll date. Who knows?" She had not seen anyone since the divorce, whereas Dad had been seeing different women from his Chicago high school for years. I found myself mostly happy for him. Hopeful he'd remarry, even. But would Mom ever date? I wanted that for her too.

"Mom." Telling her might be a horrible idea, and Court had said I should end it, now. The age difference between me and Jason was understandably concerning to her, but even Court had to admit that his texting a week after that abominable elevator fart was promising. "Mom," I repeat, because she's in her own world again, "I like, I might go on a date but I don't know." Even though no one can see me, I flip my hair to the side. When it forms a big wad of blond, I'm hotter.

"A date!" she says, still excited (catching up to four sentences ago). "That sounds fun!"

"Jason's older, though."

"K. How much."

"Eee, he's thirty-eight," and then I nervous-laugh, "Hahahha." Before she can chide me, I go on into the good parts. "He owns restaurants here. In New York City. Which is so like, crazy and like, cool. And in Massachusetts too. Pizza shops, I think."

"Oh," she says quietly.

"And a used car dealership. Yeah, yeah. He's really nice and I feel comfortable around him. He drinks algae every day, so he looks twenty. Three. They work! And this is like crazy—Gisele Bündchen was at his restaurant when I was there."

"Oh, oh—" she's doing that thing where she trips over her words. "He— Oh wait . . . the sorry, uh, the white fish? A dish there?" This is why talking to her sometimes feels impossible. I try again.

"I said he drinks algae—"

"No, the other—"

"Gisele Bündchen?"

"Chordata family?"

I'm lost.

"She's a supermodel. Who are the Chordatas?"

"Chordata. Word for fish. Scientific. No of course, I'm thinking of the *Halichoeres bivittatus.* Short and wide. What did you say? Giselola—"

"Gisele Bündchen."

"No, that's not it. *Halichoeres bivittatus* with pelvic fins—resides in the Atlantic mostly. I can't believe I remember all this. I haven't done zoology in thirty years. You know I worked at Harvard—"

"K, never mind."

"ANNA, I THOUGHT YOU WERE TALKING ABOUT A FISH THE RESTAURANT SERVED!"

"You're weird! Don't yell at me!"

"ANNA! Stop," she says, like I'm hurting her. "Don't, don't."

"I have like no idea what you're talking about. I gotta go." My impatience with Mom has weaseled in, but why does trying to talk to her about my life end up in her thoughts on theology or science—?

"Don't be like that. I thought you were talking about something else. So sue me."

Now I'm about to yell. "How do you not know her name, Mom? Her husband is Tom Brady."

"Ohhh. From the Red Sox. Okay! Okaaay. Yes."

"PA-TRI-OTS!" Now I'm yelling.

"I meant to say RED SOX. I mean PATRIOTS." And just like that, it's a fight.

"You don't listen. I'm trying to tell you something important that I'm interested in."

"A thirty-eight-year-old, you said. I'm listening." Suddenly calm now, as though she always was. I mirror her. "I like him, though. He seems like a nice person."

She makes sounds of approval before offering, "Trust your gut, Anna. And honestly, I'm not surprised you like Larry. You always were an old s—"

"Jason." My cellphone chirps. I ignore it.

"An old what?" I ask. "My phone was beeping."

"Soul."

"Aw." This makes me feel good. "Thanks, Mom."

She goes on, "I don't think men care about age. They don't care about a lot of things. You're beautiful. You are beautiful, and men see beautiful."

"You're beautiful, Mom!" I wonder if she knows that, because she is. My female elementary school janitor always told me that.

"No. My friend Tilly was the beautiful one."

"I know who Tilly is. Your best friend when you were little."

The soft embers of her voice ignite. "Tilly had a thing with so many men of different ages. Even her first cousin."

"WHAT? I don't wanna know about this."

"Good, because I don't wanna talk about it!" Like I forced her here but was leaving her all the blame.

"Wait. I have to know now, Mom. Dammit. Tilly's *first* cousin? Are you sure?"

"As the sun is gaseous."

It takes me a second to register that that meant yes. Mom goes on, "Tilly was beautiful. All the men liked her, the boys at school. That's men, Anna. Related or not. Why not her cousin?"

"Because that's, like, fucking gross!" I search for a way to make this conversation feel more normal. "Was it hard for you that she was so popular? In school, not with her relatives," I clarify, glancing at my new roommate's bed about fourteen inches from mine. Perfectly made now, but last night it was tousled by her and Devon Frasier.

John from CAP21 would look at me and my roommate and

know she'd had sex and I had not. What was it about the difference? I keep thinking *sexy* in mind when I walk; maybe she doesn't have to keep it in mind. She just is.

Mom is still talking. "And I think Tilly liked him back. She did!" Mom kind of yells like she's arguing with herself. "And her cousin, her cousin, *offered* her a place to stay in Montana—a respite from fighting with her ex-boyfriend. Tilly's cousin—"

"I know who we're talking about."

"And she went. She left. She accepted the invite."

"Wait, so the fact that she lived with him is why you say there was something romantic?"

"I wasn't blind. I visited."

"Ew!"

"What?!"

"Mom! Did you see the cousins kiss?"

"No! They would have never in front of me."

"Oh. So how did you know? You asked them?"

"Nooo. No," she answers, going down deep and low, like this idea existed for ages but sat out of bounds.

"How did you know, then?"

Clearing her throat like a teacher, she hits the ball back. "My gut. And knowing men. I've never told you this but look at your situation. They don't care about age or family ties. Attraction is attraction, and Tilly was beautiful. Like you."

My stomach rumbles over itself and I picture Jason, twenty years older than me. He wasn't my cousin, at least.

"Listen to your gut with this older man, Anna. That's all any of us women have really got."

"Yeah." *Beep-op.* "Sorry, Dad keeps calling. Maybe I should take it and make sure nothing's wrong."

"Oh. Dad? We are getting burgers tomorrow."

"What? Wh—?"

Bee-op.

"—ust as friends. We—"

Bee-op.

Her words are covered by the beep but the next thing she says overpowers the beeps with ease: "—Can we all talk together?" she asks. "A three-way?"

"Fine. But don't call it that." She's laughing, but it's more like giddiness than awareness.

Merge.

"Hi, Dad, you're on the phone with both me and Mom." Before he can get grumpy about this idea, I continue, paving the path for a good conversation. "Mom said you two are getting burgers?"

"Ha! Hello, Janet!" Dad speaks like he has a gigantic smile. "On Fridays. Every Friday? Is that right?" he states and ends with a feel-good chuckle.

"Hi, Peter." Such amicable tones have not shone their way through in ages, maybe ever. At least not in my presence.

"Yup," Dad continues, "we, uh, got burgers on the way—ha—home from dropping you at college."

"And it was nice," Mom finishes his sentence. "Right, Peter?"

"I agree, Janet," he said like the lawyer at the other end of the table, problem solved after contentious litigation. "So, your mother suggested we do this every Friday. I agreed."

"All I had to do was leave and now you guys like each other. Just like camp."

After more niceties, Dad mentions how he's planning on buying a house of his own soon. His new job is going well and the other town where his apartment is is fine and even though Scituate is pricey, he wants to move back there. Plus, he can put his carpentry skills to work on the weekend if he buys a fixer-upper. "It'll be like a second job."

It wasn't a bad idea. If this one went well, he'd continue doing it again and again. Start a flipping company. Back to his carpentry roots. This idea I liked. I could see him being happy.

Mom agrees and says she is planning on staying in Scituate as well.

"Friday burgers at T.K.'s?" he asks her.

"Friday burgers at T.K.'s, Peter. See you tomorrow."

They wouldn't be the first divorced people to get remarried.

Lips and tongues move together in a rhythm only we know. Even though I've done this a few times, I'd not yet reached the destination. But I dare myself to put a hand down his pants and brace for results. The stiffness of his metal fly was too challenging and the adamance of his elastic waistband intimidating, like I'm entering someone's mystery bag without invitation. I feel like I'm stealing, but how is this supposed to progress otherwise? To ask feels weird. You are just supposed to go. Like in the movies.

Before reaching whatever is inside his pants, my brain wonders if it will be a warm cucumber or applesauce wrapped in underwear, the latter making me feel like a trespasser. If I ever graze balls, it's a mistake, their geography is not yet well known to me.

Cucumber. Carry on.

Taking his palm from my left boob, I place it on my four-times-shaved vagina. It would never be bare enough; he didn't need to know I had hair. My obsessive shaving wasn't a new thing but a trend I'd begun in secret, starting sophomore year in high school, a good six years before this moment, before what I hoped would have happened earlier.

At fifteen, in the privacy of my shower, I'd cut my pubes with the family scissors usually reserved for wrapping paper and wrapped them in toilet paper like something precious before burying them at the bottom of the trash. The whole event left me walking like a penguin for almost two days—I had never been itchier. I was sure I'd made the biggest mistake of my life. In retrospect, I may have been allergic to the shaving cream.

Now nineteen, and it's finally happening with Greg.

Greg who always called. I never did much to earn Greg's attention.

Two months earlier, after making out with Jason in Sarma's bed, my gut told me *weird* (and Mom had reminded me to listen to that), and when I couldn't get over the feeling of his rough hands on my smooth back, I knew it was done. Court had been right too.

Weeks later, my roommate got me invited to a ball at West Point. The funny thing is we didn't attend the ball together, Greg and me. He was with his person and I was with mine. I remember thinking *That guy over there is great and that girl is perfect for him. I hope I have my thing like that someday.* Two weeks later he'd found my AIM screenname and explained how his date was a just a friend and I explained back how mine was just the same.

Four months later, Greg hasn't let me disappear into the girl you see here and there when you're in the city. He asked me to be his *gf* soon after and now he writes me cards and surprises me with flowers. He laughs at my dumb jokes and I laugh at his. Greg's twenty-one, not thirty-eight, and I'm nineteen and in my second semester at college and Greg's in his junior year. He keeps his promises.

Greg is who I am trying to have sex with for the first time.

He diddles the outside of my thong before taking the same hand back to the boob. Interesting. I wish there was a subtle sign I could give him to come on in. But maybe he feels the same as I do, in need of more direct permission. We both are shy.

"Um," I whisper, and I want to continue, "Do you have condoms—a condom?" But I can barely say more without feeling awkward. I wish I could be confident. So instead I say his name again in a whisper, but not in a breathy, moaning way. More like waking someone up at a sleepover.

"Greg. Greg."

"Anna."

"Yeah?"

"What?"

"Hi."

"Hi."

I make myself just say it, "Do you have condoms?"

"Yeah," he whispers back.

"You do?"

"Mhm," he vibrates out, while we kiss.

"Cool," I say.

We make out more.

I try again, "I'm glad you have condoms. For tonight."

"Mhm," he says after a second long pause.

But five minutes pass—making out is great but now I'm confused.

"Wait, you *do* have them?" I'm still whispering and trying to add in sounding sexy but I've asked too many times now to be normal.

"Yes," he says, less kindly.

This makes me pull away. Greg looks at me in the eye. I crinkle my nose.

"Why do you always make a face when I look at you?" he asks.

Crinkling my nose again, I say, "Why? Is it weird?"

"It's cute, but you don't have to do that," he says.

"Okay." I try to stop but it makes me feel too naked so I do it again and ask, "Why aren't you getting the condom?"—grievance settling into my voice.

He doesn't know what to say. "Well. Are you sure you want to?"

"Have sex?" I really really didn't wanna have such a literal conversation about this. I hoped it would naturally roll into having it, like others told me it would. Like it did for everyone else who has ever talked about it.

"Yes," I muster.

"Really? Wow," he lands back.

"Wait," I answer. "Why—why— are you saying that? Why are you asking me that?"

"You're—" Greg starts.

"Just tell me—it's fine." I laugh, bracing. "I can take it."

"No. I dunno." And then he goes there.

"You're just not wet at all," Greg continues. "You aren't making sounds. And I don't want you to do something you don't actually want to do. Just because you're feeling pressure or something."

The bottom of my boat falls out and I'm plunged into the freezing ocean—sinking down to the fish who go on swimming, undisturbed by my presence.

I hold my breath. "I, I do want to—to do it. Actually. But I'm not—" The truth is that I didn't know that that was supposed to happen. No one told me that that was supposed to happen. That I was supposed to do that. How is one supposed to know?

Greg sees I want to say more and adds, "I don't want you to feel like you're doing something wrong, AK. I just noticed, I hope you don't mind me saying, you're not really breathing, either."

Nodding small, I try not to be defensive, but this is hard because a part of me is angry. I'm thinking how I always hold my breath. That's what my acting teacher says. Trying to let my stomach go instead of sucking it in feels almost impossible. Like falling and you'll never reach a floor. I can't think of many things worse. How my acting teacher, Larry, says it's important to cry and access emotion which, growing up, was always accessible but when it had gotten hard with my parents, maybe I pushed it all away, wanting everything to stop.

"I—I—" is all I'm really saying now.

Maybe it's his kind tone that helps me through the insult. How my worst fears of being sexually wrong are confirmed. Trying to open up, I answer, "I didn't really know, I guess? Which probably sounds weird. Um. But . . . it's . . . uh . . ."

I don't know what to say but I keep going: "It's—well this is interesting cuz—it's also a problem in, um, acting class."

"It is?" He sort of smiles, which is nice because I know I'm sounding naïve.

"Yeah—" I keep going. "I—I'm always holding my breath and holding in my stomach, but—"

"Oh."

"Yeah," I say. "And—I'm trying to figure out how to be more connected to myself. And like, honest . . ."

He nods softly, knowing what to say back. "I want to, AK. I'm not like, less attracted to you or anything. I'm super attracted, but I just keep thinking I'm the only one who's turned on or something, so—"

And now I know how to speak with conviction. "But that's not fair. I am turned on, I'm loving it, I am. I just I guess I'm not showing it and I don't know why—."

"You're not doing anything wrong," he says, probably thinking I'm defensive.

"You said that. I know I'm not."

"Well . . ." Greg searches for what to do, feeling pressure. Like I'm pressuring him to have sex. Great. Finally, he delivers it. "I just am like, I dunno, getting in my head and it'd be nice to wait more, maybe. If you're okay with that. If you really wanna do it now, we can."

"Oh my god, I'm not gonna, like, force you to like, have sex with me!" I laugh, not in a nice way.

"No, I don't mean it like that—it's your first time. I've only done it twice."

"With two people, or two times?" I ask again, instantly jealous.

For a sec, he doesn't answer and then says, "Both."

"Oh. Right." But I don't think I really knew that.

"It's all a lot," he finishes.

Maybe he's nervous too, so I nod. I'm petting his hair because of how he said "It's all a lot" so sincerely, like a lot is weighing on him as well.

Then I touch Greg's temple before kissing his cheek and silently tell myself to breathe, while wondering why I have to tell myself and why my body doesn't know how to do it automatically in sex or otherwise. I wonder if it ever did.

Greg moves hair out of my face, holds the edge of my jaw, and kisses me back. We breathe in each other's air and it's different but I don't mind.

He looks at me, loving, and I crinkle my nose.

"AK." I know what he's saying and I try to stop but I can't. I'm falling in love. Maybe I'd have sex for the first time with someone I'm actually in love with. If I could breathe and get wet. Love had been the goal after all. Maybe it wasn't too much to ask for.

A month later, a cooler full of beer sits at the foot of our bed and the playlist I'd made for my first time blasts from the portable speakers he'd brought. Maybe it's in case I'm so loud and expressive that the other army guys in this hostel don't hear us. Wondering if I'll orgasm for the first time, I remember Court telling me that I'll know when I have one.

While foreplay happens, it's not that different from before, but

I am breathing and making little sounds instead of none. At first it made me feel corny, dumb, fake, but the feeling that followed was an undoneness, scary at first but, slowly, fulfilling. When you're doing this, you can't think about the angle of your own face as much and what the person looking at you thinks about it. When you're breathing, the insides of your body can jiggle around enough that you could become wet. And this time, through the awkward moments of the tasks before sex, the pressure feels reduced. We had both reassured each other we would know when the right time would be.

Greg asks me if it's okay to get the condom. Scanning my brain through the sex checklist: I took my birth control that morning, had a plan B pill in my bag for tomorrow, and a condom.

"Mhm," I say, all whispery, like I'm eating the best ice cream. As Greg moves his back toward me to grab a condom, I check my vagina and it's happening. I say "I'm wet" in my head and wish there were more subtle words for these things, and a lot more to choose from, but I push that out of my mind to be in the moment.

And we have sex. At first it's slow and careful, but toward the end there are a lot of fast pumping motions which makes me feel flustered and full of energy and I let out sounds and wonder if I'm orgasming.

I'd know, people said. *Maybe this is knowing. Yes, I'm louder now. This is it.*

At the same time there are either fireworks or gunshots outside and I am sure that's my final sign that we both orgasmed.

After, when I look at him, I feel like I'm falling into him. My butt is pressed into his lap and he sort of turns me toward him. Looking into my eyes, he pushes strands of soft hair out of my face and I notice how kind his half-moon eyes are and how his cheeks point up to them like two sunsets, halfway down. I wonder if I've ever felt this safe before. A feeling like peeing my pants, but in a good way, seeps through my body.

He looks under the covers at all of me and I'm happy he is, but quick to suck in and move my hips here and there so I look okay.

"You're so beautiful, AK."

I could cry. "You are. You are handsome." *And the nose crinkle.* "I can't stop doing that. Sorry."

"It's okay." He touches my nose lightly and then kisses it. He tries to stare into my eyes a lot and this makes me nervous but I'm not sure I've ever felt so seen and even though there are still feelings of discomfort, it's mostly nice and I never want it to stop.

Our bodies braid together like a single lace threaded through all the holes of one sneaker that come together, secure at the top.

We try to watch the TV on the wall as though this night isn't super meaningful to both of us. I look at my hands and wrists and feel the beginning and end of my toes, even if I can't see them, I know where they are, and right now I like that they live here, next to his. I try to picture my own eyes, forehead, cheeks, and lips. And my ass that I can't see. The bottom of my feet. Would sex make me look different? Would I be able to see it in myself? Would I ever see myself accurately? Suddenly I remember my body feeling huge, and then small, as a child. Something I'd forgotten.

"When I was little—Greg, can I tell you something weird?"

"Yeah?" he says, attentive.

"Whenever I had a fever, the weirdest thing would happen."

"What made you think of this?"

"I'm not sure. Looking at myself?"

"Ha. Go on."

"What I remember— This sounds so weird but like, my fingers would get really long. Like *really* long. And my body would feel as tiny as a toothpick or get huge like it was going to fill up the whole room. My bedroom dresser would be gigantic and any sound would be higher, louder, in fast-forward speed."

"That's . . . insane."

"I hated it. I know! It's weird to say out loud. I have barely told anyone this because it sounds crazy. But it was one of the worst feelings of my life."

"This really happened?"

"Yeah. And when we asked the doctor, he said it's something called Alice in Wonderland Syndrome. Happens to some kids when they have fevers. Makes them see the world differently. And their own bodies, even. It's brain inflammation. Apparently, it happened to my dad too."

"Wow." He doesn't know if he was supposed to laugh or what.

"My body always did weird stuff, I guess."

"I don't think your body is weird, AK." I want to make a gross face to punctuate the moment but I'm too embarrassed to be gross right now. I just long to hear him reassure me.

And he does. "You're perfect."

I'd hoped he'd say perfect, unless it was a reason to break up with me. "Too perfect?"

"Ha. No. Perfectly imperfectly perfect."

To me, perfect means normal, and all I want is to be normal, with Greg, in this moment, for the rest of my life.

Chapter Twelve

"DAD!" I PICK UP the phone fresh off scene-study where I played a mom who lost her child to the system before a social worker confronts her about the cigarette burns.

"Call himmm," I'd yelled in character, crying. "Call him," begging the social worker to dial her boss to give the child back.

After the class clapped, I thought about how my real-life dad had been ringing and I'd failed to return it for the last week.

Now I lean against the building and pick up.

"Hi, Angel!"

"Hi!"

"How are you?"

"What's wrong?" I can hear it immediately.

"You know my voice that well, huh?" but he pivots. "How was your performance?"

"Good, but how are things with you?" I respond.

"Well . . ." but then finds something to say that's great: "My high school girlfriend is excellent."

Dad had been in touch with another lady from his reunion who he started seeing after a breakup with the prom queen.

"You have to stop saying that. It's weird. It's really weird. Just call her by her name."

He's laughing a little. "What? I just know her as Prom Queen from high school."

"It sounds strange. Like you're living in the past. It's cringey."

"Well, I didn't call to be psychoanalyzed."

"Sorry. So what's wrong?"

"Let's start with what's right, shall we?" Dad goes on to explain how the house renovation is going well. After Mom had sold the family home and given him his court-ordered share, Dad had done what he'd said and bought a fixer-upper in Scituate so he could remodel on the weekends, in addition to his new nine-to-five. He'd resell the house and make a profit. Maybe it'd even become his new career.

After being laid off from his last job at Shaw's, he'd found a new one. "How's the new job?" Dad laughs like I hit the nail on the head, so I walk a block away from University Place to get away from the noise.

"They, uh, they let me go!" but his delivery is like he won something at a carnival.

Leaning against an academic building, I drop on the sidewalk.

"Oh! Congratulations!" landing his joke and we laugh before getting serious. "Gosh, I'm sorry." *I wonder why this keeps happening.*

All the loans we have flash through my mind and his new house payments and renovation costs. But he reassures me that he doesn't want to work somewhere he's not appreciated.

"It's good. It'll be a good thing." I try to figure out why but don't ask. He answers anyway, "Finally gives me time to finish my book."

"That's true. 'Belfast thinks I'm deaf!'"

"You still remember the opening. Ha." And then he pauses. "How did you know something was wrong, sweetie?" And then his emotion slips in: "You just know me that well?" He doesn't wait for a response. "Well, Anna. The other thing is, I uh—I uh—is this a good time or should we do another call? You got class?"

Art, Performance & Society in five. "Nope, I don't have anywhere to be."

"Well, I, uh"—he laughs—"went to the doctor because it was burning when I urinated," he says. Another medical talk.

"Yeah—sorry—you told me about that," I say, and then wait again.

"Well, I have prostate cancer." And he goes on to explain how it's common and treatable and how most people live for at least ten years after diagnosis and many live much, much longer and that his high school girlfriend can probably come for the surgery so he'll have support. This time I don't say anything when he calls her that.

"But with my job loss, there goes my good insurance, so it won't be covered because I'm going with the more radical choice which is to remove the whole prostate—COBRA would cover radiation—which I'm going to do also, but with my current insurance it won't cover both. You know, both my parents died young so I'm not fuckin' around with this, honey."

Biting my bottom lip, "Mhm," I say.

"I always thought I wouldn't make it past my twenties, but now that I'm old, I gotta live to meet my grandchildren! Remember to enjoy your parents while they're still here." This was sort of a mantra he'd begun long ago. "Frank says it's commendable how I'm dealing with it all. That he would crumble under this stress."

I can't figure out how to respond.

"This kind of cancer is very common, sweetie," he says again. "But it's also a helpful reminder that we must enjoy life as it comes because any of us could be gone at any time. But I want to meet my grandchildren!"

"I know, Dad. You will."

"My parents didn't. That's why I'm spending ten K on this surgery, okay? Mom would have loved you. You would have loved her. You there?"

"Mhm. I want to help you pay for it."

"You focus on paying for yourself. That's help enough."

"Well, I'll come home for the surgery." And he doesn't argue with that. I tell him I'm proud of him and I'll be there to support all along the way and then I ask, "Can I tell Mom?"

"Health is private. She said she doesn't wanna talk to me anymore, so."

"Oh. What happened to burgers?"

"Don't ask me. Mood switch? You know your mother."

"K."

"She told Sue about wanting to divorce me before she told her husband." I can't help but picture a scene I wasn't there for but heard about—my dad following my mom in the car out of paranoia but instead of arriving at another man's house, Mom pulled up to Sue's. Probably to vent. I wonder if they'd gotten into all this history during burgers.

"Can we not talk about my mom."

"Please. Please!"

A small part of me is angry at her for saying she didn't want to talk to him anymore, but a smaller, undeveloped part of my brain says how not talking makes more sense. They were divorced and I was in college. They didn't have to keep in touch. But maybe, like me, he'd thought they could get back together.

"And we will figure out the money thing. I don't want to default on my loans or lose the new house. I want you to stay at NYU. It's an investment in your future. The people you meet, connections." I don't like when he says that because it makes me aware I could have to drop out.

Plus I'm not networking, I'm training.

"Dad, I'll find out if there are certain diets for cancer. Because think about our environment, food, toxins," I say.

"Now you sound like your mother," but he's enjoying it. Doing nice things for him always makes him feel better.

"What stage is it?" I say, pretending this question hasn't been burning since the beginning.

"One. You really don't have to worry. The best thing you can do for me is be successful, you're my greatest accomplishment." The antidote to his discomfort was my success. I'd do everything I could to give him that.

Tons of people with fake bloody knives and *Scream* masks roam the sidewalks. It's Halloween in New York City and I've been hired off Craigslist to prank an unsuspecting guest at their party. I hope I make a lot of money; the terms were never explicitly discussed.

Men in suits open the heavy glass doors of the lobby in tandem, like they were expecting me. Inside there's an additional man in a suit, who grants me access to the penthouse elevator. I didn't know this kind of thing existed. It opens into their apartment—level PH.

Inside are about twenty people dressed in black. The home is modern and white, white and white, with massive walls and tall ceilings. There is a large bedroom off the living room, and a second floor opens to the roof. I have no idea how many rooms there are in total. I follow a caterer and see a den being decorated with an open casket and an actual human who wears a robe but tells me they will be naked with Dylan's Candy covering their bits. And then another person all in black, loads candy in and says Dylan is on her way. Caterers and bartenders and decorations all go everywhere.

Willa Ford spots me and she looks so incredible I can't believe it—by now I understand she's a sort of famous New York socialite with thick red hair, blow-dried to feel random, like fire around her porcelain skin. Her nose and pony eyes go up, pointing to her brain, which moves fast. She's smart. At first glance, Willa's spouse is more troll than husband, mostly in the teeth. I learn he is a loaded movie producer and so is his father.

The husband's fingers grip the zipper on Willa's skintight leather suit and she slips in her pointed porcelain teeth, noting they are a genuine danger. Blood drips perfectly from the edge of her mouth and her husband can't figure out how to fix her suit so I offer to help. He has no idea who I am but appears relieved to have me do it.

Once her outfit is fixed, she sizes me up. I'd borrowed a friend's orange and cream shift dress from some expensive store and paired it with white knee-high pleather boots. I hope winged eyeliner came out in the seventies, especially with my hair feathered out like Farrah Fawcett.

Willa reminds me of tonight's plan and for the eighteenth time I ask if she's sure this whole thing won't be too mean. She reassures me that my target is a man-slut. Plus, he has a good sense of humor. Fine. I'll just do my best and hope to be rewarded.

Guests pour in. Being a party plant in this situation is awkward and I realize how knowing absolutely no one makes it hard to talk to people. I've underestimated what it will be like to begin casual conversations with rich older people. So instead, I'm a random creature hovering around the naked lady with candy or the other naked lady with sushi.

Finally the target arrives and I zero in. Richard Manaklin, serial ex of celebrity women, and magazine editor. He walks in with a cute date, and this I was not prepped for. When I interrupt Willa, pointing out the potential foil, she says a date will mean nothing to him and tells me to do my thing. But every time I get close, I slink away, scared. Willa has to step in and introduce me as her younger cousin. I assume my role as "Kim," and Anna disappears.

I'm flirting. More overtly than I have in my entire life. And he's flirting back and it's like a little miracle. This is how people do it. Damn. Focusing, I finger the small plastic bag of baking soda in my pocket, and on cue, another party hire named Jodi, who doubles as the hostess hired to open doors, sidles up to us. Jodi is in full sequence à la Moulin Rouge and threads sarcasm in all her words. She flirts with Richard but her flirtation is more mean than mine. She even talks to me like I'm an idiot and I wonder if it's part of the act or her real feelings. Regardless, I marvel at the ease and effectiveness of it all until she's saying "bathroom" a second time and I remember how that's my cue and excuse myself and try to tell them with a straight face I'm going to do cocaine.

"I'm doing cocaine. Meet me in the bathroom." And then I wink.

Richard's eyes go big and he nods fast. *Damn, I'm good.*

I wonder where his other date is.

The bathroom tiles are a little warm. Is it possible to put heaters in your floors? No. The building would burn. Must be heavy traffic.

I assume my final position on the floor and stay still, as I take a vial of fake blood and pour it from my nose, hoping it will spill naturally and form a puddle between my cheek and the toilet. I don't think I've botched it but it's impossible to tell from this angle, frozen on the ground. Knowing they could show up at any second (or anyone else for that matter, since I left the door unlocked for them to find me), I throw the blood vial somewhere, anywhere, hoping it won't be seen, take the baggie of fake cocaine, and drop it just out of my hand, powder spilling onto the floor. Perhaps it's not the correct trajectory but it will have to do. The bathroom door opens.

"—I know but that's what holidays are like, for," I hear Moulin Rouge say.

"Ahah no you're right." Richard speaking now, and then—"Holy— Oh my god."

"Oh—my god," Jodi mirrors back. Gasps.

"Holy G— Oh my god." Silence goes on forever and then Richard finds words and they are, "We ha—have to go. We got to go. Go—"

"Okay. Okay. Richie." Jodi tries to slow him, "Wait. Oh my god," she repeats again. But their voices get farther away and I wonder if we've messed this up. They weren't supposed to leave yet. I'm not sure what to do. I never got my third cue which is *Let's get help*. But finally their voices get closer again—

"We can't just leave her there, though—"

"I know but, no, I know," Richard responds.

"That's wrong."

"I get it!" He is absolutely panicked.

"That would be wrong," she says to him again.

"I know! I know." But he has no idea what to do.

"Should we—I dunno, get Willa? Get help." I hear her say, before their footsteps clamor out again to somewhere else.

Is this when I'm supposed to get up and wipe the floor clean and run to the neighbor's apartment, throw on a wig, and disappear? Not thinking he was going to say *We have to go and leave the scene of the crime*, in so many words, I find this bit distracting. Figuring "get help" was close enough to our cue, "let's get help," I dash out, passing a rando who isn't disturbed by the bloody sight of me because it's Halloween. I keep on, into the hallway before knocking on the neighbor's door as planned.

Staring in their bathroom mirror, I wipe my face and eye the short, bleached, bang-ed, wig that Willa got for the switcheroo. And there is Willa, opening the bathroom door, exhilarated.

"Oh my god, Rich is freaking out," she yells.

"He is? He told you? He said to Jodi 'We have to go' and then he tried to leave!" I'd told myself that I wouldn't mention this part but it's the first thing I think to say.

"Piece of shit. See, I told you he deserved this." She's laughing. "Well after he tried to leave, he finally came up to me and said, 'That blond girl, your cousin, and she had blood coming out of her nose and I said 'Where, Rich?' I acted like he was crazy and then I said to him, 'Slow down, there has been a lot of drinking, buddy, it's been a long night. Show me where you saw her.' So he brought me to the bathroom and he pointed to the floor and said, 'Right there, there was blood. I'm so sorry. Have you seen her?' "

"So like, *now* he cares," I say sarcastically, trying to be cool like her.

"Well"—she starts laughing again—"He goes, 'She was bleeding right there.' I said 'Richard' "—Willa starts helping secure the short wig while she goes on with her story—" 'Richard, *that* bathtub? Are you saying she was in that bathtub?' and he starts to tell me no but I go, 'RICH. The tub is filled with ice and fake blood and limbs and stuff. I think you're seeing stuff, baby. You're going crazy.' " She's laughing again and continues, "So he's basically crying after that—I almost felt bad. *Almost.* Oh my god,

Anna, you did such a good job." And then she gets back to business, "K, we don't have much time. I told him I was looking for you. I'm going back in the party now. Okay? So wait three minutes, then you come inside too, grab a drink or something, just like you're any other person, a different party guest, and then I'll cue you and you'll reveal yourself and we'll explain what happened. Oh my god!" She squeals. "It's perfect. It was perfect. I think Page Six is going to write it up too."

I laugh with a big smile but through it I add, "I—I almost feel bad. Rich—Richard'll be fine, right?"

"No, me too actually," she throws back but is already gone.

"I hope he's okay," I call after her, feeling a ton of different things but also proud and relieved that I'll probably definitely be paid. Fuck. I should have confirmed my rate ahead of time.

Walking through the party, I feel alien all over again and spot a circle of people surrounding Willa and Richard. I wonder which guy in the group might be the newspaper writer. For a moment I can't remember how I even got into this situation, a high-end party plant, but remember: *Craigslist.* Where anything goes. Would my parents think less of me or respect the grind and what were they doing? Handing out candy, mailboxes and pumpkins already smashed. For some reason I think Dad might be proud of me tonight, maybe even both of them, but I do feel kind of dirty.

Gnawing on a gummy in the shape of a spider, I try to blend in while listening. I see Willa wave me in early. So I just say my next line and hope it's correct, "Ma'am, Ma'am, have you seen a blond girl in an orange dress? Winged eyeliner? Didn't you say you had?" I hear myself say, wondering why I sound Southern.

"Me?" Willa answers, also on cue. I don't think I fucked it up. Now everyone's listening, though, staring, all the party energy pointing at us.

"Oh," I say dumbly, walking over to Richard, who looks terrified. "It's me." And I pull off the wig as planned, revealing my long dirty blonde hair and true identity: threesome-cocaine-girly.

Richard stares and I watch his face travel to and from eight emotional destinations before landing on all-white. Then I wonder if Rich has ever met with adult humiliation before. From the look of it, I'm guessing no. But this thought makes me feel worse, actually. With a final drool and a laugh more sad than funny, he claps for a long time, inviting me to take a bow, calling me Nicole Kidman. Five minutes later, Richard has left with his date.

Willa hands me cash.

Three thousand and twenty-five dollars.

This is what I'd earned the whole summer, waiting tables four nights a week. She invites me to hang out for the rest of the night, and I try but I still feel like a plant.

After thirty minutes, I go back to my dorm room, and when I try to describe what the hell just happened, it sounds like a lie. In the morning, Page Six publishes an article about the prank and I'm referred to as "blonde actress."

It's been ten months of us.

I'm on a train with Greg, traveling from upstate New York back to the city after spending another weekend getaway with his friends and their girlfriends. I'm on edge.

Last week, I had a series of secret breakdowns but when he asked if I was okay, I said yes and gave him the cold shoulder instead.

We'd spent the day with Greg's friend Ryo and, as his friend put it, his "future wife," and I'd felt hopeless we would ever be them. They were so certain of each other, Future Wife and Ryo, and said "I love you" a lot. They also detailed how talking about absolutely anything was essential, even poop. This meant you really loved each other.

Mom asked about my BMs but never Dad's. Never in front of me. Greg and I had never talked about poop either. This idea messed with my insides. The math was not good.

On the way home, after poking around for Greg's stance on it, he said he had no interest in poop-talk with me. Inside me, the second bomb went off.

Exiting the car I was barely able to look him in the eye.

"You okay, AK?"

But I felt like I was going to burst and I couldn't answer verbally. Nodding small, I held in the tears and shut his van door.

Jetting to the shared bathroom inside my dorm, I let out a silent moan. My face is already soaked and my ribs attempt to weave together even though they are supposed to stay separate. The sensation brings me to my knees but my knees feel like weapons against tile. Instead I opt for the soft curve of the dry tub and snuggle down in it, holding myself.

"Don't come in. This is the bathroom." I'm eight, but I see it in my memory like it is happening again. "This is the privacy zone." We'd screamed at each other for hours. On the other side of the door was my mother and I was in the corner of our old bathroom, a junior in high school. Or second grade. Both. Too easy for us to get here; Mom in a rage or a panic, finding something wrong with my tone, homework, whatever.

At some point I'd realized that the bathroom was the only room in the house where "stay out, Mom" was tolerated for privacy. The one she wouldn't enter. From the safety of our bathroom, I'd hear her moans or something thrown. My brain avatar would throw stuff too, pickle jars and jam jars, and then get to work on myself with the glass. The fantasy of physical pain distracted from the loud warnings of emotion, how the roof was about to collapse. The little monster inside, telling me to run while this version of Mom blocks the exits.

But in the bathtub of my dorm room, the cries aren't hers. Mom is in Massachusetts. The sobs are mine. These old feelings came with me like a backpack I didn't mean to bring. Fuck, I'd lugged it all the way to New York City? I'd been so sure to leave it at home.

Except something new opens, pounding past my fantasies of pain, a bundle of words that come at me in a whisper:

"I'm incapable, I'm incapable."

"I'm incapable of." I nod small, eyes shut.

"I'm incapable of being . . . loved. I'm incapable of being loved." The final puzzle piece slides into place. In a fetal position I repeat it, porcelain feeling like a mattress, "I'm incapable of being loved. I'm incapable of being loved. I'm incapable of being loved."

I'd always thought this intensity of feelings didn't belong to me. That the outbursts belonged to my mom or dad or both. And when I left home, I intentionally didn't move with them.

I thought I was different.

Unlike Mom, I make my sobs silent, but my roommate finds me, rubs my back, and bears witness.

Coming back to earth, I understand that beneath the pain, the analyzing, the freakouts, are the growing feelings I have for Greg, ones that may not be reciprocated, a painful thought. With a history of sometimes loving people more than I felt loved in return, this moment is particularly terrifying. But my roommate has seen my lowest point and now I can't pretend it never happened. I resolve to tell Greg how I feel and if my fear comes true, at least I'll know to move on. Stop letting him close. Maybe I am incapable.

So on the train from upstate New York, I have new words to say out loud. And maybe he doesn't love me back. Better to know so we could stop this charade.

"Greg," I say, finally.

"What's up?" he says with a smile.

Long silence. Our train speeds on.

"Yes, AK?"

"I . . . want to—" but then I go mute.

"AK?"

"Greg. Ha-ha. I want to . . . tell you something."

"I can barely hear you," he says.

"I— Never mind."

He kisses my cheek and looks out the window again.

"Greg," I say, again.

"AK," he says back, again.

"I want to tell you something"—louder this time.

"Shoot."

"I"—he stares at me and I try to go on—"can't. I'm scared. We've almost been together for, like, a year," I push out.

He smiles—"What are you scared of?"—and I shrug in a very intense way. Looking him right in the eyes, imploring him to understand, to heal me. I say, "Well, I'm scared of what I want to tell you."

"What is it?"

Fast, I answer, "Don't make me say it. You know."

"I have no idea what you're talking about," and then he spots something out the window and says, "Look at how beautiful that river is."

I'm unable to pretend I'm looking at a river so I keep going, "It's ugh—it's—okay—it's three words."

Smooth, Anna. Jesus.

I actually have a book open in my hands so I'm staring at that too but I feel like I'm being hunted, even though his eyes are welcoming.

"You want to tell me something that's three words?" he asks. I stare into him like a baby deer begging to let me live, *don't make me say it.* But he waits.

"Okay." I take a deep breath and stop myself from crying. Why am I so freaking sensitive? Keep going, Anna. "It's about how I feel about you."

"Okaay," he says, now slower.

"And it's three words. I said that already. Don't make me say it, Gregory, please."

"I'm sorry, I'm confused." He sounds suddenly abrupt.

"I—" Why is he doing this? Even if he doesn't feel the same. "I—"

He nods and then I freeze. Literally. Like, mouth open. Thirty seconds later I muster, "That was the first word. Next word starts with an *l.*" When he doesn't say anything, I meet his eyes again but there is no recognition.

The train makes a noise. "Next stop Poughkeepsie," says the conductor over the intercom.

"The second word is 'love,'" I hear myself say.

Well, now I've totally given it away. Goddammit. But I can't keep it in forever. It was eating me. Panicking me. Consuming me. If he doesn't agree, what will I do? This thought makes the physical pain wake up. I'm saying it.

I squeeze everything in me so I don't break. "You."

The train slows, inching to a stop, and the loudspeaker guy says "Poughkeepsie. Watch your step and have a nice day." Everyone rushes to get up and Greg does too, grabbing his bag from overhead. Only his back is to me.

At least you know now, I tell myself. *You know how he really feels. It would never get there. Fine.*

Greg stands in line behind his buddies until the train stops with a long escape of air. The doors open. He twists behind him, bends down face to face, eye to eye, and whispers, "I love you too, AK." Our lips touch for a split second.

Once the train doors close and he's out of sight, I cry for a long time, hoping the mantra I'd harbored for so long was also behind me. If I could accept Greg's love, maybe one day I could also accept my own.

Six months later we agree that this is what being deeply in love feels like, and Greg and I are discussing marriage. But he would be graduating from school soon and traveling the world for seven years, the amount of service he owed. If he went to Alabama, Korea, we'd be long distance for two years while I was still at NYU and then, after I graduated, would I follow him?

"Well," I ask back, "it's not *no.* But what about my dreams? Would you follow me anywhere too?"

And he tries to be supportive but can't help saying, "How realistic is becoming a professional actress, though?" I'd be lying to say it didn't hurt. "My mom was a professional singer, AK, and then she had us and taught voice lessons from home. What about something like that?" I had my own worries, like what if he changed and became someone I didn't know after shooting guns in the service, angry, bitter, sad? What if we ended up hating each other?

After a year of this same circular conversation, we acknowledge it can't work forever but vow to stay in each other's lives, even just as friends. No matter what happens, I beg for him to fly rescue helicopters instead of the Blackhawks with ammunition so he stays more or less the same, and he makes me promise that if it isn't going to be him, that I find a guy who better be perfect, because that's what I deserve.

Chapter Thirteen

THE HOLIDAYS IN SCITUATE are beautiful and this year is no different. Dotted lights line pitched roofs, bumpy with snow. Our high school friends are united too, home from college.

On Monday I will wake up early to take Dad to the hospital because, after putting it off for as long as possible, his prostate surgery was finally here. I'd also applied to an acting program in Amsterdam and had booked a Subway commercial where I said "Sure!" so I was actually getting real money, making a trip abroad possible. It had only taken twelve years of auditioning. I'd offered to give some earnings to my dad because he'd stopped making house payments and was trying to sell quickly to avoid foreclosure, but he wouldn't accept it. And honestly, I appreciated that. Plus, I had enough credits to graduate early, which would save us a bit in tuition. That was something.

Tonight, however, is an evening to be as young and reckless as possible with my four best friends since middle school, all of us now in college, going to a party in a city where none of us live. Anything could happen.

We catch up on one another's lives. Court is still dating her high school boyfriend even though they are long distance. They had been on and off since middle school and the two of them really could get married. Her parents had also been high school sweethearts. Alyse was extremely single and mostly hooking up with Division One football players at Berkeley, finally appreciated. Emily was dating someone serious from Union College, and Nora was partying and not caring about finding "the one," which we've heard is exactly when you find "the one," and excelling at her competitive university. I admired how none were obsessed with marriage, not even Court. I wanted to be like that too. To stop thinking about who it would be. To stop trying to be so responsible. I'd be taking my dad to the hospital in a couple days. Tonight is a night to be young.

Bud Light, flip cup, and dancing fill the apartment of some person I don't know. I'd been working as an executive assistant during winter break at an editing bay in Boston, and the assistant editor, a senior at BC, had invited us here.

After three beers, I'm grinding to music with a cute guy in a button-up who is high school friends with Mr. BC. Everyone calls him Griffin. I think it's his last name and Griffin is making me laugh. He kisses me on the dance floor and I do it back. We chat and kiss more and he learns I study acting.

"Yeah, I just auditioned for this summer acting program in Amsterdam. We'll see!"

He looks intrigued. "You're an artist. Cool. I'm a cop. In Boston. Just started a few months ago." I'm intrigued too. Why I keep going toward men in uniform, I'm not sure. *Don't overthink it, Anna. This is one random night.* We make out again.

"OooOOOooo" say my friends, like the studio audience from *Saved by the Bell.* He asks if I want to go into the bedroom down the hall. I hesitate but nod. Live a little.

Don't overthink.

Five minutes in, the kissing is fast and furious and all my clothes are off. My underwear is down. He is taking his off too. I'm reminding myself to breathe, wondering if being totally naked together implies that I want to have sex, because I don't. I tell myself, *No it does not.* I don't want to assume! This subject never came easily to me. He may not be ready either. And then I feel it inside me. I back away, aware of what is happening,

"No no no," I say quietly, while making my lips smile. He doesn't respond but keeps moving. "No no no." I try again, smiling less.

He speaks, "C'mon."

"No—" and more forcibly, I move him off me.

However, he isn't listening still and for a second, I wonder if I'm about to be raped. Am I being raped? Is this rape? This isn't rape. I make my voice more forceful and activate my biceps and shove him off me while still trying to smile and laugh, as if to say, *This isn't a huge deal but get the fuck off. Don't worry, we're still friends, I'm not mad. But get off me now.* This goes on for thirty seconds? One minute. One second. I don't know. I know he stops when I push him harder.

While we put our clothes back on and stand on different sides of the room, I can't not say "Sorry." Plus I don't want him getting mad and changing his mind.

But I keep holding my breath until I'm back in the party, surrounded by my friends. When I tell Court what happened, I say how I don't want it to be rape and it doesn't feel like rape, so it was not rape. But then again, it was not not rape. The bottom line is that having a discussion to decide whether or not something is or is not, is fucked up, it is a loss, but I just want to party right now and not think about that moment again or the endless times this conversation has been had between one hurt woman and one trusted friend. If you're lucky, that is.

Dad drives into Boston at 4:32 A.M. and plays Neil Young. His nervous hand sits on my nervous leg. I'm not sure if something within me is different or if it's his grip, maybe both but I move away. Still, he doesn't take his hand away until I shove my leg harder and finally, it falls to the side. Just as quickly, I feel bad but Dad looks unfazed. He's probably got a lot on his mind.

One hour later we're sitting with the surgeon as they go over the procedure to remove the prostate cancer. Dad asks about impotence and incontinence and the surgeon warns that he may not get an erection again. I try to think about something else when this part comes up.

The doctor goes on to explain that if they could salvage a lobe during surgery, it would make everything function better. It just depended how large the cancer is and if it has touched certain nerves.

"Top priority is removing every bit of it, so if a lobe is in question, because I'm a more conservative surgeon, I will take out the lobe. My goal is for you to live longer. We need good margins. I will accept nothing less." This makes us smile. Dad holds my hand and squeezes. I squeeze back.

Despite the early morning hour, the family waiting room is abuzz with donuts, coffee, and people. A nurse hands me a buzzer exactly like the one they give you at Olive Garden. When it lights up and vibrates, I'll know Dad's ready. I find a seat, pour myself some juice, and take two free donuts on a napkin. They taste like toasted sand. I eat both and my mind wanders.

What if the buzzer buzzes, and I go up to the nurse and then she tells me the patient died in surgery? I bounce my leg. *Or there was more cancer than they thought and it spread. There was nothing they could do.* Suddenly it felt so dumb to be here alone, to be the one holding his phone and wallet. The third donut tastes like chocolate dirt. *Are you his wife? He didn't wake up from surgery, I'm so sorry.*

I'd drive his car home, my soul in a million little pieces. There would be little reason to go on myself. I wouldn't survive.

In real life, the restaurant buzzer goes off, just like at T.K.O. Malley's.

Approaching the nurse's station, I go weird: "The thing went off, sorry, but I think my table's ready, just kidding, my dad is, I don't love these buzzers for a hospital, thanks."

She doesn't react but studies the number on the contraption, compares it to her paperwork, and asks for my name.

"Anna Konkle."

"Patient?"

"James Konkle."

Nodding and double-checking a second form, she points at one of the many red phones placed strategically beside armchairs.

I sit in the lounge chair she told me to, mind wandering again, away from my doom spiral and toward curiosity bordering on disgust as to how this futuristic operation came to be. How it works. And is it necessary? The red phone elicits images of nuclear bomb activation.

The red phone rings.

Dad's doctor tells me he's optimistic that they were successful in excising all the cancer, how the surgery went great and they were able to leave a lobe and one whole nerve, which would give Dad a better chance of continence. He would need pads or diapers at least for the short term. Possibly the long. The cancer is gone, so this is wonderful news.

I can breathe.

Soon a nurse provides a room number and I walk through the hallways reading the numbers on each door but forget which one I'm looking for and get lost. So instead of numbers I'm looking at faces. Face after face. Some alone. Some surrounded by a bouquet of family. One teenager with their mother. The frail elderly person who looks like they haven't opened their eyes in years. A couple, and one is on their phone.

His backpack laid over a chair catches my eye and I want to keep walking, I'm not sure why. Instead, I stop like a normal person would. I go in slow, entering a gelatin room, but the softness in his sleeping face draws me in faster.

The wires all over him with the beeping make me need to see Dad with his eyes open.

"Dad." His eyelids flutter and we are hugging but I'm almost floating, careful not to touch the wires.

"How are you? The surgeon said it went really well."

"Really?" His eyes are fully open but he's a couple dimensions away. "Good."

I go on, nodding, "They kept a lobe, too, so you have a better chance of everything working, I guess. And a nerve. And they believe they got all the cancer."

He laughs small, like when you win five dollars from a scratch-away, and nods, but slowly, like he's underwater.

"The morphine is working." Dad's hair without mousse lies messy on his forehead and reminds me of a child. He forgets I'm here, enjoying something like chocolate dissolving on his tongue.

"I've never been this high before." But he goes quiet, serious. Maybe asleep. "Yes, I have." Without opening his eyes, he laughs from somewhere deep. I can't help but appreciate this side of him. The one that doesn't always treat me like a kid. The one who does life the way he wants to. The funny one. For a moment, this makes me feel like he's one of my best friends, and then something tells me to run.

Maybe it's just seeing my parent physically vulnerable like this, like he could go at any moment. Through the emotional ups and downs of our lives, I thought I was prepared. I'd seen my parents in all sorts of vulnerable states and thought this would be a piece of cake.

After Dad had given me permission to share this with Mom, she had offered to come with. In the moment I'd said *no no*, like the very idea was ridiculous, because she wasn't even welcome, but really I figured I didn't need her.

But if he asked me to reapply his mousse right now, I would've been too shaky, the little teeth of the comb poking through his skull. I need another adult. But this moment is not supposed to be about me. *He's just out of surgery, c'mon, Anna, Jesus.*

Continuing down the short checklist he left me with, I call the girlfriend to tell her how it all went, but when she picks up, she sounds surprised, like maybe they aren't boyfriend and girlfriend after all. Or perhaps talking to his daughter is a new step in their relationship, unapproved.

Despite the awkwardness, I like how normal she sounds, and I think maybe it could be nice if he got remarried now.

The next call is to Gary, his old friend from Vermont. I give Gary the good news, how surgery went well, Dad is alive, as though I'm Dad's mother. And Frank and Mary too. When I hang up, my chest is shaking.

I'm almost embarrassed by how uncomfortable I feel in this moment, but whenever Dad's eyes open, I make sure to smile. Gary will pick him up tomorrow, so he tells me to take the car and go home. After a long hug, I leave.

Later that evening, alone at Dad's place with bad overhead lighting and the unfinished porch, I bake two vegan lasagnas, wrap them in plastic and sticky notes with the reheating temp and time, and leave *The China Study* on the counter, a book about Eastern countries having less cancer and why. I think about how long he has smoked, noting this is the next thing to discuss, but for now, eating differently is a good start. On my thigh, I see his hand and hear the doctor's warning of incontinence. *I need to pick up the diapers.* But I'm not ready to be anybody's mother, certainly not my dad's. Not a wife either. Something inside insists that it's my job to stay and take care of him, to move in, even.

I buy the pads.

But I do not buy the diapers.

Maybe I'll go somewhere far away instead.

Chapter Fourteen

"We know you're in there."

Kate and I have been knocking on the middle part of her door for a full minute. Traditionally this is rude, but my new friend has been hiding in here for days.

"Chicken, love you," Kate yells and we knock, louder.

I add, "You're da bomb," using old slang because I know her less well.

"Wait?" I whisper, pigeon-laughing. "Are we being psychotic?" Kate shakes her head.

"We love you."

"Yeah, we do."

Something about expressing outward love toward a person who won't open their door makes me laugh again.

Plus, we are high and in Amsterdam.

Kate and I met a year earlier through a friend at CAP and decided to travel Europe together before the International Theater Workshop started in July. After years of suffering through dance and vocal nodules, I'd finally left musical theater. Tomorrow we have clowning, movement, and self-directing in the afternoon.

"Open up. It's the last day of the weekend, Chicken. Wanna make sure you're good."

The door moves hard, like we shouldn't be here, like we've disturbed the beautiful beast and the beast is Maya.

"You guys. Oh my god."

"Oops, hi Chicken," Kate coos.

Maya tucks her long dark hair behind both ears. She blinks. The jean shorts she wears look bulky-expensive but her white vintage shirt is paper thin, either a couple dollars from consignment, or strategically holey and designer.

"That was insane. You guys." Maya looks nervous but laughs from her throat.

"Sorry," I say, thinking we should go. But she leans into Kate's head rub instead. After a second more, Maya peeks down both ends of the hallway and lets us in before locking the door behind.

One lit cigarette sits against her makeshift ashtray, a simple drinking glass with an inch of water, next to an open window. This has been her seat for the evening, smoking alone. I find it hard to imagine that someone with such swag and talent could have bouts of anxiety that keep her inside. But I also respect a need for solitude, if that's what it is.

"No, yeah, it's—in part because of a UTI—if I sound weird, I smoked earlier but I'm not high anymore but yeah, that's probably not, like, helping anything, mentally." For some reason, this makes us all laugh. Then she goes on, "No, but I'm on my third round of antibiotics, it's so annoying."

"You're in pain?" I ask and she nods, hard.

"That's awful. I hate UTIs." Maya had just been in Italy and met her boyfriend. I was familiar with the hellish feeling of having to pee after you just peed. I say as much and add in to be cool,

"We were in Italy before this too." But we were eating pizza. She was having sex.

Maya's mind moves fast, onto the next. "And like this program is so, I don't know, intimidating, isn't it?"

Kate agrees.

I nod. Everyone had to audition and there are only twenty-five of us. It felt like a lot to live up to.

"I just don't want to go to class, sometimes," Maya continues. "You all are so good." How can a person dominate each prompt the teachers give us and still feel so unsure of their abilities? When we were in an acting class that unexpectedly collided with storytelling, directing, and improvisational writing, she claimed to be paralyzed and then directed her group to tie strings to her limbs, standing in an extra-large doorframe, making herself a puppet. The simplicity and execution and inventiveness far exceeded average. She was always exceptional.

Which is why sometimes one can't help wonder if Maya's self-doubt is more bit than truth. Except as I get to know her, I note how each side is more genuine than the other. At times I'd like to rid her of any insecurity, except Maya's self-doubt may be an important part to her art. Kate and I watch her puff down another cigarette and ask what she did yesterday, when everyone else was on mushrooms.

"In my room. I was here."

She'd called her mom and her new boyfriend, Enzo, from Ischia.

"I don't know. Enzo's twenty-eight, I'm twenty-one, and now he wants to move to New York? I love him, I really do but I don't know, that's a lot. And I didn't come to the park yesterday because a month ago when I did mushrooms with my friend from high school, I threw up the entire time. Like, I couldn't again. I'm over drugs maybe," she says, inhaling.

When Maya talks, it's like she's our actual age, twenty-one, and I'm eight, wondering if I'll be like her when I'm older. While she's over drugs maybe, I'd been cliché tripping for the first time yesterday, all over Vondelpark, getting rained on and telling the trip leader (and anyone else who would listen) that our skin is akin to petals, drying quickly, versus these clothes, akin to nothing a flower would wear. My shirt still damp, the shrubs already dry, therefore everything was bullshit and it was my birthright to be naked. This was my first time doing any drug other than weed and it was exquisite, like an internal reset button pressed, except I never want to do it again because who wants to ruin perfection?

"You're a purist." Kate gets it.

"Am I?"

"In a good way." And I check around to make sure that's definitely good. They nod.

"You are, Kate, growing up with no TV. Maya too, comfortable here alone. I'm honored you like, opened the door and let us in." And I am.

"Ohmagod, you probably think I'm such a weirdo," she asks without asking.

"No," Kate says. "But also, Chicken, we love weird." These two have been friends for years, both studying at the experimental theater wing ETW since freshman year. NYU's naked studio, the one rumored to be wasting their parents' money to have orgies after taking massage-class. But here, in Amsterdam, there have been no orgies. That I've been invited to. As far as I can tell, the biggest difference from CAP is that the art generated is not driven by results but process. Experimental theater is neither an obvious path to riches or an agent. For me, this is an announcing, *I'm doing art for art's sake.* The closest you could get. A rejection of becoming currency, your face and everything else for sale. In those ways, acting sucks! *Look at me, listen to me and if I'm enough me, pay me, clap. If I'm not, silence, poverty.* And if they don't, you don't. God help us actors who grew up in dysfunction. The rejection too deep and too real, applause drowning out self-loathing, without healing it. To embrace alternative art feels like opening a door to a rowdy party before realizing the party is home. We talk about this. We talk about expectations.

Maya's eyes are watering. Kate and I realize what an intrusion we are but can't leave without offering hugs and calm words, and maybe she needs it, because she asks us to stay.

"Maya! I'm the fraud!" I say. "John Early and I have a scene and we make out and I have a gun and I feel like such a bad actor."

Maya says I never seem nervous or afraid. "I don't? I feel it. You don't seem that way in the moment! Ever. I'm so scared." It's easy to admit.

"I am. I'm terrified."

"Me too sometimes," says Kate, but it doesn't sound as crippling for her.

"For me," I add, "it's like middle school after all the separate elementary schools came together. You all know each other and have done this work before. I felt so lost at first. I still do. But it's getting better." It actually was.

Something about saying "middle school" makes Maya softer. She shares with a different vulnerability about being a kid. She was one of the only nonwhite girls in her wealthy private middle school. Many wore Prada clothes and carried Louis Vuitton bags, and growing up in Los Angeles, a lunch table could be a couple kids comparing how much their dads pulled in at the box office: One hundred million, two hundred million, and so on.

"We were fine." She goes on, "But my dad was, is, like a jazz drummer, not like a film producer. So we were good, we weren't poor obviously but compared to them sometimes it felt like it." She shakes her head. But this makes perfect sense, "And I'd bring lunches to school—sorry I'm rambling. I'll stop." Kate and I shake our heads to say *No, keep going.*

"Well, I brought a packed lunch always. My mom is Japanese, born in Japan, so she might like, pack sushi or like fish or pickled radish carved into, roses—."

This makes me think of Court's mom, for the name but also the action.

"—and it's hard to explain."

"Were kids mean?"

"No, mostly, no. Like, there were times kids were jealous that I had sushi, but other times they'd ask me what stuff was. And maybe I heard 'ew.' If that makes sense. I mean maybe some kid said gross once, but mostly I was on edge that they were going to."

"Once is enough to change things," I say.

Maya nods like she's wondering if that's true and goes on. "Most kids were white and I'm half. And, I dunno, I felt it."

"You are perfect, Chicken."

"I agree, Mai." And I do.

"You guys too. No I get it though," She says, back in the past, like she still loves those kids. "I was also, like, on the edge of this group of these popular girls, I knew I was on the edge but I'd made it in. I thought. Barely, but still." We all laugh, relating at some point to *barely.* "I even made my mom buy me a Kate Spade purse but we couldn't afford it—"

"I tried too but I never convinced them. Be proud you were successful."

Maya nods. "So I got the purse, I still feel bad about that because I made my mom, I *made* her. We got in a huge fight about it."

"So many fights," I say, thinking about my house.

Maya looks at me and we really see each other for a sec.

"Soon after that, my friends all hung out without me and I knew it was over. But it like, killed me. At the time." She says this like touching the edges of old distress, still sharp.

"God, it's hard," Kate says, maybe about life.

We go over the details of what being left out looks like, to try to find a reason for her, but eventually land on the idea that everyone at thirteen is inside their own crisis, trying to survive. Eat or be eaten. Maya is still back in seventh grade, so I go back too, putting my hair behind my ear like I'm thirteen again. And resting my arm over my belly. I can't help it. At twenty-one my body feels okay but I'm in middle school and everything is wrong. Like there's sand in my undies and they can't be changed.

Maya is really opening up now. "I, I cried for days. They had each other and each other was not me."

"How'd you survive?" I ask earnestly.

"I made my own group. My real friends. So weird it can still hurt, like what's wrong with me?"

It's easy not to question what I'm about to say. "Nothing. Whenever I go home, I see people from middle school, high school, during Thanksgiving or whatever and I revert right back. It's so fucking formative. That time. You are no longer a child, growing up is happening to you whether you are ready or not." I'm finding something. "And no one has the tools to interact properly with the growth, but we must pretend to anyway." The unfair complexity of this hits and it's funny too. "I was called um, Icebox and literally last week a guy I kissed one time in high school texted me at like two A.M. 'hi icebox.' That's eight years or something since that rumor started. Kill me. I got the knot and stomach flip, I can feel it right now."

"What's icebox?" Maya asks.

"My school thought I masturbated with an ice cube. Even now talking about it, my heart—why do I still care? Like, my person won't forget."

"Yeah."

"Yeah." Kate's heard my story already so pets my hair, explaining for me, "Anna hadn't even kissed anyone or masturbated. She just put ice in her underwear innocently."

"Like a weirdo nerd in fifth grade, and it turned into this rumor."

"Oh my god. If people found out I was masturbating . . ." Maya says, "When I actually started, I might have died, I'm not kidding, because I was like, twelve, I think."

"Guys bragged about jerking off at twelve," I say. "It's so messed up." And I picture that at a school lunch. How normal it felt then, totally unaware of the contradiction.

"I started in late high school? I wish I had earlier. Ha," adds Kate.

Maya laughs. "I only orgasm from masturbating."

Kate nods. "Still not from sex?" Maya shakes her head.

Their openness is like the tip of an epiphany. I've never heard women talk about masturbating. I'd only heard them deny it.

"Interesting," I say with admiration. Maybe this changes everything. "I don't even now."

Kate and Maya have a million questions.

"You've never masturbated?"

"Wait wait wait."

"Have you tried?"

"Tell me tell me—"

I try to answer, "Not really. Well, I've tried, I guess. Like a couple times."

"A couple times?!" Kate yells. "I just used this vibrating lime-green pillow when I was home, it was great."

And we laugh, deep and hearty. She goes on, "Don't know what it was actually for but it worked," and lifts her eyebrows easy like an old man smoking his fifth cigar.

"C'mon. Stop," Maya says, also like a Russian with tobacco. "That's all you have to do?"

Kate nods and shrugs like it's easy as anything.

Maya's eyes go wide. "I'm more complicated. Specific porn."

"I've never watched porn," I say, curious.

Maya does the hand motion of masturbating in the air really fast like her vagina is floating. We are laughing again. Relief comes from somewhere, talking about it all openly for my first time. When thoughts settle, Maya hones in on the biggest question of all. "But, you've orgasmed, right? Anna?"

"Hmm," I say, nodding, "Uh—"

Their eyes get wide.

"No. Yes. No, I have. Well, I think I have. Yeah."

They tell me beyond a shadow of a doubt that I would know. So, probably I have not.

I insist, "No, I'm pretty sure I have. I just can't do it for myself. And I didn't lose my virginity till I was nineteen, so I'm still like, discovering things." My cheeks might be red. I'm not ready for a cigar. But they are silent so I go on talking. "Yeah, I, I bought a vibrator but I have no idea where it is now. It didn't work." And push away the memory I'd never intended to share.

"What? Wait." They are locked in.

A few months earlier I'd bought a waterproof dildo from the internet. It was purple and it vibrated and that's the only part of it I used. It brought me to my knees in the shower. No farther. I tried to stay with it until I couldn't. No out-of-body experience. Nothing undeniable. Just an *Off* button and the quiet gather of wobbly legs off my shower floor.

"You needed to do it for longer."

"I did it for so long."

"How long?"

"Five minutes?"

"Five minutes on your knees?"

"Pretty much. I was shaking."

"Shaking on your knees."

"Yeah!"

Maya and Kate are hysterical. The image of torturing your own clit, on all fours, for too long and stopping with nothing to show, is funny. A few seconds later we are cry-laughing.

Hours pass.

Maya has cut us both bangs with scissors she brought from home and she lets me borrow her leather jacket. It feels like we're talking about everything we aren't supposed to.

"My nipples are basically just my breasts. They barely get hard," Kate offers.

"Let me see," Maya says, like she's asking for the remote. Kate lifts her shirt and waves her double D boobs against her petite body like an anime character. She's a different species than me with my small perky ones, nipples almost always hard, which I complain about, and now we are all showing one another our breasts.

Maya complains that hers are too pointy.

I admit how I have to pluck hairs from mine. I'm half animal. They admit they all do this. I'd thought mine were broken.

"And am I crazy or do we have the exact same boobs," I say to Maya. We look at their profiles for a long time in the mirror.

"Oh my god," Maya answers.

We stare from every angle and it is uncanny.

During our download session, Maya and I toggle from having overlapping experiences to being the direct inverse of each other. My background in goodytwoshoedness is the opposite of Maya, who dabbled in more direct rebelliousness by high school and started smoking at fifteen. I'd never even tried a cigarette.

On the other hand, both of our dads' names were Peter but her dad was a successful musician and my dad was struggling. Both our moms had us when they were forty, after their first marriages, and we each had half brothers who were much older, Jamie and Taichi. And when Maya was secretly masturbating, feeling like a pervert, I was rumored to be masturbating and treated like one.

"God forbid girls masturbate," I say, like I've evolved into a feminist in minutes. But seeing our shame on her made me angry that we carry it. "Our vaginas are magical and we are shamed for them. Sorry. To be able to grow a child in your body *is* wizardry."

"Wizardry is sort of a guy term, no?"

"To be able to grow a child in your body is sorcery. And scientists still can't replicate it. There's so much mystery. It's supernatural, almost. Spiritual. Religious. Separation of church and state, *hello*? So, imagine that a thousand years ago. We were deemed magical, as we still technically are. We are witches, in a sense, I think. Right now I think that. My mom says stuff like this and usually I laugh at her but she's right. And we probably ruled the world. But because of our power, we were perceived as threatening to those who couldn't grow babies, so they needed to control us, and to do that they made us feel shame about everything, especially related to our sexuality and baby making. All the magic parts."

They are nodding. A joint gets passed.

"My mom is really amazing." And I mean it. Maya and Kate honor their moms too. How impossible each of them is but also how astounding. We basically figure everything out and keep smoking until the weed is gone.

We are sisters.

Going to bed in the quiet of my own room. I feel as though six layers of shame have been shed. What's clearer is how much extra I've been living under. I can see the packaging that has housed me, containing us with an ingredient list that might include slutty, gross, seeking male approval, and always alone. Only worth something if others said so. But maybe I don't need to be packaged at all.

Lulling toward sleep, I picture that naked seventy-five-year-old woman from a beach in Barcelona and instead of feeling weird for thinking about her, I keep watching, *remembering how the honesty of her aging body made me recoil, embarrassed on her behalf,* but the longer she walked around, her head held high, the more ashamed I became of myself and my first reaction.

Her shoulders hit the air behind her like wings, orange skin oiled up like expensive leather, swinging tits in front, big smile and soft hips—slowly she became gorgeous. My admiration for her grows bigger now and I squeeze my own body tight.

Four seconds pass and in them, it feels so simple to love all the complexities of myself. And I try to remember to never forget that this moment is important.

Two weeks later, in the upstairs studio where the light comes through, we present our final projects knowing the summer intensive is almost over.

Our prompt was to use personal experiences and tell a story with a beginning, middle, and end within a complementary frame.

John Early's turn. Throughout class, he'd talked about growing up in Tennessee, knowing he was gay in a largely Christian state, but with religiously progressive parents who were both pastors. So the frame for his performance is John proselytizing as a youth pastor with ultra-conservative beliefs at a mega-church, with the same charisma and headset mic as Britney Spears.

It's hysterical until it's very sad. Everything you want one of these pieces to be. Rachel Bloom goes next, creating a children's fairytale musical—based on the complications of falling in love with her high school music director, one year older, during their production of *Into the Woods.*

Terra hosts a cooking show but it ends up being one for an audience of people with eating disorders. Each story takes my breath away, each one better than the last.

I, on the other hand, do not have a plan.

The night before, I had not slept, trying to compose what I would be doing. By morning my mind swirled in possibilities, each progressively worse.

In the middle of someone else's piece I sneak into the bathroom stall downstairs to take a moment to myself and also to shit, probably from nerves.

In the other stall, I hear Maya clear her throat.

"Hi. It's Anna."

"Hi. It's Maya."

"Hi."

We both sound depressed. It turns out she also has not slept and has no idea what she's going to do today. And is also currently having nervous diarrhea. When we meet outside the stalls, we both look like shells.

"See, but I'm a hack."

"You are not a hack, I am a hack."

"No," I counter, "I myself am a hack."

Maya's up.

Unlike others, she has no props. She balls herself up inside her sweatshirt, stretching it until it looks like it's tearing, and she disappears. Like an alien made of cloth, she pokes around inside the wad, in all different directions, kind of tortured. Everyone is riveted and I shake my head small, thinking how this bitch knew what she was doing this whole time and how effortless she makes it seem.

Her storytelling is succinct, and we learn more about her Italian boyfriend, her first time falling in love with another person and eventually she is birthed out of the sweatshirt. From one of the cloth holes comes a baby. It's new Maya, vulnerable Maya. Ready-to-really-be-loved Maya.

It's funny and sweet, unexpected and very honest. It might be my favorite performance of the day. No matter how many times you try to kill it, self-doubt will always find a safe home inside the making of art.

When it's my turn, there's simply no choice but to go. So I do. I bring us to an area of the studio between the stairs and the wall because there is a wooden box that could act as my empty bathtub. I'm wearing little clothing.

Sitting inside, I begin kind of funny, obsessively going over how Greg won't talk to me about poop, and if he won't do that, it means he'll never love me—realizing no one ever will. Not completely, not purely, and certainly not romantically. I decide to tell Greg I love him anyway. It might be a relief to know I am unlovable for sure.

The bathtub is now the train. I can barely say it. When I do, he turns his back on me, just as I knew he would. But before total abandonment, he twists again: "I love you too."

I know I haven't grasped the prompt perfectly; it wasn't a cooking show or a mega-church, or a sweatshirt womb, there really was no real frame except a vessel, but something still came out of it, like there's less of me to hide now. Another student, Tom, is crying. It moved him: that was more than I could have dreamed when I was explosively shitting on the toilet just an hour earlier.

Maybe if the artist can converse with the doubt and perhaps even perform with it, there's potential to grow its inverse. Maybe there's potential to create the inverse, to grow self-love.

Downstairs Maya and I hug, reflecting on our panic and survival.

"Yours was the best one, you psycho," I whisper.

"No yours was."

"Nooo."

"Nooo."

We laugh and she gets serious.

"I think this is gonna give me diarrhea for two days, Na."

"My doctor says I have IBS. You could look into that when you get home."

"How'd they diagnose that?"

"Do you really want me to describe my stool, Mai?"

"Yes."

Two months later, Tom who cried would become my boyfriend and help me reach my first orgasm with a simple finger in the butt. But the real revelation was that I'd found someone to talk about poop with and she wouldn't be my lover.

She was something far deeper than that.

Chapter Fifteen

A CLUB IN NEW York City has grass-covered walls and we know this because we are on the list. Thomas has just been signed to a big modeling agency postgraduation. We always knew he could do it. Tonight is the agency's holiday party, which means a room filled with gorgeous giraffes and bottles of vodka and random rich men. Thomas and I enter and dance hard, like we were born here and are okay to die here too. And we might. I'm partying like I don't have my first meeting with a theatrical agency in the morning. The first talent agent in New York City I'd ever met with.

At three A.M. I throw up in the Yellow Cab on the way home to our shitty apartment in Brooklyn.

At six I'm naked in front of our fridge looking for something. I'm not sure when Thomas entered but he's standing in the kitchen too.

"Am I still drunk?" I ask.

"Yes."

"Should I cancel the meeting?"

"Yes."

Closing the fridge, I have other thoughts. "But I can't! The morning of? That's so lame. So unprofessional—"

"Well—"

"I'm fine."

"Do you remember, I dunno, four hours ago?" he asks.

"I threw up."

"Seven times, and it began inside the cab."

"Ohhh. Really? Oh, man. So sorry about that. Seriously. That's awful. I'm gonna be late, I need to shower."

"Are you sure, Anna?"

"Lemme think this through. Email her now and look like a clown who can't keep a meeting?"

"Say you're sick, which you are. A few hours ago, you actually were sick. Like a lot, so saying you are now isn't even a lie."

"Mmm, but I'm not now. Just the tiniest bit nauseous, and that will wear off. So, option one, your idea. Option two, take a shower, get my shit together, put on some makeup, and get my shit together."

"You just said that."

"The right agent will love me for me." He's not convinced. "Drunk or not drunk."

"So, you're drunk—"

"Not drunk."

While I'm in the shower, Thomas pokes his head inside the bathroom of our tiny shanty of an apartment, letting out my steam.

"Nooo, I need that smoke. Steam."

And like a real friend Thomas shuts himself inside with me. "Why is there a mini screwdriver in the fridge?"

"Hmm." Despite knowing I put it there, I can't remember why.

"Anna." He is holding it. He is trying to prove a point.

"Why are you saying my name like that?"

"Are you sure you don't want to reschedule this meeting?"

"Crystal."

"Sorry?"

"Crystal."

"I didn't say clear."

"I'm keeping the meeting."

Somehow, I'm only ten minutes late. The skyscrapers in New York City always looked so impenetrable when you weren't allowed in. This morning they appear relaxed. Like me.

Be yourself. I practice. *I am Anna. The only child. Barely know my brother. Icebox. And everything in between. My. Self.* I trip a little.

Riding the elevator with actual professionals, I smell glass and stone and think about commercial auditions with Dad. We all check each other out behind our sunglasses, wondering who the other could be. Except I'm not wearing any so someone gives me a look like stop looking at me. Still in the hallway, just outside the office I'm supposed to enter, I catch myself in the mirror, and unfortunately my eyeliner is not as symmetrical as I thought. I shove my face closer to the mirrored glass, and wipe under my eye here and there and then spot a boog, so when the coast is clear, I rub that away too and suddenly my mirror moves, because it is a door. Cara introduces herself, and she's either a tad grossed out or maybe I'm projecting.

"Hiiiii."

"Cara. Gina's assistant."

"Oh. Awesome. Hi, I'm Anna. Um. Konkle. I'm sorry I'm late." And I look behind to make sure the door on this side is also a mirror and not see-through, but it isn't. It's a one-way, so from her side, she had a perfect view.

"Oh. You saw me fix my eyeliner. And nose!" She doesn't respond, typing on her phone. "Gina. I mean Cara." She looks up finally. "You saw me fix my eyeliner, probably," I say, trying to connect by way of my own expense.

"Sorry?"

"Never mind." I feel like I'm crashing, my confidence going home. I note how hard my heart is racing now too. Suddenly Cara says to follow her, so I do.

She walks me through halls, past offices of people in black who look like they have been up for hours even though it's still early morning. I trip.

"Whoops. Second time today. All good."

Cara looks back at me and then forward without saying a peep and keeping pace.

I trip again. "Someone should burn this rug." Cara continues to pretend I'm not here. "Cara, sorry, where are you from?"

"New York."

"City gal."

We turn a corner. She knocks even though the door is already open. "Gina, this is Anna Kankle."

I bow. "Konkle."

Gina is maybe fifty-five and pretty, but her face is tight and unfriendly. "Where are you from?" she asks me.

"Vermont and Boston." I wipe my finger under my eye again and look to Cara reprising our inside joke about the one-way mirror thing and maybe I'd add that I'm actually from the gutter but Cara is gone.

Gina wears a purple dress and her hair is unnaturally black. She is the vice president of Abrams.

We chitchat for a while and I talk a lot about Amsterdam and throw in a nipple joke, how mine are hard a lot. Next, to show her my seriousness for the craft, I detail clowning, Shakespeare, Grotowski, and Stanislavski and how all are important methods.

She doesn't ask any follow-ups in terms of craft. Which is disappointing because I'm not prepared for the next slurry of questions.

"What's your type? Anna?" She says my name like she forgot it and picks up my headshot with my résumé stapled onto the back. "You look angry."

"Yes," I say, trying to laugh. After spending $2,000 on headshots and debating whether this look was sexy or angry, eventually Thomas and I decided sexy and I have two hundred more of them at home.

"I need new ones," I say, even though these are the new ones, and my residual Subway ad money has run dry. I keep hoping the commercial will come back by popular demand, but no luck. I tell her about my role as "Subway Artist" and how I practiced my one-word line "Sure!" in the mirror over and over.

"Mhm." She moves on. "And who do you see yourself playing? What actress would you say you are most like?"

"Meryl Streep," I hear myself answer. Her head stays perfectly still, too still, as though she stops herself from laughing or launching off her neck like a rocket. But the thing is, that didn't come out right, so I try to explain. "Not like, I'm not like as good as Meryl Streep, that's not what I mean." I shouldn't talk myself down, not to your own agent. "I mean, in the future if I work really hard, maybe I could be. Yeah, I mean absolutely, with the right commitment, why not? But not . . . not now. But now? No. What I mean is, why I said that—is like, because Meryl can play any character—and I'm saying 'Meryl' like I know her! Whoops."

Gina stares at me and I make a face like a goon-clown and jump back in.

"Meryl *Streep* can play any age and I'd believe her. I'd believe her. So yeah, I'd be happiest playing all sorts of characters. I want to play men, women, old people. A baby. That last one is a joke. Unless someone was open to it, I'd be open too, um."

I start laughing but she doesn't. So I don't either.

"No, but really, men, women, different ages. A teenager. Over a career as an artist, yes to all of the above. Right? So, maybe it doesn't sound 'lucrative,' but if I'm sleeping on a mattress on the ground, making art, I'll be happy."

A few beats of silence and I find myself hoping Cara walks in.

Gina does not think I am funny or interesting or inspired.

But maybe she will if I keep emailing her for months. A couple years even. I wouldn't take no for an answer. That's what they say to never do.

When Gina and I say our goodbyes, she gives me her card. Maybe it didn't go as badly as I think. She says to email her if I'm in a project and maybe she'll come check it out. I wonder if this means she is my agent but when I email her a thank-you, she doesn't respond and at this point I'm not tipsy anymore and understand that Gina is not actually my agent. Not yet.

When I'm cast in an experimental show called *The Bauhaus* playing the role of "architecture," I give her a heads-up. *Bring a friend! But fyi the warehouse has no heat. Ha.* When I audition for a reality TV show about finding expensive toys to auction off but they need an assistant acting as the liaison between the shopper and the seller, I email. *Almost booked it!* When I'm in a play where I hold shirtless men on leashes who bark at the audience for three straight minutes, *It's a weird one. No pressure.* And when I reprise my role as an inanimate object and play the wall in the Israel-Palestine conflict, I email a few more times.

Either she was manually inputting my email incorrectly instead of pressing *Reply*, or she never wrote me back.

I tell myself it doesn't matter. As long I'm making art, sleeping on a mattress, waiting tables, and doing downtown theater, I'll be happy.

My dad has come to see my weird downtown play on opening night. I haven't seen him in a bit. Maybe in some ways that's been on purpose. I'm twenty-three. He is sixty-three and has been in good health since surgery. After a quick stint of radiation, he felt confident his prostate cancer was behind him. But he also sounded different on the phone. Slurred words sometimes. Agitated. And the older I get, the needier I think he becomes. For instance, he's been doing something new, kissing me on the lips as a greeting. Or trying. Well, I think it's new. I can't be totally sure, memory is just memory, but he doesn't seem to remember that I've asked him to stop. But maybe memory is just memory for him too. The thing is, making a big deal out of it would be far too awkward so instead I turn my head offering the cheek and try not to think about it for long.

In a strange conjuring, most of my exes end up at the same performance and are in the same room with me and my dad and my high school friends at a bar in the East Village for an afterparty.

It is uncomfortable but also feels like some subconscious wish fulfillment, an odd fantasy I've harbored in the corners of lonely nights—a quiet vision where all my old boyfriends sit in my studio apartment playing Scrabble, discussing the weather, and being general pals. In the fantasy, they are platonically allegiant to me and I am to them, our former passion transmuted into a strong desire of mutual well-being.

Maybe like building a family for the first time that's mostly pleasant and I am the effective glue.

But the reality of this apparition is far less calming than I'd hoped. The reality is that I'm doing loops around the bar, hoping alcohol will dull this nervous energy.

A corner in the back holds my friends from work—servers and cooks alike from Prune, the beloved restaurant I quit just a month ago. It had been my full-time job, but I needed a change. After this play, I promised myself I'd be done acting, at least for a while. Maybe forever. Maybe go back to school for something else. The revelation had been crushing but I'm bone-tired and it's a relief to acknowledge it.

I hug my co-workers big and grateful, sort of incredulous they have come, some of them even getting shifts off from Prune to be here.

"Thank you for being here! Means a lot," I say, meaning it far more than it sounds.

"Of course," "Duh," they sing out in unison, effortless.

"I met your dad!" calls out Samira, a sous-chef. "He's so nice!"

"Oh!" My cheeks get hot. "Good—he was nice, he wasn't weird?"

"No! Not weird." Erin's a server at Prune too and continues, "Funny guy—very nice—I had to like turn my head fast when he greeted me. Ha."

I pause for a minute, thinking.

"What do you mean?"

"Oh, he went to—" Samira gesticulates toward her lips.

"He tried to kiss you on the lips?" I finish, wishing I was unable to. They laugh, probably uncomfortable.

"I'm so sorry," I say, "I— I— He's, uh—a hippie, and uh, all my family friends, like, of his generation kiss on the lips. Like all the couples." I laugh to myself and try to find my place amid the panic and go on, "Oh my god I'm making them sound like swingers. They aren't! But he just sort of— Maybe he went into that hippie headspace for a second but . . . I'm so sorry. That's so weird."

Noticing my spiral, they reassure, "I thought it was funny! Nothing happened, you don't need to worry about it—"

I'm wringing the bottom of my shirt in my hands. "No I do! That's my dad who tried to—not okay—"

"You aren't your dad, and it really isn't a big deal. Promise," finishes Erin, and Samira agrees. "If it was, I probably wouldn't have mentioned it."

Then I say "Okay" many times, mostly to myself. Inside, everything moves.

Hugging hard, they congratulate me and head out. I wonder if they are going to another bar where we won't be.

Ordering a third Manhattan, I take it back and see my dad talking closely to Court and Nora. I squeeze in as Dad puts an arm around my shoulders. "I'm so proud of you, sweetie. We are so proud of you." I inspect my friends' eyeballs for signs of their own discomfort. When he finally walks away, I lean over. "Tell me he didn't try to kiss you on the lips?" They look less surprised by the question than I would have hoped but say no. It's becoming the sort of night where the bar is wobbly and the black corners of the room swallow everything.

Trying to pretend Dad isn't here, I talk to my exes. But a darkness flows over me, like maybe I poison everything. Or choose the wrong people like my mom says she does. Or I'm destined to be single forever like my dad.

I see Dad speaking to a man at the bar and I watch him laugh harder than I've seen him laugh in a long time. The other guy is around his age, a bit belligerent, and kind of seems like he wants to fuck my dad. Dad seems into it maybe. I don't know. Or maybe my brain is playing tricks. They talk closely, laughing and drinking for a while.

I'm drunk. I turn back to Court and Nora. "Um, my dad is being so weird tonight, right?" They look at each other, giving away the cards they had probably planned on holding tight. Court says, "I don't want to stress you out, but . . . we can talk about it tomorrow if you want."

"Tell me." I say, "Tell me now, I can take it."

"I'm sure it's nothing, or, well, he's been through a lot, moving into that new apartment, and he just told us about that whole cop thing."

"Cop thing?" I ask.

They look at each other and she continues, "At his new apartment."

"I have no idea what you're talking about," I say, "but his new apartment seems shitty, maybe? That's so mean, but I dunno, I'm definitely worried about him. Something is off."

Court explains, "Yeah, he said that the, basically, the other night there was loud banging on his door at at like 2 A.M. or something."

"Okay . . ." I answer.

She goes on, "And they were banging and going, 'Anthony, open up. Open the door with your hands up. He said back something like, 'Anthony doesn't live here.' But they said it again."

Nora finishes for her, "And your dad opened it and there were two like, policemen with their guns drawn, he said."

"WHAT?" I imagine all the things he could have done for them to show up there. Somewhere in my brain, this had always been a concern. But I'd always been concerned about his safety. Not others'. "Anthony?"

"And they screamed at him, 'where is Tom or Anthony or

Dante or someone—'" She looks to Nor. "I can't remember the name, do you remember?"

"Carl?" says Nora.

I'm panicked inside. "Meaning they weren't asking for my dad . . ."

"Yes, whatever the name is, let's say, Carl—it wasn't Carl, though."

Court nods, quickly, "We can say Carl. Carl is fine," and she shifts back into the high-adrenaline recounting. "'Carl, hands up.' And your dad said, 'There is no Carl here. You have the wrong apartment.' And then he said they left."

"The cops left?"

"They just left."

I'm confused. That's the end of the story? They say, yes, as far as they know. Attempting to first sit with my capacity for empathy, I reflect audibly on the terror he must have felt and wonder if the apartment complex in Brockton is legitimately unsafe. But quickly it becomes more about me and him. Why didn't he tell me this story? Why did he tell my friends? Maybe he didn't want to worry you, they say. *Maybe,* I consider. Then I realize that his story makes absolutely zero fucking sense. Cops came to his apartment with their guns drawn, looking for Carl or Anthony or someone, but left without entering or searching the place because some guy told them they had the wrong apartment?

I peek over at my father, he looks even more amorphous than before as he's talking, closer now, to that same older white man at the bar with the martini.

Somewhere inside you, all you really want is to truly know your parents, and now this feeling that my dad, my childhood best friend, is a complete stranger, the idea growing like a weed, roiling in my stomach, acid as fertilizer. Then I am blindsided by a further thought, that maybe it's my fault. That because I'd been trying to live for myself all these years, going as far away as possible, trying to draw boundaries without even knowing what that word really meant, that my absence, my insistence on doing things for myself, had ruined him.

I'm next to Dad.

"Hi," I say, pointedly.

Smiling absently back, he says, "Hi, sweetie."

"Who are you talking to?" I question, deadpan.

He chuckles, too happy, and then answers, "Don't know! He got me a drink. Nice guy." I wonder if he knows the nice guy is maybe trying to sleep with him. "Nice," I say back and smile with all the energy of a tin can.

Dad laughs. "What?"

"Nothing."

"What?"

"Nothing."

"What?"

"Nothing. Just wanted to make sure you're okay." and I do.

"I'm good. Right now, I'm good. It's been a"—he laughs instead of cries—"an interesting few months but I'm with my daudau right now in New York City and you're waiting tables and paying your rent and making your art. I'm just very proud of you. Get famous already so you can take care of your pops in my old age. I can still be your manager."

His eyes glisten. I'm too scared to tell him I'm probably quitting. And he seems good for a moment. This makes me feel warmer. Maybe the cops were idiots or racist and maybe Carl was a man of color for instance, so they took my dad's white privilege as authority? When Dad said, "You have the wrong apartment," a statement that cops with their guns drawn wouldn't take seriously, perhaps in this case, they did and they left. Maybe he's telling the truth. I don't know. But I urge myself to not bring it up in this moment. When I'm drunk. Maybe we both are. I just want him to be good, for it to be simple, so badly.

And then he tells me, "You know, I haven't mentioned this yet, but Justine broke up with me because of her daughter."

"Oh." He'd had a new girlfriend for a year now. The first not from his high school but a local, just a few towns over. I'd even attended their Thanksgiving and her kids seemed suspicious of me for a reason I didn't understand.

"Yeah. It's, uh—it's really frustrating," he explains, "because I really love Justine. We have no problems. We've never had a fight."

"That's what you said about your last girlfriend."

"Yeah, it was true with her too." He says the next part like he's just put something really obvious together. "Maybe it was your mom's fault we fought all the time."

"Ha-ha," I say, obviously faking a laugh. He goes on to talk shit about Mom again, no matter how many times I've asked him not to. This is a major problem between us at the moment. I try to move on. "Continue story, please, thank you."

"Anyway, Justine's daughter had been through stuff when she was little and so that's, in my opinion, why this all shook out the way that it did. But you know, Justine has five kids . . ."

Dad goes on to explain that during the most recent family get-together, he was invited and Justine's whole family was hanging out and how they're a hard bunch to win over because all five kids love and miss their dad. But how he really gets along with the grandkids.

"You really love little kids," I hear myself say, "always have."

And he says, "Best people at a party are the animals and the children. Does that make me a loner or authentic? You tell me. I could talk about the weather with an adult or pretend to be the weather with a child."

He goes on, "Anyway, I'm sitting down next to the fire, you know, cross-legged, and Jill's daughter, Justine's grandchild, who is two, comes up to me, up to *me*, and sits on my lap."

I wait for what else he has to say. I try to be patient but my heart pounds.

"Jill comes over and rips her two-year-old off my lap like I've done something bad. Talks in Justine's ear for days after and Justine tells me she has to break up with me, even though it breaks her heart. But just because something happened to you, *Jill*, doesn't mean every adult male is a pervert. That's actually extremely sexist."

The director squeezes my shoulder as she passes us, heading out for the night.

I throw on a big normal smile. "Thanks for coming! I mean, ha-ha, for directing me and being amazing. See you tomorrow."

Then suddenly an ex is saying goodbye too and when he hugs me, I wish he wouldn't stop. Watching him walk out that door, I consider asking him to come back to the apartment I'm staying in. Play Scrabble. Take me with him. Anything.

"Your mother—"

"Stop talking about Mom. Please."

"Anna. Your mother—"

I turn away abruptly and then say goodbyes and go home, shaken.

Later that weekend, on the same exact day, Mom and Dad, unbeknownst to each other, text me they are moving from their present states of Rhode Island and Massachusetts to Florida. Thirty minutes away from each other. My Dad is headed to Sun City Center and Mom to Dunedin. It feels like I'm supposed to get involved again and tell them. So instead, I do not.

But between the cops-&-guns thing, kissing my friends, and this series of messages, I start worrying about my dad and tell him so, but he feels judged. I try on different tones and vocabulary to make it sound loving, because a part of it is, but nothing really works, and instead I hold back angry words that will fester.

I need to know: Was he always like this? I desperately miss the dad that was a deity, my hero. Did he die? Or was he never born and I wised up? When he starts to throw quiet insults, like the ones whispered at Mom when she yelled, I decide it is the latter. The pedestal is falling.

I picture him tapping a cookie against his teeth to catch every crumb and wonder what it means now.

Chapter Sixteen

Maybe this is a horrible idea, given my fraught state, but to be gone from Dad any longer feels selfish. I'd waited too long before seeing him last time in New York. That was clear. He was weirder now. Maybe a distance problem. Definitely lonely and therefore needy. In any case, if I push it, he could go full hermit.

Except Dad picks me up smiling from the Tampa airport and looks pretty normal, giving me a hug. Even still, my body stiffens. When he goes in for a kiss headed for my mouth, I turn my cheek and say, "Stop." My tone is sort of mean, no eye contact either. In the car, when he puts his hand on my thigh, I move it away and get visibly angry without offering words to explain it. Over the fried fish at dinner, I barely speak.

At least I'm here, I gave him that, I tell myself, knowing it's not enough. Since learning about the interaction with his ex-girlfriend's granddaughter, I've been in my head a lot about our past.

I can tell he's hurt by my iciness.

"So tomorrow you'll meet Deb," he says.

"Okay, neat. I've heard a lot about Deb. Looking forward to it."

He puts on Van Morrison like always and hums. I close my window and stay quiet.

Finally I ask, "Deb's your girlfriend, right?" hoping the answer is yes.

"Yes. Sort of. Basically. She is very beautiful."

"Oh. Nice."

"Deb used to fly in private jets."

"Really?" I wish status didn't come up so quickly, but lately I notice it's often the first place he goes.

"She did. Ex was a dick, but yeah. Debby might come over tonight but depends when she gets out of her art show."

I don't ask what that means—is she a painter? I skip it. Tired of keeping track of all the girlfriends' history over the years. Instead, I withdraw again. "I think I'm too tired tonight. I want to go to bed."

"Oh." He meets my frostiness and one-ups me, "Hey, how much money did you save from that Subway commercial you did? I told Debby you made forty K on that. She couldn't believe they pay so much. You have some left, right?"

Whenever my dad brought up the one commercial, he tells people how much money I made on it, despite my asking him to keep it private and saying, how would he feel if I went around telling everyone how much he made.

"Dad." *Tone.* "I've asked you so many times to not share that with people. And I don't think I'm comfortable telling you how much I have left." This annoys him.

"Why?"

"Why what?"

"Why don't you want to tell me? It's gone?"

"Fine, yes, Dad. It's gone. It's been gone. It helped pay for Amsterdam, and it's expensive to live in New York."

"Gone? Really. Wow."

"The forty K came slowly over four years of the ad playing."

"Still. Forty K. Wow." He's pissed. I'd wasted my money. "Could it play again, the ad?"

"Doubt it." I'm tired of the passive-aggressiveness. The criticism. The dual-ness of his absence while also feeling controlled.

"See, this is why I was upset when I saw that receipt for those sunglasses you bought yourself."

"That was four years ago! Why are we going backwards? I'm not going to talk about the sunglasses I bought with my own money. Mind your own business. Please."

"Yeah. While I'm still paying off a loan for you to go to NYU. You're welcome."

This had happened more and more on the phone and was maybe part of why I was seeing him less.

"I'm thankful for the loans you took out. I am. Mom took a loan out too and so did I. Which I'm still paying back. Every month. But she doesn't hold it over my head." He rolls his eyes and wishes he could do it harder so instead he rolls them again, but this doesn't stop me. "And Dad, just because you paid for part of my college doesn't mean you get to tell me what I can and cannot buy for myself, forever. Or am I forever indebted to you?"

"Maybe." Mom always said he was controlling, which he would turn back on her.

"Do you know how many kids there were at NYU that didn't have their parents' credit cards? None."

He scoffs. Which is fair. There were lots, but it felt like many more who put fancy meals, designer clothes, partying, whatever, on their parents' card. Maybe it made me feel jealous, so sue me. "I tried to say thank you by using my waitressing money or nannying money or whatever to get you hotel rooms to come for the weekend to New York because I felt bad I got to have the experience, and you didn't. Or concert tickets. Or whatever. You didn't chide me then. I've been working my ass off and if I buy $395 sunglasses, years and years ago, by the way, please don't make me feel bad."

Long silence. He is very unhappy with me and this makes me unsure of myself.

"Dad, I'm sorry. Okay? But we skipped the fact that you told Deb how much I made and you did that with Frank last Thanksgiving and I'd really like that to stay private. Please. From now on. Okay? I know you didn't do it to be like, unkind." Olive branch.

"Fine," he says, quiet and still unhappy.

I look out the car window at long expanses of swamp. The streetlights are different in his neighborhood and outside the land is wide. Inside the car doors get closer like Alice in Wonderland Syndrome.

"I think I'm getting sick."

"And tomorrow night, I invited the neighbors over to meet you."

"Did you hear me? I don't feel well. Wait, for real?"

"What now, Ja—Anna?" In his mind he's speaking to his ex-wife.

"Dad. I told you a few times how I don't want to have a party that's about meeting me. Maybe next time. This is a short trip, we've been arguing more in the last couple . . . years, I don't feel like pretending otherwise and I'm not in a great place. Visiting is about reconnecting, right? Not your neighbors."

He shoots his head toward the window looking like someone slapped him. But I'll be paraded around. I know it.

I go on, "And I'm sorry. But let's just spend time together." I used to love being his prize and now it's way too much. I want to belong to myself. I want him to mentor me on how *not* to define myself with the expectations of others. But I worry he seeks it out on my behalf and I suspect, for himself too, like osmosis. I want to be worth something to him for all the opposite reasons he wants to show me off at his neighborhood party. Plus, whenever he praised my education or the dumb theater I'd done, it didn't feel like he was just proud of me. It felt like I was his fabrication. A fraud we were hiding behind. Or maybe loudest of all I heard, *Pay me back. With kisses on the lips.*

"I can't cancel." That's all he says.

I try to ignore it and believe he'll see me. "I'm sorry, I know it's hard but I'm not feeling jovial or like things are simple with you right now and I don't want to pretend, if I'm being honest, the idea of a party makes me feel icky. I'm sorry."

"I can't cancel," he says again. His jaw knits up and down like it's been wired shut but he's trying to work it apart. This pisses me off because he told me he was going to host this party a month ago when I booked the tickets and I begged him not to. These are the things we spoke about. I wanted to believe that the old Dad who took really good care of me, or who I thought took really good care of me, was in there. That he wouldn't force me to do things that felt icky.

He tries to toggle into chillness and hits my thigh. "Angel. It'll be fun," and he puts in an old CD.

"You got this for me. Remember? You said it was our song."

It would appear too unhinged to plug my ears.

"Savage Garden. 'Truly Madly Deeply.' Remember?"

I wanna stand with you on a mountain
I wanna bathe with you in the sea

It's too much. I want to go home and grow up. Now.

The party with Dad's neighbors ends up being extra awkward as I arrive almost two hours late. Earlier, I'd sought serenity at a faraway nature reserve, ending up in swampland with barbed fences, perhaps to protect patrons from gators. In actuality I'd mapped myself an hour out to a rural prison. I didn't get out of the car. On the way home, my GPS got more confused. When I'm back outside his place, I watch the lights on and strangers through the window, eating hot dog nubs on toothpicks that Deb probably made. And a man who looks like my dad. Who I had texted saying I got lost, and who wrote back "Take your time," which made me feel guiltier.

Once inside, Dad tells me it's totally fine I'm late, that a second with him is enough. Sure thing, he displays me a bit, arm around my shoulders, but I waddle instead of strut and wiggle out of reach. When I meet people, he tries to find ways to brag about a waiter figuring out her acting career. So I share shittier things about me to deflate it, like how I need to go to therapy and that I'm quitting acting because it's not working out.

During cleanup, I study his face while wiping down the coffee table and accidentally have a heart-to-heart with Deb, who tells me that she knows my dad can be weird. He must have told her about our fight.

"What are you girls saying about me? Watch it, Deb, watch it." He wants a flame but she picks up a fly swatter. It'll do.

"Peter, just relax. I'm saying—" She almost has a Southern drawl but it's cut with a little Valley Girl and pitched up an octave. "I'm saying, honey—"

"Yes, sweetie?" I like how he looks at her with deep admiration instead of at me.

"Peter, I said you were weird! Honey. Okay? You are. You

fought with Anna yesterday and then you said 'We all fight with family sometimes,'" and she puffs up the side of her bleached hair. She turns to me, "And I tell Peter, 'You're a tough guy Peter. You're no walk in the park. You get harsh and set in your ways and a little weird and very very cheap.'" The last part makes me laugh. I like her. She's funny.

"Hey. I'm not cheap. Okay? I'm frugal." He likes that she is talking about him like this and he turns on a vacuum that looks like a ghost. It was his parents' vacuum and he reminds us it's over fifty years old. Deb and I crack up.

"All right, ladies," Dad says. "Even if I was wealthy, I'd still be a practical spender. I should have been."

"Wealthy?" I say.

"Chaa. I'm a lot smarter than all the other guys who got promotions and then I was too white, too male. Other people got the jobs I earned."

"Dad. You probably thought you deserved to be a CEO—smart enough to have one hundred million dollars. Right?" Then I add that he acts like it was a position stolen from him.

"Yes!" He almost laughs but is actually yelling. "Yes I fuckin' do think that!" He sounds angry again.

"Dad! That's insane. What makes you entitled to that? Do you know how many intelligent, amazing people live on nothing? You weren't cheated out of anything. And you gotta stop saying stuff about affirmative action and women. It's racist and sexist."

"I am not— I'm a fucking Democrat."

"I didn't say *you* are. I said what you're saying is."

"I did protests, rally on the green in Burlington 1970!" I try to tune him out, but a part of me wants to get into it with him. His layers are unpeeling in front of me. What is at the core?

Tell me who you really are.

A little later, when he follows me around the kitchen putting away the ice cream I'm scooping before I scoop it and cleaning the counter like I'd defiled it, I study his face again. He *is* weird. I never thought of him that way before, but other people do. Deb is right. I'm only here for two more days and we have plans, but something is telling me to take space. I don't listen.

We're inside the Frida Kahlo museum.

Surrounded by self-portraits of a woman in emotional and physical pain, Dad isn't present in the viewing. I'm not sure if I'm spinning out or seeing him clearly for the first time, but I think I notice him looking too long at a young girl with a skirt on. I feel like I'm coming out of my skin. Perhaps Dad, the most significant male figure in my life, represents an accrued distrust of men and my body. Uncomfortable in myself before I could even remember. I pray it's projection.

On the ride home, it all comes up.

"You know, Dad, this isn't easy to talk about. But"—*keep going*—"a couple of my friends at my play that you came to told me when they said hello, you tried to kiss them." I feel scared but remind myself that it's my right to say this. To ask. Maybe I will actually be heard. Maybe my fears are worse than reality. So I plow through, probably sounding pissed instead of brave. I'm not too familiar with this part of myself.

"Yeah?" he answers, smoking a cigarette out the cracked window. Humid air pours in. Not what I expected to hear.

"I'm not done. They said you tried to kiss them on the mouth." There. I said it.

"I did? No, I didn't."

"Really? Two different women I work with told me that you did." His eyes are looking wild like my mom's did on certain nights. "And they didn't say it as a mean thing. They said it . . . nice. But it bothered me."

"Court and Nora? I certainly did not. I don't think I did, Anna. They are adults though."

The last part of the sentence hits funny. "Though? No, not them. The friends that I worked with at the restaurant. Their names aren't important." He's not totally with me right now but I wonder if it's on purpose. My words are hurting him deeply. I can see that, so I try to bring him back. A bit.

"They didn't tell me to make me feel bad. Or for you to feel bad. They said you were really nice and then laughed and said you tried to kiss them hello. On the lips."

"Oh."

"Did you?"

"It's something I could have done. They are adults, Anna."

The way he says "Anna" like I'm an idiot, pisses me off.

"Okay, no. No. They are my friends. It's not okay. Let's not think of them as a random adult you just met." Or actually, let's. That didn't make any sense either. I try to imagine him as a human resource manager and all of his layoffs begin to make sense.

"They are my friends. My peers." I'm already trying not to cry. "I don't like—ugh—I don't like when you've tried to kiss me on the mouth. I always turn my cheek." Maybe this is the thing I've been really wanting to say. "So yeah, I don't want it either. And I don't want you to ever try to kiss my friends on the lips again, okay?"

"Kids do that with their parents."

"What?"

"Some kids kiss their parents on the lips."

"Okay, sure, but I'm telling you now I don't want to. I turn my head away every time. I've told you to your face, 'No.' But you try again the next time." This really gets me. It hurts way more saying it to him.

"I—I—didn't know you didn't want to!" His words are angry. "You didn't tell me."

"I have, actually. I tried not to make a big deal of it. And now it's my friends too. It makes me uncomfortable, Dad." Maybe I'm overstating it, but I will repeat it calmly until he responds properly, like a dad should. "It's inappropriate."

Now I am sensing rage, which is rare from him, reserved for nail polish spills on carpets. Missed exits on Vermont highways. Mom. "They, your friends, could have told me if they didn't want to."

"No. No. No. They shouldn't have to. They are my friends, and if you do that again I will not bring them around you. Or you won't come around me. Okay, Dad?" Every time I say "Dad," it hurts more. Like the old one is dying.

Now he hits a new interval.

"This is ridiculous, Anna, back in the eighteen hundreds it was normal for that to happen. For kids and adults and adults and adults. The kissing. That's—that's what happened—"

I'm trying to keep up but I feel like I'm sinking. It's all going fast.

"Dad. Dad. The eighteen hundreds? What are you talking about!" I'm panicking. "Listen to yourself. I get that you and Mom kissed your Vermont friends on the lips. It's consensual, you're hippies, free love, blah blah. But you kissing my peers on the lips makes me uncomfortable. It's weird. It's not okay."

In the back of my mind is the thing that happened with his ex and how her adult daughter didn't want her two-year-old sitting on his lap. But I don't bring it up. Or how he hardly ever kissed Mom. But maybe he can read my mind.

Because now he's incredibly loud.

We circle a rotary, the sun setting over a Scientology building in Clearwater and my father is spit-screaming, at the top of his lungs, *"I AM NOT A PEDOPHILE I AM NOT A PEDOPHILE I AM NOT A PEDOPHILE I AM NOT A PEDOPHILE!"*

The cells of my body scatter. The shoes I am wearing are flip-flops, not ideal for running. I eye my seat belt and unbuckle it.

Outside our car, a mother walks her daughter in a stroller and the tip of the sun's edge is at the black line separating it from the ocean. Staring, I wonder what it would be like to be her baby instead of his. To be in a lineage, one of the sane ones, born of another sane one, out not to run from something or someone, but to watch the fucking sky and be fine.

The way we sat on the couch. How he put me to bed every night. The dark room, my puppet Monkey. How his living room is covered in framed pictures of me like a museum. He was nice to Jamie before I was born. Happier with Mom when I wasn't there. *Mom and Jamie,* she'd told me, *against me and Dad.* How he told me a million times more than he told Mom that he loved me. The immense focus on me. And the girlfriend, her daughter, her grandchild. Had he been sexually aroused when the child was pulled off? Gross. It doesn't ring a bell in my history with him, but maybe I've been blind. I think about how he can't get an erection any longer because of his prostate removal and hate hate hate how I know that. I've been so scared of my own sexuality my entire life. Why did I never feel comfortable in my body? Why had I been unwilling to breathe with Greg? The time Dad walked past me naked when I was maybe eight. Had that been on purpose? Were these normal things that happened in most families? When I was changing in my room and wanting privacy, saying he'd seen it all before, *You know I changed your diapers.*

But we had been so close. We had been. He was my best friend.

He gave me joy that I didn't have around my mother. He was Dad, Daddy, Pops, I was Angel, Sweetie, Baby, the thing in his entire life he was the proudest of. He was my lifeline for my entire childhood. And now, in this rotary, he is gone.

Everything leaves me and I leave everything.

I AM NOT A PEDOPHILE I AM NOT A PEDOPHILE I AM NOT A PEDOPHILE.

This sentence is the death of the person I believed I knew. I flash to a memory of him telling me "Pedophiles should be killed" when I was nine.

Now there is a silence and it's much louder than the yelling.

I couldn't be farther away from him, on the edge of the passenger seat, almost inside the cup holder on the car door.

I'd always thought it was my parents' relationship that fucked me up. If I could just steer clear of becoming them, I would be okay. But I am fucked. I am unwell. Somewhere within my life, in the dark recesses and the bright rooms, I've been damaged.

This is finally as clear as the Florida sun setting on the ocean.

More silence for what seems like hours. I'm not crying, though, just staring down, pretending I'm no longer here.

"I'm sorry I yelled," he says, finally, in a normal voice. But to me, it's like he is at the other end of a long hallway. I want him to stay there, please. I don't respond.

"Anna. I'm sorry I yelled." I look straight ahead. My heart bangs around the walls of its cavity telling me to get the fuck out of this car. After he takes my silence as an invitation or necessity to speak for ages about how things have been hard and how sorry he is, it's too late. I am not in his car in Florida. I am not his daughter. I see now that my father vanished and maybe he was never here, my image of him only a relic of a dumb, youthful brain concocted to idolize the strongest guardian or else I would have died.

We pull in to the driveway of his condo and he makes small talk to himself about nothing, attempting to pretend that whatever just happened never did. Before he's fully in Park, I open my car door and put my feet on solid ground. I barely have phone service here. The last thing I want to do is go inside, past his bedroom, the ghosts calling out from the floorboards. I beeline into my white bedroom with the Ikea bookshelf that houses my private high school journals (did he read them?), I grab them and throw my shit in a duffel bag, hide it under a chair, and walk straight back outside.

"Anna. Anna. Where are you going?" I hear him call behind me.

I'm leaving and I'm never going to see you again. I don't say that aloud.

"For a walk," I say as I leave.

My movement is continuous until one bar of cell service comes back and I sit on a bench and dial Mom.

After some explanation I ask it. "But Mom, do you think anything happened to me?"

She's less taken aback by my question than I'd hoped, and she pauses. "I don't think so."

"Think, *think*? You don't think so? It's okay. You can tell me."

"I . . . I don't think so. I didn't see real signs of that."

"He's obsessed with kids and animals. Is that a thing? That's a thing," I add, doing math.

This time she answers quickly, "He was obsessed with you, yes. And he loved animals and loved you very much. From my vantage, from what I could tell, he was a good dad. A horrible partner but a good dad. One weekend I had to work he said he didn't want to babysit you."

"I dunno. His living room has like thirty framed photos of me, okay? I'm barely exaggerating. And he doesn't respect my boundaries, doesn't even hear me say them." My close friend was in therapy and I was dabbling in her vocabulary. Plus, I was reading a book about unhealthy child-parent relationships. Perhaps cracking the spine had tainted this trip from the beginning. Didn't matter the publication hadn't been packed. "I've been reading a book about emotional incest"—I hate saying the word "incest" but go on—"emotional. About being emotionally violated or being treated more like a wife or husband by your parent when you're a kid." I go on unloading and it's heavy and doesn't feel fair to throw it on her, unsuspecting, but she takes it. Which is nice because I can't stop. "It was with you, too. You treated me like your husband, the way you screamed at me and then made me hold you and tell you everything would be okay, that I loved you. Sleeping in your bed until you stopped shaking. That should have been an adult's role, your husband's role, not mine. I was a child. I was eight." I say it like I am eight, these ideas still new to me.

It had taken me decades to say these sentences to her. Or to myself.

She starts crying hard. "Oh, I'm sorry."

"Don't cry. I'm sorry." Even though I mean it. I am sorry for making her cry, but my apology makes me defensive and I reverse course, "Mom. Don't cry. It makes me feel bad, like I have to console you. Why can't I be the one who gets to cry?"

I hear her gasp like I've hit her, but she says, "Okay." And says the next part like a slap, "You cry." But softens and tries again. "You cry."

"Thank you. I'm sorry—I'm sorry."

"It's okay, honey." She doesn't know how to stay engaged without crying herself, it seems. But I note the effort and appreciate it. It actually means a lot. Her trying to be there.

"I'm scared," I say. And I realize my body is shaking.

She locks back in, "Anna. Honey. I really don't think he did." Pause, "But—"

"But?"

"But he's a very weird guy."

"He's a weird guy. Wow. Why do people keep saying that? Is he that weird? Do you think—wait—Jamie? Is that why Jamie doesn't want any relationship with him?" Has everyone known?

A lady in her midseventies power-walks by me with headphones from 1999 and says "Morning, chica, beautiful day!" I look down, like a freak.

My mom answers finally, "No. I don't think so. No." But this took way too long.

"I need to get out of here. I can't be around him. I'm scared, Mom. Am I being dramatic?"

"No, no." But she sounds like she's been electrocuted, the wrong person to ask. "I know you're scared. I'm sorry, Anna."

She's on speaker now as I search the internet for flights home. "It's too late to get one today, I'll have to tomorrow. I need a ride there."

"You don't want to let your dad—"

"I will never be in a car with him ever again," I say, interrupting, and then I search "car service" like my life depends on it. The only car that is available is in Tampa, forty minutes away, and it's less *big company*, more *man's name*—Devon—and he has one three-star review. I wish there was an app that connected me with drivers. *Someone should invent that.* I tell my mom that I'm hanging up to call Devon but I'll call her right back.

Instead of an old local man answering, I reach a calling service whose operator puts me on hold for five minutes while I simultaneously search for the cheapest hotel around. When they come back on the line, I've found an Eco Lodge two miles down the road and book it on credit because Mom has offered to reimburse me. The lady tells me the driver can be there in sixty minutes.

I walk back to my dad's place, where the car will pick me up, and he's outside smoking a cigarette. I am standing next to him now. Five more minutes pass and I stay like a street sign facing the road, but in the middle of his driveway.

"Anna." I hate how he says my name now. "Anna."

Nope. Not answering.

"I can start cooking dinner and I'm really very sorry I yelled at you. That's never going to happen again. Okay, sweetie?"

"I am waiting for a car to pick me up." My voice is tight.

"To go where?" he says, seeming to imply that there is nowhere to go.

"A hotel." I move closer to the curb, afraid he could pull me inside.

"You hired a car and are going to a hotel?" he asks.

"Yup."

"I can drive you to a hotel, you don't need to get a car."

"No, thanks," I say. "I already called."

He asks me if I want to at least come inside in the AC while I wait? No. He's been watching me call the car company over and over to ask for new ETAs. It's ninety-three degrees.

An hour passes. Suddenly I've become horribly hungry and thirsty. Every five minutes, he offers to drive me again. I say no no no no no no and I wilt further each time. Becoming less confident that Devon will ever come. Finally, I yield, pulling my duffel bag out from behind the chair without explanation, and let him drive me to the hotel. But my hand stays on the car handle the whole way there. I'm not online. We arrive almost immediately because he lives less than two miles away.

"Angel. I'm sorry. I love you."

I get out of the car, knowing my intention is to never come back.

—

In my motel room, I call Jamie.

"I'm so sorry, I have to ask you a weird question."

My brother hasn't spoken to my father in fifteen years. What was so bad that could have propelled him to excommunicate Dad, who had been trying to reach out? Over time, my dad often complained about the letters he'd written to Jamie and how he never got a response. Trying to stay out of it, I would mention how busy Jamie is and how I knew Jamie loved him and was probably protective of our mom. How I rarely spoke to him myself, but still we kept in touch. Now I wonder if it was something more. Had I been oblivious?

"I'm visiting Dad. My dad." I didn't want to do this but I'm heaving crying. I don't think Jamie's ever really seen me like this before. It might be the most I've ever fallen apart in my entire life, which is saying a lot. He'd seen me fight badly with Mom, but never broken like this.

I'm still going, "He just screamed, Dad screamed—sorry—my dad just screamed *I'm not a pedophile* at me. Over and over. It's a long story but it was not really relevant to what we were talking about. I guess boundaries with women came up, my friends but my adult friends, not children, though, and he just started yelling the *p* word and how he's not one, over and over and over."

"God, Anna, I'm so sorry," he says. Professionally, Jamie is a therapist now. Go figure. I wait but nothing more comes. But I have to know.

"I'm just wondering, it's been so long since you talked to Dad, my dad and like, I know he was tough, but that's a long time to not talk and . . . I don't know how to ask you this, I'm sorry, Jamie, and you can tell me to fuck off but I don't want to be blind to it if you did want to share—did my dad, did he ever abuse you?"

Pause and then Jamie answers, "You mean, like, sexual abuse?" Somehow over the phone he hears my nod and answers, "No."

I'd been so sure he was going to say yes. Earlier in the driveway I'd put the pieces of the scandal together.

"Okay. So that's not the case. That's good," I say. "That's good. I'm sorry to ask. I feel so crazy. Fifteen years is a long time not to talk to someone—It's absolutely your right . . ."

"I didn't . . ." Jamie is very measured in how he answers, "I didn't . . . like . . . how your dad spoke to my mom. Or, sorry, our mom."

"Oh."

"It wasn't right." Jamie's never told me this before.

"Right. Of course," I answer. Guilt coming over me. Grampy said that too, in his letter. But I can't help to ask more. "What about her, though? She was crazy too, though, right?" It's unbelievable to me that we've never discussed any of this before now.

"She's my mom," he says, like those three words tell the whole story. But for him, maybe they do.

What he means maybe is *Peter isn't my dad.* And I picture how this big stranger came into little Jamie's life and even though his mom would scream too, he saw Peter, his new stepdad, being unkind to his person. His mommy. He didn't want anyone screaming at her. Fair. The conundrum of our whole lives as siblings was that some guy was being mean to his mom but that guy was my dad, so to me it was my parents being mean to each other. And then when all the doors were closed, our mom was mean to me. Maybe it was simple.

"I get that," I say, thinking, "and I think he should have been nicer to you too, Jamie. I'm sorry. I just—he didn't know how to be a stepdad. Obviously. He's always told me that, I dunno—I'm not sticking up for him, but his goal was to be your friend. He said you didn't need another dad."

"Huh."

Why am I sticking up for him? "Maybe that wasn't right."

"You know I'm a stepdad now and I think about Peter a lot, because it's really hard. I love it. And, it's complex."

"You're an amazing one, though." He says thank you and I know how much he loves his kids and confirms it's an epically complicated role. He makes it look so easy.

Then Jamie throws an apology my way. One that I wasn't expecting. "I'm sorry I left you alone at the house, Anna."

That does it. I'm a mess. Nobody else could have said that to me, and I didn't realize how much I needed to hear it until this moment. "Why did you leave?" I manage to squeak out.

"Because there was too much fighting. I didn't want to be there, but my regret is leaving you alone."

"You were just a kid too, though. I don't know how to say this, but sometimes I worry that I, like, overblow my memory of it all. Like maybe it wasn't that bad. Maybe I'm just being dramatic."

"No," he says solemnly. "It was really bad."

Chapter Seventeen

I DON'T HAVE A home anymore.

After leaving New York, I'd had a car for a bit, where all my things were packed, but I sold that after I went all overdrawn last week. So now I'm kind of needing one again. And a job. But this sounds like a lot of work.

What if my dad did abuse me? What if I just can't remember? This is where I keep going and my chest shakes like there's a pole attached to an engine.

Get up.

Walk.

I'm pretty sure I'm headed to Hancock Park or Hancock Park–adjacent but who cares. Really. Everyone in Los Angeles always wants to talk about where they are and how they got here, like that SNL sketch everyone who lives in LA is obsessed with. Also, it's too sunny here. And the palm trees look like sick Muppets. But again, I don't know where I am. Somewhere in Los Angeles. Where I was before, who knows. Who was I without memories I could be sure of?

As I walk I am seven years old again, pretending to be asleep.

"Wake up wake up wake up wake up." My dad endows my brown monkey with his puppet voice and little soft arms shake me by the ribs.

"I'm awake, Monkey, I'm awake!" I say, giggling.

"Why are you awake, Anna? It's bedtime. Go to sleep!"

"You woke me up, Monkey!"

"No, I didn't. It's bedtime."

"Don't wake me up again! Good night!" I say joyfully and close my eyes and roll over. Knowing I'll be woken once again.

This was a prized memory of childhood. But was I missing something? Where were monkey's paws? I only remember his hugs around my neck and the shaking of my ribs. But maybe this is denial.

Two cars slam into each other nearby. Just a fender bender.

Everyone is okay.

My pace quickens.

My heart slams like there are two of those too.

I reach a corner where three fancy-looking restaurants link like a trio and I cup my hands around my eyes and I push up against the glass to look in.

It is so different than in New York, here everyone smiles a little too much and I sense transactions during long lunches. Lunch is a part of work, not a break in the day.

But the transparency of art being transactional holds some relief. In college, that would have been betrayal. Now I see it as more honest, most of them inside chasing money first, art second, third, fourth. Tell me your real motives and I'll tell you mine.

I walk in and find the chef. He's in his whites.

"Chef. Hi. Excuse me. Sorry, I know you're busy."

Chef turns around. I try again. "I'm sorry, can I give you my résumé? I'm Anna and I just got here from New York. I waited tables there." He barely says anything but takes my one-page and goes.

I'm walking again, following my phone's directions to a car dealership, but my batteries die.

I head in the general direction as I remember it and end up wandering around for two hours until I find myself in a 7-Eleven, which I walk into like I'm lost, instantly think of my dad, and cry. The Slurpee machine is our Slurpee machine. The cheese-filled hot dogs are our cheese-filled hot dogs. And it feels like a cruel joke.

I use their bathroom after getting a code, but not till after I buy a charger, otherwise they say I can't come in. I don't mention that my dad used to work here but I thought about it.

When I look in the mirror, I see a lost girl pretending to be an adult.

Four hours later, I leave the dealership with a Toyota Yaris, my first car lease, and a fully charged cell. I call my best friends one by one and tell them what happened in Florida.

Every time I do, my chest shakes. One by one they tell me I am loved and surround me.

Court and Janna both share their memories of my dad as the cool adult. The yummy pancake breakfasts with bacon. They never felt or remember anything inappropriate. And they are sorry I'm going through this.

I'm full of shame over what I say but find little pieces of pride that these people, not related to me, are so clearly my family. Wonderful souls I gathered in life, surrounding me, no matter what I bring to them. No matter who I am or am not.

A gross abused girl.

An overreactive adult, too hard on her struggling, desperate father.

When my dad calls, I hit *Ignore.*

When his texts turn into incessant apologies, I scan past them.

And when the emails turn into blame, I skim and call friends.

Despite the gaping hole, I still have a family.

That's something.

Am I starting over or running away? Somewhere in the past months I'd faced myself as a baby. I was shaky and cold and crying.

But trying to grow up.

When I get back to Maya's, I have a car and the general manager of that fancy trio of restaurants has called to schedule an interview.

She's made dinner. We eat whole fish and pickled radish.

"Come on, let's go," Mai says.

We do. We go to Korean baths, an LA specialty. Inside the bathhouse are women. Maya describes the onsens in Japan. How families bathe together and that's the culture, which somehow brings me both unease and deeper comfort.

Maya tells me to take a shower before we enter the shared bath. "Gross not to." I agree, and we clean in a large open room. There is no privacy and yet solitude here is plenty.

Each bath is labeled *warm, hot,* or *extra hot.*

We choose hot.

It's nice knowing what to expect before we get in.

When we get bored, Maya dips into the ice plunge and I sit in the steam room until my face feels like it's wet fire.

She gifts me a scrub here and we are in one big room, with massage tables covered in plastic and Korean women dressed in black lingerie. They take salt or sugar or something coarse and rub it all over my body. Hard.

I want to tell them to stop until the burning gives over to scratches, the good kind, like what I imagine an animal craves.

They use a pitcher dipped over and over in water to clean off my sloughing old skin.

Their job is hard. It takes strength to do this again and again. There are no windows down here. They speak to each other in Korean, smiling and laughing between the seriousness of scrubs. After, they bow to me and I bow back, really meaning it.

I bow again. I'm very grateful.

Since Florida I've been so afraid of big noises and big feelings. Maybe before Florida, even. The smallest poke can set me off. Now my body feels stripped of layers and prickling like it's alive. It still belongs to me. That's what my skin is saying. And it's actually not fragile. There are a million layers to slough and get rid of with water, and there are a million more left.

In the care of fake Korea, Maya and I eat a second dinner, soup and seaweed and noodles and bulgogi and hot rice. In front of everyone at the café, I sob.

Maya holds me.

When we leave, cold LA air hits us through her windows. We turn up a song from the year 2000 and blast it so my thoughts go away. We sing at the top of our lungs, belting without thinking of technique. I believe I'll be ready to chase joy. At some point.

I'll get to work.

I'll use my hands.

I'll call a therapist.

I'll be with friends.

I'll laugh a lot.

When the time is right, I'll get a dog.

Maybe even a partner. Maybe. Maybe not.

A second of hope.

Just a second of this as we drive down Wilshire Boulevard.

"What do you want back?" Seth asks. His office building reminds me of a strip mall.

I'd been seeing Seth, a therapist, for a few weeks now and I was talking about a letter I had written to my father and planned on sending.

"What do I want back from a letter I write him? A letter back."

"That's a good start," he says, trying not to laugh at my literalness.

So I go deeper. "I want him to tell me the truth."

"In regard to what, exactly?"

"Was I abused? Was anyone hurt? Did he—ugh, I hate saying it—molest me?" And I laugh inappropriately.

Seth nods, brows furrowed. "And if he answers and says no, will you believe him?"

It's a good question. "I don't know. But I should ask, right? Seems like I should ask, like—'Did you ever hurt anyone?' To just sit here and wonder and never ask feels like I'm stalling. In limbo."

"Interesting. Okay. For what purpose?"

"You think I shouldn't?" It's obvious he thinks I shouldn't.

"No. I'm never going to tell you what to do. Just exploring."

"What you think doesn't matter, that's what you say."

"Right, it's what you think." I want to roll my eyes but I don't.

"Why ask?" I say, posing the question to myself again. "To call the authorities if he says yes? I don't know."

My therapist nods for a while, thinking. "Do you think someone who is a pedophile is a monster?"

This takes my breath away, but the answer comes easily. "No. I don't. I don't think anyone is a monster." Except for a few exceptions, and I think about killing Hitler before he was Hitler. "I think most or all of them experienced the same abuse and then they repeat it. I hope that didn't happen to my dad. And what if some people are born with that? That's a really sad thought, torturous. Pushed into the shadows because asking for help wouldn't feel safe, I'd imagine. Which isn't an excuse for any of their actions. It just seems like pure torment. I can have empathy for that."

Silence. He nods.

I go on, "I don't know much about his family. His childhood. He never talked about it. I get the idea that maybe he was slapped around, as he put it. But that was the culture then, as he says. He never elaborated on what happened."

I think for a minute and then add, "Oh, and he was very sick as a child. He had sores down his esophagus so he couldn't eat real food that wasn't liquid. He had to swallow iron powder. It was a mystery illness. At some point they learned it was a form of herpes. Which now out loud sounds strange." That stays in the air for a moment and I wish I could take it back. I go on, "That's a lot of suffering, especially for a kid. He couldn't go to school. I don't know. They hoped it'd resolve the issue, but it didn't." I think about how some serial killers experienced a lot of pain as a child.

"Wow."

"I know." We sit in that for a moment before I continue, "It resolved after a couple years and didn't come back till he was really stressed and not taking care of himself in his twenties. I believe that's why he moved to Vermont. To heal. Start another life. Ditch the van. I never met his parents, they were already dead, both from cancer. My dad always said he would die young too so I should enjoy my time with him."

"That's not a caring thing to tell your child. How old were you when he said it?"

"I can't remember a time when he didn't. Seven maybe?"

"That must have scared you." My chest gets tight but I don't want to cry the entire session. I barely know this person. But maybe this is part of letting go. "Huh. This is a lot. You've taken in a lot. So I wouldn't want you to skip this processing part. Idea: What if you write him letters but bring them in here first? We can read them out loud if you feel like it or I can just read it in an email, whatever. But you don't have to send them until you're ready. If you're ready. Until you know what you want in return."

I consider this for a long, quiet beat. "I want to send one now, though. It's weird. I want to get through this moment. To get to the next step. I feel in limbo. I said that, but this—"

"Estrangement."

"Yeah yeah, this estrangement feels like I'm being crushed."

Seth is quiet for even longer than usual.

"Would your dad ever respond to a letter by telling you this is your fault? And how would you feel if he did that? Would he say, what happened to us was"—Seth underlines the last two words with a boom of his voice—"'*your fault*'? If something sexual happened, could he blame you, in other words?"

This immediately makes me cry. "Yes. I think he could. That scares me."

The other day Dad had sent me a random email in regard to his harbored anger over Mom and I guilting him for smoking, choosing an example of when I was nine, threatening to Scotch tape a school picture of myself on his cigarette pack. It was something I'd seen in an anti-smoking video at school.

Seth nods again, oddly familiar with this area of work given how I chose him pretty randomly for his price and location. "I guess what I want for you is to get to a place with a letter, with your own statements and self-expression, so they are complete, so that no matter what he says in return, you are receiving healing simply from what you write to him. Then, anything this imperfect human who loves you and who is flawed says back to you won't break you. That's what I want for you.

"Have you heard of Al-Anon?" he adds. I have not.

He explains that this is a group built for family of alcoholics but how it might be helpful for me too. And then apologizes that time is up. I pick up my coat and purse.

"Keep writing those letters. See you next week."

Two plush chairs sit across from a TV executive at some production company. Maya and I wear too much makeup and I wear all her clothes.

"So, you raised the money on Kickstarter?" The exec has a slight Southern drawl, and I wonder how long she's been here and what her aspirations are. Fingering the TV-lot pass, I sort of don't know how I'd answer my own question if it was turned on me. What are my aspirations? I don't know, but Maya and I made a web series for six thousand dollars that we raised on Kickstarter. It had made a teeny tiny splash, more like a dribble, and so we were taking meetings now. This was going to be the last hurrah before going back to school for something else. I guess my aspirations are to just go one step at a time.

"This part is crazy!" says the executive, not knowing if she likes it or not. She is on YouTube and plays a clip from our web series where Maya is playing a Japanese prank show host and I'm a male Ashton Kutcher wannabe, wearing a 2005 nonsensical headphone mic thing, connected to nothing, because I'm also a gamer and the headset makes my character feel important.

"My name is Cory." He is very muted and self-conscious in a short blond wig.

"And I'm Tomokusan." Maya's is extraordinarily animated and positive, with a bowl cut.

Tomo and Cory are an unlikely pair who love each other and met when they started gaming online, despite speaking different languages. Cory loves Tomo and his culture. This episode of our series is called "Slam" and it's a fake seven-minute pilot for a prank show. We cast Maya's real mom who walks down the sidewalk as an unsuspecting pedestrian until we run over and pull her skirt down.

In the next prank, Tomo and Cory slam someone's coffee out of their hands as they exit a café. Then a camera crew runs out of the bushes and Tomo and Cory hug the guy who got pranked. Our friend Jeff Ward plays this idiot. The clincher is that the dumb pranks get progressively more intense, so in the middle of the night, Maya and I, as Cory and Tomo, take it further by wearing diapers and white face paint and sneaking through people's windows, lying in their bed with our eyes open, touching their noses until they wake up to meet our eyes and scream, running out of bed.

It was dumb and funny and all preplanned, medicine to my soul, but watching it back sitting next to a TV executive even feels nice too, like we'd hacked the system. She laughs despite herself. And we laugh too. Playing characters with Maya feels right on a cellular level and makes everything okay in certain moments. So for now, I won't go back to school to become a teacher or study art therapy. For now, we will play rejects as much as possible and write for each other and I'll wait tables as little as I can while still paying for what I need and nothing else will matter.

I write a notecard that says NO PRESSURE, JUST PURPOSE and pin it to my wall. I don't want to get sucked into running toward a success that doesn't feel authentic to me. Toward everyone else's approval. To being the centerpiece in a parade that marches. I'll take it day by day and enjoy the days as best I can.

The executive tells us that she thinks we are very funny but has no idea what to do with us. And that's fine.

We go outside and I smoke too now apparently. I'd been so hard on Dad about this my whole life and now we puff and reflect on how playing rejects feels like coming home. When our stomachs start nervously churning like they did in Amsterdam, we remind ourselves to click into what we love. Sometimes it feels like we have one mind, me and Mai. And decide our goal is to play the biggest rejects we can muster, as authentically as possible. And then we have the same thought at the same time: middle school. If it didn't suit anybody else, it didn't matter.

We were on our path in the right direction.

Becky raises her hand again. She insists on speaking at every single meeting, which is probably why a veteran named Bob rolls his eyes, but Becky's been through a lot.

After a year of being in LA, I find myself here at least once a week. Sometimes twice. Al-Anon is a twelve-step program, technically for people who have someone they love with an alcohol addiction. But here I am without that, sitting on these cold folding chairs in a church room by another 7-Eleven in Silver Lake. Most people here seem quite well adjusted and that's really comforting. Some don't. I guess Becky's an in-between.

"Hi, I'm Becky," she starts, like always, shoving hair away from her eyes.

"Hi, Becky," twenty-five of us say in return.

"I'm really grateful to be here today. I, uh—oh yeah, today is my dad's birthday so . . ."

Yesterday was my dad's birthday. My chest shakes. My therapist recently named this feeling as possible PTSD. *This could be that then Anna, okay.* Naming it helps.

Becky continues, "And I called him."

Ooohs and ahhhs ring low across the room.

"I know." She does a huge exhale like she's been holding her breath since yesterday's share. "He picked up. I put a timer on my phone, ya know, like I planned. So I knew when I had to get off the phone."

She pokes at something in her teeth and pushes her hair back again.

"I told him I had a work meeting. Boundaries. Learned that trick here, thanks. It's so obvious, a timer, but when you think that you are responsible for someone else's well-being, just getting off the phone when they want to stay on can feel impossible. And then I'd blame him. But why not blame me for lacking boundaries? I could hang up. And it's *my* responsibility to do it kindly."

"Mmm."

"Mmm."

"Yes."

"Awareness, Acceptance, Action," she says. "Stay on your side of the street."

This resonates. I want to blame my parents alone, but why not take partial responsibility? There were so many corny terms and slogans here, but I need them. They help.

Becky's two minutes are not up. "And that made me feel safe, or saf*er*, calling, like I wasn't going to get entrenched in his fucking shit. I wasn't going to like, sink on a toilet boat in his diarrhea sea." Everyone laughs. Weird humor has ample support here, which is nice. "And what's crazy is, I kind of actually like, enjoyed the fucking phone call! The call started as obligation, but then it was, I dunno, actually good. My dad's voice"—she takes a big inhale and lets it out with her next words—"didn't set off gross goosebumps for the first time in memory."

For me, something about the words "goosebumps" and "dad" and "gross" set off more shaking feelings in my chest. I guess I know what Becky means.

"And I was truly"—she stops herself, emotional and amazed—"truly able to say 'Happy birthday, Daddy' and mean it."

This brings her to tears.

I had sent my dad a brief text yesterday on his birthday. And I had sent a gift with a very short card. But it had been a year since our estrangement, and we still had not spoken. But I was working on the letters.

Becky goes to say more but an alarm chimes, a real one, and the leader says, "Thirty seconds left."

"Thirty seconds, I hear that."

And in her last moments, Becky recites Al-Anon slogans:

It's not important for me to comment on everything I hear. It is important for me to let go and let others make decisions for themselves. Easy does it. Keep an open mind. A mistake a day keeps my perfectionist at bay. Today I will endeavor to enjoy my humanness.

Unable to see my dad age or change, to note new wrinkles or the widening of his double chin or track the quiet inclination of my own DNA, takes a toll that I feel viscerally. Something is missing. It takes a lot of work—therapy, Al-Anon—to decide that this loss is okay.

I walk out into the sunlight from the church basement, and I can compartmentalize. I wait on people at the restaurant.

Pay my very few bills and try to get ahold of my debt.

Hang with friends, go to parties.

I may not be immersed in every inch of life but I'm getting through.

I feel pain but I do not want to hurt myself.

This is okay.

In moments when things get too quiet and my thoughts get

too loud, I feel like I'm pretending he no longer exists. Not that Dad died, but that he was never here. Or that the person who had been my dad officially left long ago—packed and boarded a plane that landed in a dimension I could not enter.

Without him in my ear, I was free to traverse dark recesses of my mind and memories, moving the spotlight from places regularly traversed to the edges, searching for anything repressed.

But over time, after lots of looking, I don't see any.

I don't see any physical violation. I don't see any sexual abuse.

The memories of my mother's tantrums, however, her breakdowns, are readily accessible.

Later that day I look into the mirror.

You're an adult now, Anna.

You aren't being abused.

You are allowed to have boundaries and ask for them nicely.

You can't make anyone do what you want.

Knowing that Becky had a relationship with her father, as she put it, a triple-threat abuser, I believe I could get there again, too.

And my relationship with my mother had room to grow, too.

Fixing their relationship was not my problem to solve, and being the glue trying to hold them together had never worked.

I wouldn't try to fix anything anymore.

I would expect something different only because the difference would be within me.

If I gave something different, maybe I'd get something different.

Maybe not.

But I couldn't let any of it be my entire world.

Not again.

Chapter Eighteen

We've been filming an episode of another web series all day, except this time it's not ours. I took the day and night off from waiting tables to help—groups from college take turns holding booms, pressing wardrobe, keeping schedules like makeshift ADs. Then we take turns acting in each other's stuff.

The house I've been staying at has been torn apart and put back together today and now everyone is exhausted from a long stretch of manual labor and playing pretend. But we are still full of adrenaline and laughter, and from that, an unhinged creative energy lingers into the night.

This has led to smoking a little of the strongest weed I've ever had in my body and I'm a lightweight. Which is how we've made the last-minute decision to drive somewhere we've never been before.

We are going up a mountain but I'm convinced we are going to careen off the side and I can't stop laughing. And screaming.

Sam Zvibleman, a director in LA who is friends with a lot of the NYU kids and won't tell people his age, is sober and driving us, thankfully. Jeff Ward, a friend from Amsterdam and NYU, tries to calm me down but I'm not listening.

"He is going to drive off the mountain. It really feels like that. I'm begging for my life." I'm also hysterically laughing because of how embarrassing and honest my screams are coming out despite me.

"No no no no too fast! WAHEAGGHHH!"

"It's not fast!"

"You swear you aren't? RASGHHAHHHHHH." I sound like an animated bird getting hit by a plane but I'm almost sobbing too. "Holy— You poisoned me with this strong California weed, Jeff. You smoke this every day? Jesuahhhhhh."

Sam is hysterical now too.

"Look the speed limit," I say. Sam waves his hand to look at a sign that says speed limit 20 mph.

"And look, Anna." I do. But then I scream again.

"Shhh. But the speedometer, limit's twenty, I'm driving ten." Sam laughs out.

It's true, he is. "Oh my god you are. Why does it feel like this though? It's so twisty. Are you pressing gas on the turns?"

"It's not twisty. And no, I'm not."

Jeff is in the passenger seat and has been buried in his hoodie, eyes almost glued shut, because he's laughing so hard he stopped making noise.

He gets himself together and tries to explain, "He has to accelerate a little during a turn. That's what you're feeling." When I'm not screaming, I'm smiling, which is maybe why I'm not horribly annoying yet or maybe I am and they are good at hiding it. Either way, I appreciate it.

I eye the speedometer again and Sam's highest speed is twelve mph.

"Oh. You aren't going high—fast. I mean fast. You got me high."

When we get to the top of the mountain, there is Griffith Park Observatory where you go to look inside a building to see . . . fake stars, which feels strange, but I try to stop overthinking everything. *Why would we go inside to see stars?*

"Alex is meeting us," Jeff says.

I'm staying on the couch at their house. Jeff and Alex are roommates.

Something shifts warmly inside me whenever I hear Alex's name.

"Oh, Alex is coming." Gulp.

For some reason Sam was just dropping us off, probably relieved to get this psycho out of his car and back to editing.

And there he is. Alex. He smiles at me.

I smile back and think, *Don't like Alex.*

We are walking.

Do not like Alex.

But he's next to me in this star museum and his shoulder is grazing mine. Every time we are around each other, it's like we are made of magnets.

Stop it, Anna. Alex dated that friend from college.

Plus her name is also Anna, so that would be weird.

And she is lovely. And would be hurt.

Do not like Alex.

While buying tickets inside, Jeff says his hips ache.

Earlier in the evening he told us he might have something called Bamboo Spine. I think it was his delivery or the timing or probably just the weed but everyone died laughing. So, trying to make up for that, we suggest getting him a wheelchair. We do this seriously because friends laughing earlier hurt him. Jeff insists he doesn't need it but when I bring it to him and tell him that he must use it, he listens and sits, at least a bit thrilled.

After I wheel him around for about five minutes, I find what I enjoy most is leaving him places and letting him roll down ramps by himself.

And when there is a star installation on a wall, I face Jeff inches away from the opposite one and go to look at the installation myself. Soon this makes me laugh again and I pee my pants. Alex is dying next to me. We have the same sense of humor.

Don't like Alex.

When Jeff gets tired of the two-note joke, we watch him try to maneuver the wheelchair alone but he does so poorly, hitting the wall, and I pee again.

Driving back down the mountain, we agree that this was one of our favorite nights since moving to LA. I don't say it, but it might be my best one. And later, Alex buys me a Happy Meal and I think about my dad and our fast food for a second but instead of it enveloping me in pain, I send Dad good thoughts and respond to a text that he sent from the morning asking me how I am.

Good. How are you?

Back at the house, the guys take forty-five minutes to choose the movie we are going to watch. They never seem to want to sleep in their beds, either, which is such a relief because I never want to be alone at night with my thoughts. Jeff falls asleep on the chair in the first ten minutes of the movie after ripping a bong and when Alex wakes him up, Jeff is angry, denying he fell asleep at all. When Alex shows him a video he just took of Jeff sleeping, Jeff harrumphs off to bed.

"Are you tired?" he asks me.

"No, are you?"

Despite filming since six A.M. and now it's two A.M., we aren't tired.

My gut tells me to go to bed, but this couch is my bed. When Alex asks if I want a shoulder massage, I say yes because at least it's in a public space. We won't make out. But it is my bed.

He kisses my neck.

And this time, my body says yes too.

Before it goes further, I have the wherewithal to say that I feel bad about this because he dated a friend. But how I like him. He feels bad too but says that they've been broken up for more than a year and that life is messy sometimes. Life is messy. I'll have to tell my friend. But so be it.

Perfect was out the window.

At least I knew that and could still breathe. Maybe that was something. The other thing was our laughter. It had been a while since I'd spent time romantically with someone who was so funny.

He would be the funniest one of all. When we go to bed that night, Alex and I are laughing.

When we wake up, we are laughing.

For the first time in a very long time, I feel comfortable next to someone.

The whole thing is not overly intimate and it isn't too separate either.

On one hand, it'll be easier if this is just a fling.

But on the other, I never want it to end.

A couple years later, I am at his family home for a Hanukkah Christmas combo and we have adopted a dog. My life consists of writing passion projects with Maya on the weekends and working as a professional actor on weekdays. We're on similar paths, both doing TV procedurals on FOX and NBC respectively. I've been able to pay off my loans. And I'm surrounded by a gorgeous chaos that I've always wanted but never thought I could have.

"Alex, honey, can I get you anything else?" Lynn, Alex's mother, asks. He has his arm around her. It's so easy for them to be like that.

"I'm okay, Mom."

"The farm, I forget what it's called, but the local farm up the street that just opened . . ."

"Jacobson's," Danielle, Alex's older sister, says flatly, like she doesn't care if their mom hears her or not, which is an if because as humans do, Lynn has lost some of her hearing.

"It doesn't matter," Lynn says to herself but then turns back, remembering, "Oh, it has the honeybee on the sign because they sell honey."

"Jacobson's." Danielle tries again.

"Bernie's?" says Lynn.

"It's not Bernie's," John, Alex's dad, says too loud. I'm sitting in the blue-striped chairs in the living room, bare feet on cold Malibu tile, and decide to speak up. "Um, I think Danielle is saying Jacobson's."

"JA-COB-SON'S!" Danielle yells.

"Jacobson's, Lynn. JAY. COBB. SUNS," John pipes in again like he's been saying it for years even though he just joined in.

In my mind, Alex should be mediating because he's closest, but Alex does nothing. Like none of it's a big deal. Like a pronounced *back-and-forth* doesn't put him on edge. Like there's nothing to mediate. Maybe there's not.

John gets up to grab himself orange juice, possibly annoyed it's not already on the table, and then out of nowhere gets a sideways kick in the spine.

"Jesus. Christ."

"Fire Dragon spew lava times one billion. NOW," six-year-old

Edward chimes in, buried in his own imagination and gives another lateral kick with his tiny strong foot into John's spine.

"Jesus," John says again and laughs despite himself, clearly loving the idea of this small kid beating him up, and takes on his own character, Grandpa Nemesis: "Wrestler champion in Pittsfield High School activate . . . destroy grandson. GO!"

And Edward giggles like a Tickle Me Elmo. John wrenches his grandson to the floor, "I'll squeeze this SOB like a grape until he pops." In response the kid holds nothing back, truly dedicated to destroying Grandpa John.

"John, John—don't hit the table, John," chides Lynn, also appreciating the moment.

"GET THAT BASTARD," yells Alex in some sort of supervillain voice. "THAT OLD MAN'S GOING DOWN. SEND HIM BACK TO HIGH SCHOOL. HE'S GOT NOTHING ON YOU, POKÉMON."

Face buried in John's armpit, Edward tries to yell, "I'm not Pokémon, I'm a sledge slinger!" I peek at Alex, who looks at me back smiling.

John's foot hits a stool and makes a loud noise, but nothing breaks.

Still, Samantha, Alex's other sister, runs out of the bathroom with her hair half done, despite using the powder room for just under two hours, and wants to make sure everyone is okay.

"Fine. We're fine," John yells. And goes back in.

"Wait. Sammy. How are you not ready yet?" She makes a rascal face and runs back to finish. Alex laughs.

Edward's little brother, Kaleb, wants in on the violence even though he's not yet two, and his dad, Scott, trails after him, too tired to run (though Scott will later claim that he was never too tired and always outran them and always will).

Kaleb watches inches away from the human ball of grandpa-grandson and stands like he's invincible, unafraid of a leg hitting him in the face. It hits. Now he's wailing. Danielle picks him up, inspecting where he got knocked, kissing it and rocking him. Scott yells at Edward to be careful and Edward yells back like a teenager, "Stop, Dad."

Again, wondering if I'm supposed to do something amidst the pandemonium, like help in some way, I start cleaning up the dining table, but Lynn tells me not to. To sit down. To relax.

That is what Alex is doing, now cradling our dog, George, like a baby, unconcerned. Suddenly Kaleb and Edward stand over their uncle, watching him hold this huge animal. "I can't believe he lets you do that," says Scott, and Edward echoes his dad's statement like he thought of it himself. Kaleb bends down and pets George's nose, and George licks his.

"Yup. He does this all the time," I hear myself say with admiration. "George loves it. Alex too. It looks crazy, but. . . ." No one's really listening to me. Scott reads a book, Danielle feeds Kaleb eggs, Edward keeps trying to kick Grandpa John in the back, despite John actively ignoring him. Lynn cleans up every last crumb with the vision of someone half her age without showing an inkling of resentment, while Alex trails along sort of helping, though he isn't doing much because she won't let him and it's clear, this has always been their way.

In the living room chair with absolutely nothing to do but take them in, I admire the ease in which this family seems to move. Any arguing, gone in a second, maybe even performed for fun.

Alex sits on my lap, but then we switch. George sees us together and takes his cue to join. The three of us stack on top of one another like a wedding cake. Alex moans in discomfort. I jump and land, crushing him more. The animalistic sounds make George lick every pore of his face like the most in-tune LA facialist. Kids tear into the presents topping the family coffee table like the varnished stump of a Christmas tree. Sometimes I worry it all could vanish.

Dad's on his hands and knees, balling up our used wrapping paper, and eating pieces of orange and chocolates out of his stocking. The Christmas record by his college acapella group plays.

What if he is by himself on Christmas morning while I'm here, in wonderland? The idea makes me nauseous. My mom's with her fiancé, Jack in Rhode Island, but what if Dad's totally alone? I sent him a bunch of gifts but never called him back. I've also written him five letters I haven't sent. One of them asks if he abused me. If he says no, do I believe him and then visit for Easter?

Every draft feels like trying to compose the right song for the most important funeral. In the third one I asked him if he was "minor-attracted," a result after googling non-pejorative terms for pedophiles. Most folks would rather be called a serial killer. My chest shakes, wondering if my own father had been hurt as a kid. The Konkles didn't talk much about childhood. My mom told me she had almost been abused by her friend's father but left before anything happened. That's all I knew.

These ideas punched at me, punched at my memories, no matter if it was a holiday—holidays made it worse. But had I been personally hurt, or was it a father short on boundaries, who should've listened when I'd asked him not to kiss me or put his hand on my leg? Was this about me being "sensitive" most of all? Or emotionally beaten down from all the nights of my mother's mental breaks, alone with her? What had happened in Florida sort of triggered something burned in long ago. The fact that my chest knocked told the story that I had endured some level of physical harm. But years later, I know that I'm someone who happens to feel things, anything, quite deeply. For whatever reason, this is me.

Edward rips open a Batman figurine. Kaleb, Paw Patrol.

Kids are full of so much trust and depth and resilience, so much decency, the best of human beings—to be a toddler and watch your parents fight for the first time, with those big eyes and that open soul, is profound. *Mommy and Daddy don't always like each other. Should I yell with them like a game of pretend? Or run away? Or make new neural pathways for pain to flow real easy?*

Drafting letter after letter for my dad, I tried to give my little self the credit she deserved. I tried to stay with her in the secrets. The more I poked at the dark, quiet nights with my dad, when he would put me to bed alone, I could only remember him playing with the monkey puppet who would wake me up while I was pretending to sleep.

The very contemplation around this subject brought me such shame and made me feel like I was carrying a secret, even though I hadn't found one. Maybe the wondering in itself had become the actual shame that just felt like a secret. I kept playing through the tapes in my head, trying to figure it out. My mom had chased me around the house. I was never allowed to have physical space. Maybe hearing my mom say that she thought he was sitting inappropriately with me on that couch cast a shadow on everything. Perhaps it had begun growing when I was little during all the fights but bloomed full force in Florida, sitting in the passenger seat as Dad screamed *I'm not a pedophile.* But maybe *he* was scared to death by the accusation. Maybe he was a man with a strange style of communication, a man who had recently gone through a breakup for reading a grandchild a book on his lap, and then admonished for greeting my thirty-year-old friends with mouth kisses.

Maybe he was just a broken-down man short on boundaries, with one finger lost, multiple firings, no prostate, a life that hadn't gone remotely the way he thought it should have, and nobody around to talk to. A wife that left. A stepson who wouldn't return a call.

Maybe he snapped.

And then his daughter, who had been his best friend, and he hers, wouldn't call him back either. And today on Christmas, not enough wrapping paper to ball.

I owe him a letter. I'll be brave and I'll finish it.

We exchange gifts.

My boyfriend holds my hand.

I wonder if they will ever know each other, Alex and Dad.

By then, who would he be?

Ten drafts later and a few years after the Florida car incident, I finally have something to send, a letter that I don't need him to respond to.

> Dad, I'm extremely glad you told me about
> your health change because I love you
> + care deeply about your well-being.
> Irrelevant to that is that I miss you.
> I've been scared to write you until
> now because I was scared of how
> you might react. But now, I feel
> more afraid of not sharing my truth
> with you, so here goes—
>
> When I first wrote you about this,
> After the argument in Florida, I didn't
> go deeply into detail + I quickly gave up
> partly because I felt blamed for

how I was feeling. And I was
extremely fragile.

I think we have been having tough times here +
there for a while now, beginning more
obviously in high school when we didn't speak
for a couple months. Our communication
has been off + on through the last decade,
very difficult.
Some things
have changed in my life + I see I do take some
responsibility in our difficulty. With that said,
you do too, and it's been a frustrating
path because you're my dad and though
I no longer expect perfection or really,
anything close to that, a role model
for our communication + communication
in general, would have been obviously
preferred.

I have found it difficult post-divorce,
talk, money talk, my physical boundaries,
my work talk, all difficult, frankly.

I also want to express some of the many
good things you've afforded me—levity,
unconditional love, art, generosity, deep
thinking, fun + so much more.

Unfortunately, in recent years my
experiences with you have been severely
tainted with difficulty.

One of these things being that you have tried
to kiss me on the lips countless, really
endless
times, though I have told you no.

This shattered me. If my own father
wouldn't listen to me, why would I
expect any other man to?

When I had friends, my age, tell me
you greeted them by kissing them on the
lips too, again, I felt shattered.
That same intrusion I had felt + tried
to shake off, was doubly apparent to
me. Your intrusion on them + defensiveness
around it, destroyed me further, that's
just the truth + but moreover
I have felt the same intrusion as
I resisted + despite that, you persisted
every single time. Not
wanting to do that isn't something
you "forget." This has been deeply upsetting to
me. My expectation is that you should have heard no +
stopped.

Then when I moved to LA + spoke to you on
the phone, you would sometimes sound
slurred + say unpredictable things.
This was difficult + I wondered if you
were doing okay. I didn't like talking
to you in your unpredictable state.

Not knowing what you might do
if I might be blamed for something.

Then later, in Florida, you opened up
about the reasons for the Justine
breakup: Mentioning that Justine's
daughter felt you couldn't be trusted
around her young daughter, frankly,
scared the shit out of me. In one
sense. I assumed this was very
difficult for you. Personally it brought
up feelings of despair in me—your
daughter—not feeling heard when you
would try to kiss me, walking into my
room when I was younger, changing clothes, citing
you had changed my diapers so
you had seen everything anyhow.
And perhaps, more innocuous-sounding stuff
like talking about my work . . . you have
always been more pleased with me, interested, available,
loving
with performance stuff of mine, when I acted
well, sang well, get a good part. Or
maybe you just gave me more attention
in those circumstances, when typically
you drove away + left, all too often
in the middle of some fight with Mom.
I think it would be nice to feel like
you care about me, without work needing
to be involved. Or money. So that's
a bit into why I stopped wanting to

discuss work with you. I needed to
stop pursuing my aspirations to please
you + to do it for me + myself
alone. Ironically, I think of you often in
my work because of tools you have
given me to do well in it. In
business + otherwise. But that's kind
of the role you assumed by being my
dad + though I am grateful, I
don't want to feel like I owe you
something for it or want / have to pay
you back. What I would like is
some iota of a simple, safe,
parental relationship. Simple sounds nice.
Not sure what that would look like or
if it's possible but if there's something I don't want to do
or talk about, you won't get angry at me, but respect me +
keep me safe.
When we drove home from the museum,
both work + kissing my friends came up

And I snapped because with you
I often feel like the only
boundaries I'm allowed to have are
the ones you're willing to give. I yelled
and I'm sorry for that. Now I have more
boundaries + I do my best with them
to make sure they are not contingent
on someone else's prodding. I think I
thought if I yell / explain one more
time about how this all hurt me +

how inappropriate it was, somehow I
would become safer, because you
would finally agree, but of course, that's
not how life works. And then you
started yelling, the angriest I'd
seen you in years "I'm not a
pedophile, I'm not a pedophile."
And unfortunately that memory was
burned in my brain forever + has
scarred me, to say the least. It looked
like a psychotic break + I ran, shaking,
wondering who this other person was
who snapped out of you. Wondering why you
would yell that at me. Reeling from all the
times you put your hand on my thigh + I
would ask you not to. Remembering
when I was little, you saying
Pedophiles should be killed + have the
death penalty. Wondering if more
inappropriate things happened that I
didn't remember. Wondering if you were yelling
 because
that's how you really felt?

This is a summary I guess
of some of what I've been grappling
with for years. This shattered me:
anger, sadness, grief. I said that already.
It's been my work to get emotionally
strong enough for many things, one
of them being to share this with you.

Sending you strength
+ love,
Anna

I send the handwritten letter by mail, prepared to be blamed by an angry father and to possibly never see him again.

About a week later, I receive an email from him. I click it open:

"Hi, Anna—I've read and re-read your letter and written an initial email as a first thought. I'm going to sleep on it and re-read it in the morning before sending. Just want you to know I am processing your letter and taking it very seriously. Thank you for putting your thoughts and experiences down on paper and sharing with me."

That's it. He doesn't sign it. My chest shakes again but there is nothing sharp this time. His reasoned note surprises me and I hope it's a good omen for the next one to come. And it is.

His next writing arrives in the mail.

Dear Daughter,

I thought I'd handwrite you back and also use snail mail.

Firstly, I'd like to take a moment to appreciate your honesty. Being so candid with me could not have been a simple task. Though it was hard to read and I felt very sad you would question some of these things, I can understand it.

I'd like to address your letter point by point.

In terms of saying "I've changed your diapers, I've seen everything anyway," I do not recall but am not questioning your recollection. If that's what you said happened, it happened. The truth is, I did change your diapers and was a very present parent for your younger years but I understand that this made you uncomfortable and I should have respected your boundaries more. In terms of my outburst in the car, I also do not remember it as clearly as you do. But I know that I felt I was being blamed for something that I was not and a feeling of not being seen clearly or for who I am, is deeply embedded and painful. And yet you did not deserve to receive my screams about it and I understand that must have been very scary. Lastly, there was no abuse, sexually especially. And I'm sorry you even had to question that. That must have been very painful and it's painful for me too. I'm sorry.

In terms of your brother, he did not want much contact with me since the divorce with your mother. I do not know why. I wish that he did, but I respect his decision. And your mother is your mother. Who knows what she has said. And finally, I did not know that your mother would get upset at you after I left for the beach or wherever, post argument with Mom. If I had, I wouldn't have left and in retrospect, I should have known I was leaving you with an angry parent in those moments and I should not have done that.

This is heavy stuff. All for now. Thank you for sharing.

I love you always, I'll do better.
Dad

And at the bottom is the animated picture of the little guy with the big nose that he always draws at the bottom of his notes.

This is enough.

A few months later, we are talking on the phone, and when I say that I don't want to talk about something, we don't. Mostly we don't speak about serious things at all. He wants to go to Italy and is planning a trip with his ex-girlfriend, Justine, the one whose daughter had the issue with him. Knowing he and Justine are in a good place again makes me feel relieved. As we mend things, he builds me art out of wood: A handmade side table with curved legs and a yin and yang symbol expertly placed in, with both blonder and darker pieces of wood layered into it. And an irreplaceable jewelry box, with green velvet inside he cut and laid. The top is inlaid with my initials, bulbous and intentionally imperfect.

Progress, not perfection. From time to time, of course, we find ourselves going in a slightly heated direction, but now I know to hang up. Kindly. Without getting into anything. "Oh, Dad, call from my agent. Got to go." And we talk the next day and it's all easier. He finally self-publishes his book, *On Bolton Flats,* but doesn't offer me a role in the movie version, doesn't ask to be my manager. It's all a bit simpler. This is a new kind of love, maybe. One I never knew before. One with boundaries and taking responsibility for my own shortcomings instead of just blaming all of them on my upbringing or on him.

It feels old and new, like neither of us is the same as before, but we still know each other deeply.

Chapter Nineteen

"So how about . . . you visit me in Los Angeles. That would be really nice. That would mean a lot, Mom," I tell her. "You know I have my place now with Alex. We have a guest room too. You can stay with us." I didn't want to beg, but she also deserved the facts.

My mom starts her sentence with a meditative "Mmm," considering the different ways she can respond, and lands on challenging me directly, "Anna, your tone sounds like you might as well be saying 'Fuck off and die.'" I laugh because she's right. I'm not exactly emphatic about the visit.

"Well, I don't want that, Mom. You just never visited me in college and it hurt my feelings," I say, trying again.

"I did!"

"Barely, and only after I begged! So it's kind of annoying I feel like I have to ask you to visit in LA. I've been here like four years and you came out once for a nanosecond."

"Anna," she says, saying my name like I pulled out one of her nose hairs, "I was working, what do you want from me?"

I'm about to get angry back but instead say, "Listen, I can't talk long—ten minutes—I have a meeting, but can you FaceTime?" This reminds me that I'm not trapped in this conversation. It's a choice, and I'm responsible for my own behavior.

She answers, a little thrilled and definitely surprised, "I thought you'd never ask!"

Mom pops up on my phone screen, her face full and round like Diane Keaton's, with deep wrinkles everywhere that look extra beautiful on her. Since she hit her early seventies my mom gets endless compliments about how gorgeous she is. And it's true. Most people didn't mention it to me when I was younger, except my dad occasionally, but mostly my janitor, Marge, which I've still never quite wrapped my head around.

Mom's hair back then was matted and black or a little red and sat against her forehead, glued there from running around to patients' rooms and pulling a sheet over a person's head after they died. Then she would commute home, make dinner for me almost every night, and then fight with my dad and yell at me while still somehow making sure I did my math homework. There is something impressive about that.

In one sense she made my life hell, but she was also the only person keeping it going. The birthday parties, the dinners, signing me up for camp, the babysitters, taking me to meet all the first graders in my new town of Scituate, giving me a chance to make new friends before being alone all summer. It's not her fault it didn't work and I'd ended up with the Amys. How she managed enough of a long-distance relationship with her son, Jamie, that they still talk a few times a week to this day and seem to have a mostly functional relationship. The more space I got from Dad during our estrangement, the more I realized how little he had been responsible for my day-to-day. Whether it'd been intentional or not, he'd made her into the bad guy by default. He didn't cook as much, he didn't wrap gifts, he didn't do the back-to-school clothes shopping or the homework enforcement or the dentist or pediatrician appointments or getting me out the door or staying home when I was sick or any of that stuff. He did what he wanted to do for the most part. He was so full of music and alternative intellectual thought, all of which he shared with me so generously. He took me to the movies. He took me to Starland. And I loved him for that. But he was also smart enough to whisper insults while she screamed.

At the time, what it came down to was that he was very nice to me. And next to her, this made him my savior.

But that's not to say it was fair.

On FaceTime now, I see her frizzy waves of gray with the streaks of white and gold she's experimenting with at her latest salon. At a little over seventy, she is coming into herself. Newly retired, she has more dedication to self-care and seems to feel some kind of peace.

"Hi. I wanted you to see my face so you can see that I don't hate you," I say.

"I can't tell."

So I smile big and fake with all my teeth. "I don't hate you. Come visit. I'll make you comfortable," I say. But Mom looks more undone than last time I saw her face. I pivot. "You, okay?"

And then I notice that the engagement ring is off her hand again, which is interesting because she had it back on the last couple days. It's sometimes on, sometimes off.

And then she says, matter-of-fact, "Jack left me."

"What? No." Boring Jack? Jack who never left even when Mom got mad at him? Jack who took her ballroom dancing? Jack with the La-Z-Boy he wouldn't replace even though she hated it when she sold her house and moved into his? I'd come to love Jack like a sweet and occasionally confused uncle.

"I didn't want to worry you." She tries to keep her face stone.

"Mom. I'm sorry. Why didn't you say anything?" I ask.

"You've been dealing with a lot."

"Well—I appreciate that, actually. Thanks." Over the years, she'd taken to calling me if she was upset enough with Jack, one time outside a Home Goods, just letting it roll as people passed.

"If he couldn't, Anna— if he couldn't let me pick out items. For. Our. Home," she had said very slowly, "And Pieces. For. Here. And. There, then"—finishing fast—"whatthefuckwasIdoinghere!?" I understood, but her reality could be quite far from the other person's reality, so I'd never know what really happened, and the following week she'd forget, staying together. Regardless, I'd always try to talk her down.

But now she was not just thinking of herself. I was here too.

"But, Mom, are you okay?" Her stone face nods for an oddly long time. "I don't know, not right now. I will be. I will be? I took off his ring again, because you know, Jack kept running me around about the marriage thing."

"Last time I spoke to you about it you said you didn't wanna get married anymore."

"I know I said that, but—did I say that? If I did it's because—well, maybe I didn't for a second but maybe that was for Jack. Maybe because he didn't want to."

She sounds like a little girl, and continues, "But I do. I do. And he's been getting so distant, so I said to him, 'I want to grow old with someone I can talk to. Who will speak back.' He's ten years older than me. If I stayed in this, that would mean caring for someone soon."

"What do you mean? Like caring for him dying?" I ask.

"Yes! Before he becomes my patient, and I give him everything." Maybe this is just where your mind goes when you've cared for elders your whole life. She goes on, "I at least want to feel in love." This to me is poetic. She is still searching. Part of me wants her to stop, to be satisfied, okay with a boring relationship because at least it was someone around. This seemed to be enough for many other parents. Security for her, at least. A friend. But I could see Janet's restless soul pushing back, that part of her that wanted to eat, chew, and swallow up life—a new meal served many times a day, both a gift and a curse.

She explains that they took some space and Jack had been in a hotel for a couple weeks. I'm amazed she didn't call and tell me this earlier, and to be honest, it means something to me. Though I also feel bad because I want to be there for her, but maybe I don't need to be there in all ways. Maybe she can stand on her own two feet. She can—obviously, she is. And then Mom goes on to explain how she thought the separation was leading to something positive, "but then he texted me at the end of the two weeks, TEXTED that he was breaking up with me. He couldn't even call me. And now I'm sitting here, surrounded by his furniture, HIS FUCKING LA-Z-BOY reminding me of him and us and so on and so forth."

"Well," I say, trying to be light, "go to Florida. Enjoy the good life. Keep the ring. Sell it."

"I gave it back."

This pisses me off. "Why did you do that, Mom?"

"Why are you yelling at me?!" she says like a kid.

"I'm sorry. I'm not. I just— You don't ask for what you deserve sometimes. With men. Ken, right? You and Jamie in a cabin without heat. Ken kept the house with his mistress. I don't wanna bring up painful stuff, sorry, but I want you to know it's okay to ask for things. You deserve to have standards. So just, like, say you want it back. And then sell it. Buy yourself something nice."

"Or make it a necklace . . ." she says, dreaming, or as if that had been her plan all along but when push came to shove it wasn't right. "Maybe. Well. Thank you for standing up for me."

"I'm sorry, Mama." All of a sudden, it's easy to call her that. Usually, her tears make me want to hang up, but not this time. And what I say next, I mean, "You have a beautiful heart and I'm so sorry you are going through this."

She thinks for a sec. "I didn't know you ever really wanted to see me, actually. In LA. Like, really see me. Thank you for asking me to your home you share with Alex. I'm sorry I didn't make enough of an effort to see you in New York. Really." And she thinks, "I will come visit you. And Anna, you should see him too. It's time."

"Jack?"

"Not Jack. Don't see Jack. He broke up with me in a text. NOTHING is what we do for Jack. I'm kidding. But really, don't call Jack. See your dad, Anna. He's not going to live forever."

"You know we talk now, Mom?"

"I know. I guess this breakup made me think of Peter. At least you're slowly repairing things with him, and that's great, but you move like a turtle. Go see the guy."

"In Florida? Florida's weird. No offense."

"You had a bad experience there."

"I'm not ready."

I get a call on the other line.

Maybe it's a sign.

This time I don't suggest a merge, or even mention to Mom who it is. I just ask her if I can call her back later.

As always, she asks me eighty-nine last-minute questions about nothing right when I say goodbye.

Boundaries mean something different to me these days. I say "Call you back" again and click *Accept* before she gets out "Goodbye."

I know it shouldn't be a big deal nowadays, but for a moment they are both on my phone at the same time.

—

I pick up.

"Hi, Dad."

"Hi, Anna. Glad to see—sorry, to talk to you."

"Me too." I'm stilted on the phone still.

"Anything new?"

"Nope. You?"

"Well. Sort of. No pressure, but my doctor suggested I come to LA for an experimental test. It has to do with my old prostate cancer. Everything is fine, they just need to identify where a stray cell has landed because my PSA numbers are up."

"Uh-oh."

"No, it's normal. It's recurred a few times. They always give me some radiation and—"

"Hormones."

"Yeah, this is just part of it, to be expected. And this experimental test is preventative, just one more thing I can do to help longevity."

"So, what's it looking for?"

"You know I don't have a prostate anymore."

"YES."

"Moving along. This experimental thing will show if that cell has landed somewhere else. And then they can remove it."

"And this test does that?"

"At UCLA, yeah. I was thinking of coming in a couple weeks. They have an opening."

"Um." *Say yes. Just say yes.* "Um." *Anna.* "Yes. Yes." He can't stay here. I haven't seen him in five years. "We probably don't have room—"

"I'm going to stay on the Westside," he says, stopping me. "Just because the test is really early in the morning. It'll just be a two-night trip. But can I take you out to dinner one night?"

"To dinner?"

"It'll be light. We'll keep it light. I'd like to meet, what's his name, Alex?"

All three of my hearts beat, but it's a sickening feeling.

My chest too, but how can I say no.

"Sure."

It was happening.

During my dad's absence, I'd done something strange.

I'd dressed a man up who sort of looks like my dad and found him corduroys like the ones real Dad used to wear. I'd located a 1998 champagne station wagon with velour seats that looked like the Ford we used to drive around in. And I'd dressed up as a child, with my thirty-year-old smallish (yet perky!) tits aggressively strapped down, going almost concave, teeth lined with braces on an invisible retainer, and through this I'd relived many parts of our dad-daughter relationship, all of it ending up on television. Or rather, not television, but a show on streaming that my aunt and uncle on my mom's side asked that I please make into a "real show on cable TV." I found the question fair, though Maya and I had graduated beyond web series and with Sam had finally written the thing we wanted to about rejects. It was semi-autobiographical and sometimes felt like some very expensive therapy, given how we'd written our parents as versions of our real parents, Maya's biological mom even playing her mom in the show. For mine, we'd hired actors, and I'd write arcs where they'd fight with each other and make up, like they did in real life. And also like real life, they would eventually divorce in the show. And even split the house in two.

Real Dad had said he was proud of me but kept his distance from talking about any of it too much. I'd gotten to relive all the good times on the show with TV Dad when real Dad and I weren't seeing each other in person. Real him had changed, and I'd written a version of the old one back into my life.

Now we're back to where this all began. When Dad flew all the way to LA for one Italian dinner.

After five years of not seeing him in person, we are next to each other slurping noodles and he's talking to Alex. To Dad's credit, he asks very little about the show, or about my work in general. Maybe he really took in the part of my letter where I tried to express how my worth to him sometimes felt tied to how successful I was or wasn't. How many points I'd earned on any given day. He really heard me, but he could say he liked the show a *little* more.

A sweet-looking couple approaches us midpizza and apologizes for interrupting. "We just have to say how much we love *PEN15*. Your show. You're Anna Kone, I mean Konkle, right? That would be, ha, so embarrassing if you weren't." I nod, about to answer, but before I can respond she asks Dad, "Are you Mr. Konkle?" He nods yes and they shake his hand.

We do look a lot alike.

At the end of the interaction I'm hugging the couple, they have been so kind. It hasn't been out long. And once they have left, my father takes it as permission to say something about the show too.

"I really love it too, Anna. I'm proud of you."

"Thank you, Dad."

He's getting giddy. "Well it's insane you play thirteen-year-olds, surrounded by real thirteen-year-olds. Wouldn't have ever said that would work. But what the fuck do I know?"

"Ha. Thanks." I laugh genuine because in the past he always knew best. Had to be the first to say it, usually.

"I knew it was a great idea," Alex says. I eye him, seeing some shared traits with Dad. "What!" he says.

"Well, it's crazy we got to make it. A lot of people said it wouldn't work. We weren't sure either. Oh. You okay with the divorce announcement being in it, Dad? And you saw your station wagon? I would have, like, asked you but— we filmed it awhile before it came out. We weren't talking much."

"Yeah. Yeah. Of course. The scene where we tell you that we're getting a divorce was tough. I remember some of those moments. But seeing it from your perspective was . . . I learned some things."

Maybe making the show, playing a version of myself where my parents fought but I had a best friend in the same room to hold me, was the gift of a lifetime. Wishing my hair would turn black came from dinners at Court's Italian table, but in *Pen,* when things are bad for Anna Kone, it's Maya's Japanese-American family she wants to chameleon into. I'd had the opportunity to process and play out my past and rewrite it as sweeter and more resolved than it really was. The show was literally a six-hundred-thousand-dollar- (or $1.3-million-, depending on the season) per-episode version of the exercise I'd done over the years in my therapist's office where I would close my eyes and picture little me in a scary memory and relive it until big me holds little me, telling her she's safe now. On set, it could be like doing the same but with my eyes open. Or the scenes could end with a version of older Anna rewriting something for younger Anna, telling her that it was going to be okay. You wouldn't see older Anna on screen, but I knew she was there when I wrote something helpful for little me. Or something hard.

Or a lesson learned a decade after middle school and applied retroactively, often forming the spine of the show's emotional arcs. Like in episode 106, where Maya and Anna steal a thong to magically get a hot ass while walking a fashion show paired with elderly people from church. That plot could stay dumb-funny, and there are lots of those moments in *PEN15* too, but the emotional stakes were always kind of gigantic; in this case not in regard to the fashion show, but to the advice an elder named Pu gives Maya when she's forced to give back the thong: *All my life I would grow older and think I was prettier the year before. I never got to enjoy my beauty but kept obsessing over it all the time. I wish someone had told me when I was younger that I was beautiful because of who I was, not what I had.*

Other times I could gift myself an odd catharsis, like screaming at my TV mom that she's a bitch but in a funny way that only a thirty-year-old playing a thirteen-year-old could do. And real Mom laughed watching it.

Next season we'd write Maya into scenes after my parents' fights escalated so that she could rescue me and pull me out of the house. I'd sprint with her toward the woods, toward magic and imagination, even when the reality was that I was alone with Moe to comfort me. In the show, I could rewrite the past. Truth is paramount, so if it wasn't holding up a mirror to the shadows of ourselves and our memories, then we were doing it wrong. Maybe next season I'd write an episode about cancer in honor of my father and how much he'd been through.

A week or so after dinner with Dad, I'm wondering how his test at UCLA went.

He'll tell me when he's ready.

The hallway outside the award show auditorium reminds me of teens in line for prom, scattered with adult chaperones, all dressed up and self-conscious. And like any school dance, I'd freaked out for weeks over what to wear. Tonight I'm a tween all over again, and the popular people are the celebrities. Everyone knows their names. The ones at the top know how to do the interviews, where to sit, who to talk to, and if they should care a lot about designers or just enough. They know how to appear they are enjoying themselves and grateful without getting desperate or hungry. They know where to put their hand on their own body during the red carpet, which we've already done tonight and it's hard. And harder not to search yourself right after to see what a loser you do or do not look like.

I click "Anna Konkle Emmys" and I don't look anything like myself, but in a bad way, and after all that dress deliberating, even though it's a beautiful one, the outside just doesn't match my inside.

Maya finds herself fresh off the photo barrage and asks me why her hands always look like doll paddles on the carpet when she's trying to look her best. "I told them to be loose. All my blood, Na, it rushes to the ends of my limbs because of like, adrenaline. That's a thing." She explains why they go numb and in directions she can't help when she is nervous. She says it looks like Barbie hands when a too-young child plays with the arms, unaware of anatomy.

I assure her that no one would ever notice, but she still makes me laugh.

We link our real person arms and I show her my photo again and tell her not to complain because I look like a penis in chiffon and eyeliner. I'm a man in a wig but nothing's real, who cares. This makes her laugh big, so I know my self-roast is unfortunately spot-on.

The real joke is that we'd tried so hard after being anarchists, playing freaks.

We get nervous that someone might see us doing an internet

search of ourselves on the red carpet while we are still on the red carpet, which would be really embarrassing.

Sacha Baron Cohen stands sullen a few people down, on his phone too, as are a lot of other celebrities. Except the cast of *Succession,* they seem alive, eyes still sparkling.

Waiting for the auditorium doors to open, I think of Dad, who all those years ago agreed to put money down for a stretch Hummer limo during my junior year. And my Armani dress from TJ Maxx. I feel bad I'm not wearing it like I promised, but it didn't look good. At least I'd tried it on. I'd wear Dad's dress when it was important to wear it.

"I think I'm going to video-call my dad," I say to Alex in his tux, looking handsome. The idea makes me nervous but I ask my body if I want to and I do.

Al gives me a nod, like *Don't overthink, just go.*

He picks up on the first ring.

"Hi, Dad. We are at the Emmys. Can you believe it? Ha."

"Hiii. I'm so proud of you. Not just for this, sweetie. But for a lot of things."

And of course just then the doors open.

"I gotta go. I love you. Sorry it's so brief."

"Thanks for calling, sweetie." He's weeping.

I smile really big.

My chest is still.

I'm unsure exactly why he's crying, but it's probably because we were apart for so long. A wave of guilt rolls into me but I try to let it go and be grateful for where we are now. Neither of us is perfect. We both did our best.

The morning after the ceremony, I'm driving toward the writers' room after a long-ass night of martinis to burn off the nerves and not enough food, plus I'm a little allergic to literally everything so my eyes are puffy from all the makeup. The phone rings and I pick up while driving.

"Hi, sweetie."

"Hi, Dad." I detect some sadness, maybe because our show lost. But it's not that, he says.

"What is it? Is everything okay?" I say, skipping niceties.

"I'm so glad you called last night. It really meant a lot." He's basically crying again.

"I am too. I wanted to—" But I'm being interrupted like if he doesn't say it now, he never will.

"I do have to tell you something."

"Okay."

His voice flows, unencumbered. "And I wanted to wait till after the Emmys to do that."

"You— Oh. Okay. That's now."

He stops himself, "Where are you off to right now?"

"The writers' room."

"Would you rather I call you later?"

"No."

"Okay, well, just a few months ago I had that scan in LA."

"Right," I say simply.

"You got nominated like, right after."

Where was he going with this? "Right."

Our dinner had been effective in opening a gate to a real relationship again. Alex, knowing him and confirming that he is not a monster, also made me feel extra safe.

Dad forces humor into his tone. "I'm glad I did. I'm really glad I did. Because maybe it'll save my life. The PSA level that was up—well, my prostate cancer is back."

"Okay. Slow-growing, though, yeah? As prostate cancer often

is." I sort of already knew this part and go on, "And is that the kind of thing they can radiate? Even though you don't have a prostate?"

"Well, maybe, yeah," but his voice is high. "Honey, that's something we'll figure out, but they are more concerned at the moment about the spots that are on my lungs."

Packs and packs and packs and packs and packs and packs and packs and packs and packs and packs and packs and packs and packs and packs of cigarettes that went into his body, down his throat, falling through his webby, soft lungs, making them black and swollen like they showed us in school. This image comes to me immediately.

But then again, some people smoke and don't get spots at all.

Reading my mind, he answers, "You know I haven't had a cigarette in a year."

"Dad . . ."

But he's not defensive, just responds simply, "I haven't. I promise. People get it who don't smoke too."

Nodding, I go on to the list of questions now lining up in my brain. "So could it just be the prostate cancer finding a place on your lung?"

"Yeah!" he says, high and jovial.

"Yeah?" I answer in an opposite tone.

"Yeah. Yeah. Maybe. I hadn't considered that. Could be."

He's almost singing his responses but not making complete sense. "Or . . . it could be lung cancer," I say.

"Yeah," he says with new candor, like your first exhale after taking off a girdle. And Dad cries long and hard.

I picture a cold stream under a covered bridge in Vermont where the rainbow trout live and think, *Let it flow, Pops. Let it flow.* The thought comes from somewhere else. A more relaxed version of me.

"Oh, Dad," and I cry with him. "I'm here for you, okay? I'll come to Florida. I'll take care of you. Whatever you need."

"Really? Thank you. I hope you don't have to do that—I don't think you will. You're in the middle of your writer's room. And Debby has been coming to my doctor appointments and taking really good care of me"—this is reassuring, and he continues—"you don't have to rush here, though I would love to see you."

"Okay." My first feeling is relief and appreciation. "That's nice of Deb, wow." His sort of girlfriend. Or not his girlfriend. Whatever. But I also feel bad I wasn't there for the appointments.

"So . . . are you . . . you've been going to doctors with Deb. You've known for a minute, then?"

"This has been ongoing for maybe two months, yeah."

"Two months." I mull this over. The test had happened a while ago. "But they don't know if it's lung cancer yet?"

"Doctors still have to do a biopsy, technically, to confirm it's lung cancer. Or what stage it is."

"Maybe we can come to you this weekend." Alex and I had been arguing a bit, but this news put things into perspective. "Would that be okay? Would that work for you, Dad?"

"That would be great." He's laughing. "That would be great, sweetie."

"Okay, good. You sure?"

"Let me check my fuckin' calendar. Clear. Come. I have the guest room all ready for you. And Monkey is waiting."

I listen to my chest. It's still.

"I'm sorry you are going through this," I hear myself say. I'm almost whispering.

"Me too, but I've had a great life."

"Don't say that."

"I just mean I'm grateful."

"I love you."

"I love you."

We hang up knowing we will see each other soon. In Florida.

Chapter Twenty

Floating above earth's ground in a four-hundred-thousand-pound steel bus is strange when you think too much about it. I try to distract myself, sipping water and eating chips, watching a little TV.

After the plane ride, Alex and I drive the humid, lush highways of Florida in the white Toyota rental car. I keep an eye on my boyfriend and his perception of the area. But he seems pleasant enough, and when I press him on his opinion of the place, he reports that he could see himself retiring in Florida. This disturbs me, but I'm happy for his comfort.

The gaggle of chain restaurants sit flat against cement like they are gathered for a party at a warehouse with fake trees. McDonald's, Popeye's, Subway, China Chen, China Wok, Denny's, Little Caesars, Checkers, Burger King, and Taco Bell sit patiently as retirees stream in and out of them like albino ants. Alex licks his lips in a way that seems like a joke but turns out is a result of authentic hunger, which makes me laugh. I remind him that my dad made dinner for us and reassure him we are five minutes away.

The entrance to the retirement community is to our right, next to a man-made pond with a single fountain nozzle that spouts water in one stream like a girl's thin ponytail. The guard gives us a hard time.

"My dad, Peter Konkle. Could be under James Konkle as well."

He answers with a twang, after a long look, "Maybe. I don't see your name, though."

"Really? It should be there." He wasn't really listening to me and starts looking at his cellphone. Alex, from the passenger's seat, says, "It's very important this get addressed. We have a family emergency we are attending to." The guard straightens up and lets us in.

We take some winding turns into the expansive community that feels like a strange little city.

We pull up to his condo and get out.

"Alex, I'm feeling, like, I'm nervous about going in."

"I know this is probably intense for you."

"Can you hold my hand?"

"Yes," he says, and takes it. "I'm here. It's going to be okay."

"Very basic reassurance. But it's working a little, thank you." We squeeze hands before getting out of the car. I see the little outdoor wooden table, the one with three boards that we've had outside each of our homes, starting in Vermont. But instead of an ashtray on top, there's a dinky, vibrant fern.

I ring the doorbell. The golden knob turns, and the cold air of his condo hits us through the acrylic screen door. The outdoor light on the side of the house glows against him, and Dad smiles.

"Hi, Dad." I'm smiling too.

"Hi, Peter! Great seeing you," Alex adds.

Dad covertly catches his breath before responding, "Hi, Angel! Alex! Come in." He tells me our bedroom is on the right. At first sight, it's home; the same white bedding with purple flowers I picked out all those years ago, and the poky down comforter I'd insisted on needing. Pushing down, I can still feel the mattress topper too. He'd splurged on it in high school, trying to make my bedroom at his place a home too.

"The condo looks great, Dad."

He'd moved from the apartment I'd run away from last time. This helps.

"Did you see Monkey?" he asks.

I'm nodding hard before answering, "Yes, I did. You'll have to do him for Alex later."

He laughs as much as he can. "I dunno about that."

"I'm not worthy," Alex tells us.

"Monkey is selective as hell," Dad adds.

The dinner table is up against the wall, topped with the same set of pots from forever ago. He's keeping dinner warm. Alex sits and says, "I can't believe you made this, given you aren't feeling well."

"It was eas—" His breath pounds in and out.

I can't help but ask if he's okay.

"Yup." He pushes out his words hard. "Easy—recipes I've made—a—a—quite a lot. Sit."

"You sit too."

"Don't tell me what to do, Angel," he says, kind of laughing.

"Sorry." I make myself laugh too. "I'm going to use the bathroom really quick. Don't wait, though."

I rush through the hall, feeling tears coming. It looks like he's in bad shape, the way he's breathing.

I shut the bathroom door. Two beetles are in the sink and I wonder if they are cockroaches, which makes me stop weeping enough to get it together. I flush the toilet for punctuation and I'm ready to enjoy dinner again. But from the hall, I hear no talking. I come back and Alex stares at me nervously while Dad's eyes are closed in his chair, gripping it.

My dad is making a sound that I've never heard before.

I kneel next to him small and put my hand on his but he doesn't respond. When he comes to, I look into my father's sleepy eyes.

"What's going on?"

"Pneumonia," he says quickly.

"Not related to the lung cancer? Or it's related to lung cancer? Or whatever it is on your lung?"

He shakes his head. "Unrelated, the doctor said." And he's ready to fight me, I can tell. Or rather he *wants* to be ready, but he looks too tired. "I saw my primary"—he waits for more breath to facilitate the end of his sentence—"doctor and I'm on antibiotics. It's being managed."

I'm treading into territory he wants me out of, so I say, "Okay. Okay, good. And you reached out and told him you were in pain today, I assume?"

"Yeah—he's uh—he's amazing, I love him. He's on his boat today—" In response to my annoyed look, Dad continues, "Doctor Modler has a boat—good boat day today! But he'll get back to me Monday."

Trying to seem less worried, I agree, "Oh, nice, love a boat."

The doorbell rings and Dad scoots in his chair but I jump up like a cheerleader. "I'll get it!"

"It's Deb, I bet," he says, his eyes happy, then, looking to Alex like a child, "She's my best friend."

"Anna's told me about her," Alex responds. "Seems like a person someone would wanna spend a lot of time with." And here she is again—Debby—face unchanged. Always a fresh five layers of fire-engine-red lipstick. She seems nervous. "Hello, Anna."

"Hi, Deb!" I give her a big hug, appreciating the presence she's had in my dad's life all these years and what seems like good influence, ultimately.

"Dad's in here." But I add softly, "Seems kind of, um, unwell, though." Debby looks nervous again and we walk in as Alex stands to greet her. "Hi, Debby."

"Ahleksss," she says. There's an added vibe to her tonight. She's flitting around the room and side-hugs my dad, who is glowing now but she seems uncomfortable. "You started dinner. You said you were going to wait," Deb chides.

I realize Dad and Debby are sort of fighting, and as we finish our beef stew on this eighty-four-degree night, he's looking down, not saying anything, and I'm sure this tension is embarrassing for him. Or maybe he's just in pain. I want to ask but Deb is talking, trying to make the mood better.

"You know the story of us meeting?" she says, and this brings a twinkle back to my dad's eye. If the pain was still there, you couldn't tell. She goes on, "I'm at the grocery store, minding my own business, and this handsome man comes up to me."

Alex and I make eye contact but look away quickly.

"And I know he thinks I'm beautiful. These old men are always stalking me. I'm running around the store trying to escape these three-legged monsters, two legs and a cane."

This makes my dad really laugh. And I see how this friendship formed. She doesn't let her successful joke slow her down, "And I can see he's following me."

"I was," he says like it's funny.

I think *yuck* but Alex is riveted, probably writing every piece of it down in his head for future scripts. "And so," Deb says, "okay—

whatever—I'm used to it. Keep your eyes up here, though." She points to her forehead.

Dad thinks this is funny again. "That's an unfair allegation," he sings.

"Ohhh, big word, Peter," she says, rolling her eyes through a flirty pout.

"Order, order," Alex jokes, buddy-buddying himself up with these two.

She continues, "And I go out to my car, and the fucker is still there! Your dad won't leave me alone!" She laughs and I can finally tell she likes him too.

Her lips lie like slugs, working hard through a strange, seductive smile as Dad still struggles to breathe. Alex and I have been here for two seconds and it's immediately a scene from a movie. She's still explaining it, "and . . . so he's very pushy—"

"What a gentleman," I add, and Dad gives me the middle finger, smiling, but then holds his stomach like it hurts again. She keeps talking, "So I say, 'Fine, give me your number.' So he does. And his email." She continues, "So then we go out to this dinner . . ."

Dad adds, "Really nice dinner, I splurged."

"It was nice," she says like *It was fine, don't go overboard* and he contests that actually it was very nice and that it cost two hundred dollars. She rolls her eyes at the idea that two hundred dollars is "very nice," and Dad takes over temporarily, explaining how after that first meal, Debby told him this is what she expects all the time. Dad told her she won't get that with him all the time but he'll treat her well and make her laugh. Debby admits that low funds probably won't work for her long term, but they can give it a try. So they did and then they broke up and now they are best friends, which they both agree on.

We start talking about the doctor visits and I learn that they have seen the primary care doctor and the urologist and the prostate specialist, but two months after they learned about the cancer, they have not yet seen an oncologist. Suddenly I realize I won't be going back to Los Angeles anytime soon. But then I remember I have to because of this show we've made about the past. About him. And like an exclamation point to my private thoughts, my dad suddenly doubles over in pain.

"I think we should take you in to the hospital. I'm really worried."

Then I realize that I have seen him once in five years and I am trying to take control of something I know he won't allow.

His eyebrow lines go together like a two-lane highway. "No."

"Dad, you can't breathe and you are in pain."

"I have pneumonia, I'm on antibiotics, I told my doctor—"

"But—"

"Anna." This is a warning and it's final.

In our bed, on the same sheets from high school, Monkey stares at me and I'm dialing my mom. With my other hand, I hold on to Alex.

"Sorry to involve you"—I'm whispering—"on something Dad-related—"

"That's okay. What's going on?"

"He can't breathe, he's in a lot of pain. He needs to go to the hospital but he's refusing. I asked him once, he said no, and then privately I said it to him again. Just like, 'Please. Please go. For me,' and of course he still said no."

She listens. "What does Alex think?" she asks.

"He said—he's sitting next to me—Alex doesn't think he

needs to go to the hospital necessarily, but no offense, he doesn't know what he's talking about." Alex gives me a look like *What the hell?* and I give one back like *What! You don't* and continue talking to my mom.

"It's very scary what I'm watching right now. It's a lot of pain, an unusual level of pain, and he's gasping after walking five steps. And he's acting like it's normal, like it's just pneumonia."

"Oh, it's *pneumonia*!" she says, like finding the answer to a hard test question.

"Or lung cancer!" I say.

"Well, he could die just from pneumonia."

"Thanks, Mom. But see, that's what I'm trying to say!" I'm spraying tiny tears. More like anxiety mist than weeps.

"Honey. What I'm trying to say, okay—you know my career was taking care of elders, and here is the fundamental truth: You cannot make an adult do something for their health that they don't want to do. Period." This is not what I wanted to hear, so I don't say anything for a long while. So she adds small, almost like she didn't say it, "Which is heartbreaking."

I hang up and put the phone down. How many lessons do I need before I understand I can't save him? He won't let me. I cry into my comforter—on the same tears from years before.

I look down and notice another roach scurrying across the floor and think how unlike Dad this is, to have bugs in the house. And not just a few. They're kind of everywhere.

He who always approached fastidiousness like a religion.

But the bugs are winning now.

"Anna."

I wake up slowly.

"Anna."

My dad is leaning on the doorframe and he can't manage to

say my name a third time so I call 911. It's sometime in the middle of the night.

The ambulance roars in and they get oxygen into my father's nostrils and I'm relieved he can breathe for the moment but he holds his stomach in pain again. Grasping his other hand, I pretend to be stoic.

We arrive at the closest hospital and he's given a room and an IV, fast. A long, thin doctor enters.

"So, what's going on for you today?" I look to my dad but his eyes are kind of glazed. I wade into an explanation—"He was in a lot of pain earlier. In his abdomen. Around five o'clock he was gasping to breathe when he walked." Dad just looks down while I explain things and then says, "Didn't want you to wake up and find me dead on a pool day."

The doctor appreciates the liveliness with the smallest of snorts. I explain how his primary told him this was all pneumonia and he's on antibiotics but he's in the middle of testing for a mass on his lungs.

"Got it. When did this begin?" the doctor says, taking notes.

"Dad?"

"What?"

"When did they find the mass?"

"Three months ago." Earlier, he'd said two. The doctor asks if the diagnosis is lung cancer and Dad confirms that it is.

"What stage?" asks the doctor.

Dad shakes his head. "I dunno. A later stage, they think."

This is news to me, and Dad adds, "They want to do a needle biopsy where they take a needle this long"—Dad's shifting from dissociative neutral to off-roading—"and stick it through the wall of my chest and into my lungs to take a fuckin' sample to confirm the stage." He says this with bravado and like *Can you fuckin' believe it.* We've left joke territory and are in angry zone. I start writing everything down.

"Yeah, that's what they do," the doctor says, unfazed. Like he knows Dad was trying to get a rise out of him. "It sounds worse than it is."

"No, thank you," says Dad.

"Well, they won't know the stage until they do that. Okay? I'm giving you morphine," Doc says.

"Thank you very much," Dad delivers back. "Don't mind if I do." I shake my head but can't help laughing a little.

"We'll get some quick imaging of the lungs and then, if we need to follow up, a whole-body PET scan, which I think is likely. I'm actually just gonna schedule that."

The doctor leaves and we're sitting in silence. I'm reeling and glare over at Alex, who's confused. I shove my head in the direction of my dad as if to say *Can you fucking believe him? Late stage?* But Alex has no idea what I'm gesturing about. Kayla, the nurse, injects morphine into Dad's IV and he melts into bed, talking about his upcoming trip to Italy, a tour with a group of older people but he's bringing his friend, who actually is his ex-girlfriend, funny enough, and so he has to be better in two months so he can go.

"I don't mind if I die after that. Just get me well enough to get to Italy and back."

I take note of his goal: Italy.

Check.

The quick X-ray confirms the mass. Masses, actually, and they suspect PEs. Pulmonary embolisms. An MRI shows blood clots in his legs and lungs. Dad's barely comprehending it all, so I keep writing it down. They administer heparin and Dad is carted out at a quick pace for another full-body scan. Alone with Alex, the first thing I need to say out loud is that I'm upset about everything I didn't know.

"And he's been *avoiding* them fully staging the cancer because he hates needles. I thought Debby was his saving grace. What the fuck?"

"You can't blame her."

"I'm not. But, wow."

When he is wheeled back I ask about doing the biopsy, inpatient. But there are more acute issues at hand, like preventing future embolisms. His stroke was silent this time, thank god, and you can't do a biopsy on blood thinners. The doctor goes on, "Get him stable, then you can do everything else."

"Sorry you're going through this, Dad," I say and squeeze his ankle. He soaks up the touch and I wonder how many hugs or shoulder squeezes he's had in recent years. Since his breakups. His oldest sister he was close to has passed, his middle sister won't speak to him since he told her she was an idiot for voting for Trump (their relationship had always been on and off, I didn't meet her until I was thirteen). Jamie wouldn't respond to birthday cards. He'd pushed so many people away who once hugged him back. But Deb had stayed. Maybe she hugs him.

I give him a bear hug out of nowhere and feel joy wash over me because I'm comfortable close to him again.

Is it because he is attached to wires? Restrained? Or because we healed something? I decide it's both and note our body and spirit's capacity to mend.

He must stay overnight. He sleeps.

On the way out, I say to Alex, "All the oncology appointments are very far out. He needs treatment like yesterday, I think. I had no idea how sick he was. Is."

"Anna. I think Peter was trying to take care of you."

This idea is annoying to me, "By not taking care of himself?"

"By handling it himself. Unsuccessfully. But releasing you from the burden."

Chapter Twenty-one

It's hot. The air-conditioning is broken in the condo. It's 4:18 a.m., my alarm is set for 6:45 to head back to the hospital, and all I want is sleep. We decide to try to fix it in the morning.

Before bed, I attempt to imagine Dad back here by himself. Alex assures me, "The best thing you can do for your dad tomorrow is sleep today. Ten hours ago we were on a plane."

"Flying," I say, distracted, staring at two odd black beads on the lampshade, "Do you think those are two beads, glued together? What are those? Is that the design? That's so weird."

Alex clocks them and says emphatically, yes, they are just two rectangular beads on a lampshade.

"It's a normal lampshade with two random black beads on the edge?"

"Yes, that's what I'm saying. It's a bad design element from Home Goods. Why do you keep repeating stuff about the beads?"

"They're not like"—I hesitate—"insect . . . eggs?"

Alex goes off, "WHY WOULD YOU SAY THAT. NO"—he's panicking, inspecting them closely—"THEY ARE PERFECT

RIDGES—THAT IS A SYMMETRICAL BEAUTIFUL BEAD."

"WHY ARE YOU YELLING."

"WELL, WHY WOULD YOU SAY THEY ARE SQUARE EGGS?"

"I DON'T KNOW. Okay. Maybe you're right and it's a bad design element," but I don't believe myself and start searching the internet.

Alex finds it first. "THOSE ARE COCKROACH EGG SACS. JESUS FUCKING CHRIST. GERMAN. COCKROACH. SACS."

"I fucking knew it. Ew. Each sac has twenty-eight to forty-eight babies. I'm going to throw up."

Alex is still yelling, "IT LOOKS LIKE A BEAD WITH PERFECT RIDGES. THERE ARE TWO. WHY DO THEY LOOK LIKE THAT. THEY SHOULDN'T LOOK LIKE THAT—" He's gagging. I'm not sure why this is worse than the birthed and grown cockroaches dotting the apartment.

I take a fork and flick them off into my paper-towel-lined palm, turn on the garbage disposal in the sink, and pray they aren't due to hatch exactly now. The grinding wheel takes them and Alex screams, imitating one hundred palmetto babies, "STOP, NO!"

And I'm laughing and almost crying, delirious, "I don't like killing things, but these must die."

The bugs in the apartment seem to have taken on an almost biblical air. I search for meaning in the infestation and find it too easily.

The next morning, I miss the doctor's rounds and learn they take place at six, not seven. I vow never to miss a round again. My dad can recall next to nothing the doctor told him, and I wanted to ask when he will start cancer treatments and if they can transfer him to Moffitt, the top-tier cancer treatment hospital in Tampa, thirty minutes away. But I can't do that if I can't speak to a doctor. Hiding my frustration, I break the news of the air-conditioning issues to my dad, who seems somewhat resigned. Alex stopped by Denny's and delivers a better breakfast. Dad is clearly touched by my boyfriend's effort and tells him so by calling him "brother," a word reserved for only two and now three of Dad's closest friends.

"Thanks, brother," Dad says again, and digs in. Seeing him hungry gives me hope. Alex takes a picture of us together, on the hospital bed. Dad puts his hand on my arm, just below the shoulder. I feel comfortable.

It occurs to me that if we hadn't come into town last night, I might have gotten a call that, after I'd seen my dad only one time in five years, he'd died alone in his bed. Instead, he has lung cancer, at least stage 3B, probably 4, a cockroach infestation, a stroke, PEs, and a very humid condo. And an ex-girlfriend turned best friend named Deb who texts me back while night-baking on Ativan. Dad is alive and in front of me. And I'm here in front of him, with Alex, or as Dad knows him, "brother."

Debby texts back again, the drug hopefully wearing off, "I was sleeping—sorry—and then making cookies cuz of the pills. How's he now sweetie?"

"Better," I text back.

"Thanks." Then, "Can I come by in a little?"

"Sure, whenever works. Room 202."

And a final answer from her, "I'll be over at noon :)"

"Debby will be over at noon," I say to him. Hearing her name, Dad lights up but goes dark seconds after. Knowing him and what he's probably thinking, I explain, "She just fell asleep last night and didn't see the calls or texts."

"Fine. Okay," he says, calming himself down. "I figured, NBD."

When Alex and I arrived in Florida, Mom had landed in Los Angeles for our preplanned visit, but when we needed to see Dad, she kept her flight to LA with the assumption that we all had: We'd just be gone for the weekend.

I call her, and she's at our favorite coffee shop, Proof.

"No, no don't put me on speak—" I say, too late.

The unsure voice of a stranger pops in. "Hello?" It's a barista.

"Tell her—" says my mom with her little East Coast accent. "Go ahead, tell her."

The lady tries to speak again, "Hi—I'm the one who gave the free cookie to your mom yesterday. I'm the barista at Proof, she wanted me to tell you that, um—"

"Hi."

The barista responds after some silence, "I'm not sure what to say."

"Oh. Oh, good. Yes. It was so yummy. And your name is Manoya?" I hear my mom say.

"Monica," the barista corrects her nicely.

"Monyica," Mom says.

"Yes, Monica," says the barista kindly, but louder so Mom will get it right.

"Monyica, Monyica pretty," says Mom.

"MONICA," I yell, and before she can botch anything more at our favorite neighborhood spot, I continue, "Hi, Monica nice to meet you, thanks for being so nice to my mom. She thinks you're her best friend now. Sorry, thanks."

"That's sweet. Jana is my best friend too. Haha."

"Aw. Thanks—you too."

"Mom," I say, and pray she gets that I need to have a regular conversation now. "Mom? Hello?"

"Monyoca is such a unique name, isn't it?" she screams into my ear and I picture her mouth too close to the microphone on speaker, basically eating it.

"Can you please— You're still saying it wrong, by the way, it's Monica, but Mom, can you take me off speaker please?"

"My daughter makes *PEN15*. Bye." And then proceeds to tell me I'm not on speaker even though I can hear every spoon and comment about the credit card tap, including when I hear that name again.

"Jana. Jana, cappuccino."

"Yup. Me," Mom starts to say, but then, "Wait, did you say caccachinah for Jana?"

"CAPPUCCINO." I can't take this. She always called Walgreen's Walgrens, mojitos mamajeetos, and Alex my first boyfriend's name, Greg.

"And there is espressa and milk in there, yeah?" I hear her ask.

With no idea if she can hear me or not, I start my small lecture. "Mom—it's a top-tier coffee place, you don't need to grill Monica or any barista there on a drink that you can't even pronounce and don't know what's in it."

"No one's grilling anything, Anna, this is a coffee shop. There's no grill here."

"MOM. TAKE ME OFF SPEAKER AND SIT DOWN AND TALK TO ME."

"I can't hear you. I'm"—and then the phone sounds like it's being flushed down the toilet and sucked up a pipe—"Sorry, you slipped. You theaya?"

"Are you like, putting on a thicker accent?" I ask. For some reason it sounds really pronounced all of a sudden.

"Putting on an accent—are ya crazy?"

"So Dad is . . . wait, did they say cappuccino for *Janna*? Are they calling you Janna? If so, why?"

Mom tells me that she decided to change her name. And she chose my best friend's name from childhood, who we are still very close with.

"Mine's just one '*n*'."

This is too much.

I instantly flash to how much it bothered me when she would change religious institutions or how she started talking about Jesus for a few years and then stopped. It used to be Spirit, though she claimed she was still the "same old spiritual bitch" she always had been.

Mom was constantly changing. I wanted to love this about her but it was exhausting.

A few years ago, about a month after she first met Alex, she told him that she never cries. After spending three days with her, he said she teared up more times than he'd seen his own mom, in the last thirty-four years.

"Mom, you changed your name at seventy-two?" Though I already know it has something to do with her breakup with Jack.

"The 'et' was closed. Janet. Jan-*et.* It doesn't match me. 'Na' is more open. Ja*na.* Jana. That's me."

"It's basically my name. That's what Maya calls me on our show."

"What?"

"Na. Never mind. But Jana and Anna? You're naming yourself me, a little, and mostly you're literally taking my friend Janna's name"—I keep going, speaking faster—"And actually, Janna's last name is White and so is Jack's, so if you end up marrying Jack at some point and you take his last name, you'll actually be taking

Janna White's full name." I'm horrified. "You began as Janet Ryan and ended as Janna White, my first best friend's first and last name?"

"OH!" she yelps as though whacking me with a dish towel—"I'm not—I'm not taking anyone's name and—if Jack and I got back together and got married"—she searches for an answer she doesn't yet have—"I won't uh . . . I won't uh, take his last name then . . . or I'll change my name back to Janet. I won't take Janna's full name! I wouldn't do that. My Jana is one *n*, hers is two."

"Right."

For about twenty seconds I think in silence of what I'm trying to ask her, and then it comes: "Do you think you're weird?" I ask genuinely, letting a tiny tone of adoration in.

She ignores me, on her own slope of thought. "But we won't get married, me and Jack, cuz he broke up with me in a text and left me and thank you for reminding me about that—he's an asshole and I'm Jana on Bumble now."

"Mom. Do you hear yourself?"

"You called to talk about your father, Anna, why don't we do that."

"I don't like that you changed your name to Jana! Don't care about the number of *n*'s either. I liked when you were Janet—I can't—get a hold on you. It would be nice to have that. To hold on to who that one person is. Especially since Dad is changing every moment. And has been over the last ten years and now is doing it even more because his body is doing stuff to him and I'm just trying to get him not to die so can you just be Janet? Please. At least with me? I can't do one more change at this very moment."

"You call me Mom anyway, what's the difference?"

"MOM!"

"See."

She swallows a few times and clears her throat before saying "Okay" and gives generic suggestions around the kind of care Dad will need when he gets out of the hospital. But as we get deeper into the subject, she asks question after question and it becomes very helpful. I try to recall everything the doctor said about the blood clots and restricted oxygen flow—she listens and waits, and I imagine all the things that made her a great nurse.

At the end of our conversation, which will become a daily check-in where I update her on Dad's health so she can guide me toward the next solution, she says, "Please tell your dad I'm thinking of him. Praying for him."

"I'll try," I say. There's a long silence, both our wheels turning. "But whenever I so much as say your name, he gets mad at me. Which I don't usually care about but right now he's fragile. Maybe if I say Jana, he'll think I'm talking about the Janna White he likes."

She manages a chuckle but mostly ignores me, deep in her own thoughts. "And if he wants me to visit—you know, when I'm back in Florida—I'd love to see him. I can help too. I'm a nurse."

"Right."

She sounds like she's dreaming. "If he'd have me."

Chapter Twenty-two

Coming out of the hospital, Dad looks fragile and untouched. He insisted on personally waiting in line at the pharmacy instead of letting me grab the pain medication for him. So he towers over the eighty-year-olds with osteoporosis, curled like cheese puffs, one behind the other, instead standing tall, scowling at his oxygen tank's blinking orange light. I panic that it could be running out of batteries but reassure myself that the hospital wouldn't give us a faulty oxygen tank as his singular source of life support.

Now he's looking more like a big tree about to fall over. The coloring in his face is off. I try to push him to sit down and take a break, but he's resentful and agitated. I imagine he's probably scared to be out of the hospital, because I am too. Hours earlier he was hooked up to a cord that pumped cold oxygen from an endless supply from the hospital basement. But now he drags a dinky tank that looks adequate only for a young person's brief scuba trip.

I can tell that he's trying to be stoic, but it's obvious that he can barely breathe. He wobbles one way and then the other, but his facial expression says "I'm fine, and if you fucking think that I'm not, you can die now. Thanks." So as older people give him the type of smile that says "I'm sorry your day is like this," he grows more and more agitated.

I look down and see that his tank is blinking now and I'm panicking.

Putting on a soft, high voice I say, "Dad, can we plug you back into the car charger? It's blinking red—"

"What?" He looks at me like I'm a stranger on the street.

"How 'bout you go sit down," I say, trying to sound chill.

"You go sit down," he snaps. "I'm. Fine." He delivers the last two words with petulance.

"So you're getting enough oxygen?"

"I'm fine, Anna." Everyone's looking at us. "Leave me alone! Jesus." Cheeks burning, I face forward so the grandmas and grandpas look away.

Eventually my dad orders his medicine like he's a top officer making demands of an inmate.

"I need it now. Go get it," he says rudely to the pharmacist.

Managing to get the medication and barely making it back into the car, he rips off his oxygen cord and I'm arguing with him, but I'm pretty sure it ran out of batteries anyway. When we walk into his condo, I plug it in and ignore everyone around who fills his tiny space. There are air-conditioning repairmen and also oxygen tank installation men. Dad lumbers in, unhappy.

"Is it a fuckin' party here? Get 'em outta here!"

A group of three are finishing the installation of the emergency oxygen tank in his bedroom. It's a manual mother lode of oxygen. And he needs it. He spots it as he walks in.

"What the fuck is this? Get that outta here. Now."

"Dad. You need that. It has to go there," I say. "Here sit, I'll put the TV on and you can take your oxygen again." I turn the knob this and way that, trying to get the number indicating how much oxygen it's outputting to glow. He sits for a second and tucks in the cannula.

"It's not fucking doing anything," he says, and rips it out again, and he's right. It says it's at two and I need it at ten, but it refuses to turn up.

His breathing is labored. "Dad, please put it in your nose. It's better than nothing."

Alex hands a credit card to the AC guy, saying, "Thanks. Thanks so much. Thank god it's cool in here."

"The pest guy come?" I ask.

"Yes. He said it's going to take a while to get rid of them all so he'll come once a week and so I bought the package. Is that fine? I couldn't get ahold of you."

"That's good. That's fine. Thanks."

From the other room I hear, "I DON'T WANT THESE IN MY BED. WHERE ARE MY PILLOWS?"

Dad throws the wedge pillows I just got him across the room. I'd bought them to mimic the incline of his hospital bed because he'd been sleeping sitting up as it was easier to breathe that way. I'd also found him a rolling hospital table so he could have meals in bed. But his home being outfitted for a handicapped person has set him off. As Alex and I enter, he's still throwing pillows across the room and yelling.

"I DIDN'T ASK YOU FOR THESE, ANNA. I WANT MY OLD PILLOW. WHERE ARE MY PILLOWS?"

I can't take it. "UNDER THE ONES I GOT YOU. I WAS TRYING TO HELP," I yell back.

I should have prepped him for the oxygen tank being installed in his house. But so much was moving so quickly—he needed an RN and a caregiver and someone to drive him to appointments when I went back to California for a few days. He needed an oncologist and pulmonologist, the best ones, and an appointment yesterday, but no one was available for a while. He needed groceries and a vacuum that worked so we could get the rest of the palmetto eggs. The list felt endless, and this didn't include the TV show I was supposed to be running, the scripts I had not written, and a production that would not slow down just because my dad was trying not to die. I'd asked, but the network wouldn't do it, plus there was the crew who would be out of work.

Alex watches like a shocked bystander at a zoo where the gorilla starts bashing its trainer's head like a coconut.

"YOU THINK YOU CAN COME HERE AND DO WHATEVER YOU WANT TO MY LIFE??"

It's too much. I slam the door to my bedroom and grip my stuffed monkey upon scratchy sheets that should have softened after ten years but haven't. Alex enters soon after. "I'm sorry."

"What did he just say about me? I could hear something."

"Nothing, don't worry about it," Alex says.

"Tell me."

"He said, 'Good luck with her.' "

"Good luck with her!? Good luck with her who is trying to keep him alive and coming to see her dad who ignored everything that was wrong and almost died the other night and who is now trying to nurse him back to health. Yes. GOOD LUCK WITH ME. Hope she doesn't fuck you up."

I'm crying because I don't mean everything I'm saying. I worry that he's right. That there is something inherently wrong with me and now he's told Alex.

"He is crazy," Alex says. "I've never seen anyone like that."

I'm surprised by the label but comforted too. "Right? Welcome to my life." And then I feel a pang of jealousy that he's never seen anyone like that.

Dad is finally sitting on the couch with his cannula back in—gripping it and pressing it as tight as it can go without surgical insertion. Wordlessly, I move the nebulizer next to him and fumble with the medicine that is supposed to become vapor and give him lots of relief. At least it did in the hospital.

"Don't break it," he says to me like I'm a fucking idiot.

"Dad," I warn.

"Can you hurry up?"

"Stop talking to me like that." My words come grave and slow.

He juts his jaw out in two different directions before slamming it shut like whenever he is mad but he doesn't say anything else and helps me with the medicine. Annoyingly, he is the one to open it successfully, but I'm just relieved it's finally working. Dad takes the vapors in like the first sips of a cold soft drink. Watching him, my iciness melts back into worry and I feel bad.

"Alex," he takes off the nebulizer mask to say, "close the fridge door. Now."

No.

"If you talk to Alex like that, if you talk to us like that, we will leave. We are in your house, using your things, because you invited us here."

He looks at me sharply, says nothing, and keeps breathing.

"It's okay, Peter. It's not a big deal," Alex says, shutting the fridge door. "I should have closed it."

Dad answers Alex's kindness with the same, "Sorry."

"It's okay, Peter."

"No, I'm sorry, brother, sorry."

The next morning, we're back in the hospital, but despite my pleas, he'd refused to go anywhere but North Bay, a hospital nearby without an oncologist. I wanted him to go to the better place with a specialty in lung cancer like Moffitt, to fast-track inpatient treatment but North Bay was it. I suspected it was because he'd wanted to make sure he was close enough for his visits from Deb and Tampa was at least thirty minutes away and could be an hour in traffic. Plus, Deb didn't drive at night. Now they're giving him oxygen and confirmed he had not been getting enough. But they are seeing fluid in his lungs, which they are less equipped to deal with at North Bay, so they will call a major teaching hospital in Tampa to see if they would take us there. I ask if they can do Moffitt instead but no, Moffitt doesn't typically take transfers, they tell me. The teaching hospital also doesn't have a spot for him and then I call because I've learned to be a very squeaky wheel in the health world—it can make a big difference. I force a spot open for him and say, "Dad, you aren't allowed to say no. This is happening. Debby will come, I'll be with you all the time, and so will the RN I'm hiring and maybe some friends from Vermont can come down or at least be on FaceTime. I have to keep going with *the show* but I'll be back every weekend and I need your friends' help and they love you and it's good for you to reconnect with people right now. So, this is happening. Being at a larger hospital in Tampa is better. They have an actual team of oncologists. It's right."

He doesn't say no.

Alex goes home to LA to relieve my mom of George duties and get back to work. I was here still holding my dad's hands. Lying on his side, he's almost hyperventilating. That needle through his chest wall to stage his cancer that he'd been avoiding has again been skipped because of a sudden, more pressing need to put a needle through his chest wall and into his fluid-filled lungs to drain them. The pulmonologist and head of the ICU, an ideal combination for us, was certain that this would give Dad the relief he needed and perhaps we could start cancer treatment in the hospital. This had given us all a big breath of hope. Plus, a new iPad had bolstered Dad's spirits. Less because of the gift, although he loved a gift, and more because of the sixties playlist we put together and the FaceTime calls he was getting from Deb and his best friends up north. He'd been sequestering himself for years, relationships deteriorating around him except maybe the ones with Frank and Mary, Justine and Deb. And Gary too. But Russ, his old best friend from Dunmore, who he had loved watching Formula One races with, who'd been the best man at his wedding, who was Janna's father, had gotten away, so to speak. They hadn't spoken much over the last decade. But Dad allowed me to tell Russ about his current plight, which resulted in them talking for quite a while and Russ saying he was going to come down and visit. To be my eyes and ears when I left for a few days and to reconnect with my dad. Even though he looks like he is dying, part of Dad is coming back to life.

He gets numbing in the area where the needle will enter. I fear he'll stop Dr. F before the needle goes all the way in, but instead he grips my hand and squeezes, saying, "Fuck. I don't like that."

And a full bag of yellow liquid pours out into a once empty plastic sac.

I can't believe all that can fit in his lungs, and neither can Dr. F, "That's a lot," but adds, "You're gonna feel a lot better, Peter, a lot more comfortable. And then hopefully we can talk to the oncologist and start cancer treatments like, tomorrow. I can't speak for her, but I will speak *with* her."

"Thank you so much," I say.

"Damn. I can breathe," Dad says, sitting up and looking brighter than before. "Thanks, Doc," he says. "Now I know why they say you feel like you're drowning with lung cancer."

"Right!" says Dr. F, matching my dad's energy.

"You're literally drowning," Dad says.

The doctor gets more serious. "Yeah."

"Well. I never wanna feel like that, Doc. Okay? So kill me if that starts happening," Dad says, sharply.

"Okay. Well, I don't think that's gonna happen, I think you're gonna feel a lot better soon."

We heave a sigh of relief together.

"I'm serious, though," Dad says as the doctor prepares to leave.

"K," I say. "I hear you. You don't want to live if you feel like you're drowning. I won't let you drown."

"Dr. F, how long do you think we have till the liquid comes back?"

"Shouldn't, but gotta start treatment soon." We nod. I'm happy.

When Dr. F leaves, I hug Dad because he seems overwhelmed.

"Thanks, honey," and he starts to cry. Then I attempt to land something I wasn't sure I was going to attempt: "You know, I feel like maybe it's a good time to tell you that Mom wants to visit."

"No," he says, comically quick, which makes me laugh hard, once.

"Okay, well think about it," I say. "She's a nurse. She wants to help."

"I don't want her help!" I've pissed him off now.

"Okay. Well, she made you a blanket. With prayers from her church on it."

"She's still doing that stuff?" He looks happy to make fun but follows with another "No."

"Dad, I can't tell her you won't take a blanket, that's crazy."

"Then don't tell her, but don't give it to me."

"You're so difficult!" I say, but I'm laughing and something tells me to keep going. "Speaking of, is this a good time to talk about something that there's never a good time to talk about?" I ask. "I certainly don't want to."

"Yes, it's the perfect time, then."

I go for it. "The social worker is asking me for—and it's not because you're going anywhere, but because this is what they do—your living will, your directives."

"Okay, shoot," he says.

I've caught him at a good moment. The Monkees play in the background and he is still breathing more easily. Expecting him to shut down or stop the conversation at any moment, I tread carefully, knowing I need his signature at the end for it to be official.

What becomes clear is that he does not want life support because he doesn't want to live if he can't do it with a certain quality of life. He doesn't want to go on as a vegetable, he keeps saying. And he explains that this is why he advised taking his sister off life support three years ago. He wasn't sure what she wanted because she didn't have a living will. He's never said this out loud before and sounds like he feels guilty about it.

I say, "You made the best decision with the best information you had."

"Yeah, but that'll eat at you, ya know," he confides.

"You did the right thing," I say with absolute certainty.

Then he chuckles. "You know, I'm glad we are doing this, honey. Because I never want you to look back and feel bad." I note that he's a different kind of thoughtful recently. Maybe it's the morphine, but it means something.

He tells me he doesn't want to be resuscitated if there is an emergency. This stops me. "Dad, if they have to do a surgery, and there's a complication . . ."

"What kind of complication?"

"I don't know! But you don't want them to try to help you live?"

His voice booms low, "Well, I dunno. I don't want to be a vegetable."

"That doesn't mean you will be!"

"I also don't want to feel like I'm drowning." I nod to show how much I get that. He goes on, "My will and all my important information is in my desk at home. Debby knows where it is. Frank knows where it is. And you should too. Deb gets the condo, but you get my retirement."

"Dad, I don't need to know all this."

"I know. You want my living will. Sorry, it comes with all this other information. You get all the art and the chairs. But I'm going to Italy, okay? That I know. But if after, things go downhill, all the art, the furniture, it's all yours."

I give over to the melting this makes me feel. It feels like I'm running a marathon and someone has stopped me to tell me that I'm not gonna make it to the finish line, just so you know, so just walk, jog lightly, whatever. It's not worth killing yourself because we aren't getting there.

Back at the apartment, I fall asleep. There's a knock. Shifting out of the bed and into the bright hallway, I push the screen door open, and there is a small boy. He runs into my arms. He's probably four years old, with blond hair and one turned-in eye. He squeezes me and I squeeze him back. The back of his head rests against my palm. He's so safe. I kiss his forehead, and he nuzzles into me. I know that it's my dad as a child. He's also my son. We look at each other and he nuzzles back into me.

I wake up to a text that says, "Honey, liquid is back."

Chapter Twenty-three

He keeps asking the new oncologist about his Italy trip and she keeps telling him that he won't be well enough to go next month because flying isn't safe and they can't get his lungs to stop filling up with malignant liquid.

He's not gonna ask, but I'm starting to think someone should, "And do you think it's important to know the zoom-out here? How long does he have, is that important to talk about?"

She nods and looks to him and back to me, "One to five years, I think," depending on when we get into treatment.

"Can we start treatment now?" I ask. "Chemo—like what do we need to do?"

"We still don't technically have staging," she says. "We've been putting out one fire after another."

"Can we assume it's 4? Or 3B, and just treat from there? It just feels like it's wasting so much time."

Dad looks down and is texting, maybe ignoring us on purpose. I hope he doesn't mind I'm asking all these questions. Recently, he's totally given over control and I don't take the responsibility lightly.

"If it's 4, it's gonna be far more aggressive. 3B, that's a different treatment course. Your dad isn't stable enough right now to start any of the treatments anyway—even 3B treatment is aggressive. He needs to be stronger to handle that. Do you understand what I'm saying? And we have to stop the liquid in the lungs."

"So what's the timeline on that?"

"I can't say. We could hope to start soonest, in a week."

"That's too long."

She's annoyed.

"He's not eating."

She writes that down and I feel justified to list everything that's going on because it's proof she isn't asking all the questions, "Yeah, he's not eating, not much. He is on max oxygen sometimes."

She looks very surprised by this and repeats to be sure, "Max?"

"Well, almost, like 80 percent," I say.

And she answers, "That doesn't really add up to the size of his masses. We should do more imaging and a full CT scan and see how it's progressing."

"Yeah," I say. "Agreed."

I was learning a lot on Reddit and Facebook groups and Wikipedia. I remember one more thing: "And he's coughing up white froth now. That started yesterday." She looks alarmed again. Do they read the fucking charts?

When she leaves, I watch him. "Did you hear that, Dad? I hope it's okay I asked."

He looks at me blankly. "I'm sorry, but I think it's important you hear it too." I brace myself: "One to five years."

"Good, I'll go to Italy."

"Yeah," I'm relieved to hear him not crumble. "You'll go to Italy," I say because I can't handle anything deeper, and then turn on a TV show for him on Netflix. Before I leave, I put the blanket on his feet that my mom made and he forgets to ask who it's from.

The camera is rolling and Maya and I, age thirty-three, swing our bodies back and forth, dancing and grinding like two desperate thirteen-year-olds trying to get the attention of the cool kids by doing something we hope will appear sf&c: sexy, funny, and creative. We play thirteen-year-olds among real thirteen-year-olds, so doing any scene can often be like being around the ghost of yourself. We sing a made-up song as our tween characters, "I'm really gonna win for the weekend weekend. Really gonna win for the weekend."

It's mostly a relief to fall away into these versions of ourselves during such a stressful time in my life, but it's also torturous. Playing this age, without responsibility and with a naïve view of the world, is like putting ice cream in front of someone on a restrictive diet, but worse. How much do I lean into this feeling of innocence during filming, knowing it's going to be stolen from me between every scene, every camera setup, every take—every weekend or week spent back in Tampa next to my dad. My phone is hidden in my character's school backpack so I can make sure there's no emergency.

It buzzes.

"Cut." I say, which I'd never do normally, but I say it again, yanking my phone out of my bag, scared and excited for it to be the doctor I've been waiting two days to hear from, the oncologist who will finally have a plan for starting treatment. This was everything.

"Everything okay?" asks Maya.

"Probably. Yes, no, it's good. But it's important I take this quickly. So sorry!"

"Hello?" I pick up the call and it's the oncologist. She jumps right in, breaking down the genetic findings.

"So, he's not a good candidate for immunotherapy." This was a newer kind of cancer treatment saving people in stage 4. It had been revolutionary, but it's not an option. Cross that off the list. I'm perched behind sets, hidden, spying the feet of busy crew running around, knowing they are waiting for me and willing myself not to feel bad. They know that things are paused because of me right now. Hidden but still under a microscope.

The doctor goes on, "I'm just gonna say it. I know we wanted to talk about starting treatment quickly, but Dr. F and I had a very long discussion this morning."

"Okay, good. Thank you for doing that."

"We went over every angle of this thing."

"Good, yes. Me too. I mean, thank you for doing that." Ugh, I just said that.

She's taking on tones of apology, "And he's still on such a high level of oxygen."

"He was maxed out last night, is what Jill said—er, the overnight nurse."

"Right. He was, yes. And we believe that's because the lungs keep filling with liquid—which is the result, most likely, of a very aggressive cancer. It's unusual."

"I figured that was why. Right." God, he's going to be so sick from the chemo.

She explains more, gently, her humanity showing through: "Ya know, we had wanted to get him to a stable place because he's been unable to begin chemo or radiation. We wanted to do both. But he's not getting stable, and at this point I'm going to have to recommend hospice."

No.

We have not worked this hard for hospice. No. I don't want to say goodbye to him. Is that what that means? No. The five years we lost. I need those back. I need them back. It's not hospice now. No.

After a little, I ask, "How long does he have?"

"I don't know. Months or weeks."

"Weeks?" This wasn't supposed to happen this way.

"I don't know, you never know with these things. But he isn't eating much."

"Right. Are you sure?"

"That he's not eating much?"

"That he needs to go to hospice."

"I don't see any other option."

Hiding my face in my legs, I hold the phone far away from my mouth so she can't hear me for a long time until I can say something again, which ends up being "Okay. Thank you." And I hang up.

And then I leave set and I don't come back for a bit. They'd have to figure it out without me. They'd have to lose money on this set. They would have to. They would just *have* to. I'm a shell. Doesn't human life matter more than work? Maya finds me curled into myself and holds me as everything that mattered leaves.

She tells me to go.

I call him from my car on FaceTime and he picks up. Dad says he likes his nurse right now and that she stays after hours and watches *Survivor* with him because she doesn't have a great relationship with her own dad.

The irony strikes me.

"Did you tell her we've had a hard time? But we got through it?" I ask.

"I haven't told her," he says.

"You should. Maybe they will fix something too."

I know what I have to do but I don't want to. How do you tell someone who thinks they are going to Italy next year, who is suffering and fighting every single day in the ICU, that all of this hard work is leading to death? The metal armor and shield, melted and recast into the final sword.

I look at his face and try to leave my body like I used to and just do it. I tell him that the oncologist finally called me. He looks at me, silent.

"And we were discussing treatment options, or we were supposed to, but she and Dr. F spoke and your health hasn't stablized enough to start treatment and it's getting worse. Because of that they think we should focus on your palliative care. I'm so sorry to tell you this, Dad. I'm so, so sorry. She said you have months probably."

I try to wait, but he doesn't say anything, so I go on. "And so, um, hospice is going to be the best option, they think you're too fragile to start treatment." And before he can answer, maybe I've robbed him of a response to such immense news, I'm not sure, I don't mean to, I'm crying, telling him we will make it great. "I'm gonna look for an ocean view, ya know? The best hospice we can find. Okay? And I'm going to be there the whole way."

And then he smiles. "Okay," he says peacefully, almost like a small child. For another moment in our lives, we cry together.

Then I start going again. "And you don't have to deal with wires and beeping anymore and being woken up in the middle of the night. The whole point of it is comfort, so we'll turn up the morphine and the music."

He laughs and says, "Jamming out to death, huh? Groovy," and it occurs to me that he's probably on a lot of morphine right now.

"I'm sorry, Dad. We really tried. Right? I'm sorry."

"It's okay, sweetie. It's okay. You've done amazing. I can't believe everything you've done for me." I can see a nurse's arm touching him.

"I love you."

"I love you."

"I'm sorry we missed those five years," I say.

"Me too, but I don't blame you for a second."

"You don't?"

"I don't. I fucked up, a lot. And I changed because you made me change. You were gone for so long."

This cracks me open, full blown. "I'm so . . . sorry."

"You had to go," he says. "You had to. I had to get my shit together."

"Me too, Dad."

I catch my breath and decide to try once more, for the sake of the family that we once were, a family that did exist, that was real, not imagined, not reducible to only its worst characteristics, that was alive, that did laugh together, many years ago.

"You should let Mom come by, Dad. You should. It would give you peace, I think." There's a long, long silence and then he says, "I'll think about it."

Chapter Twenty-four

An ocean view in Los Angeles is what I'd wanted to give him, but after a week of planning, I learn he'll never be able to leave the hospital. The amount of oxygen he needs is not available on any helicopter or in any hospice outside a hospital. We waited for his need to decrease to make the transfer but his need only grows. And now we are here.

I accompany his gurney down the halls and hallways of the hospital, like a bodyguard, ringing the doorbell to in-house hospice too many times. When no one answers, minutes feel too long, like Dad could disintegrate into pieces at any moment. Which maybe he could.

They answer the door like they were always there and warm faces greet us. He's placed in his new room. Sure, there is a view of the equipment on the hospital roof, but there is also some ocean and we can see the bright blue Florida sky. But would he like it? The place you come to die seems important.

"I like it. I like how quiet it is too."

"Me too. Right? Yeah. I like it. Honestly, this is better than the spots in LA we were touring. Seriously." And it's true.

The walls are a calming blue and the room feels more like a hotel than a medical facility. A soft chair pulls out, becoming a bed, which the ICU didn't have, and I make it up with sheets knowing I'll be sleeping here awhile.

Behind us Alex carts groceries with ice cream and cheddar cheese and apple pie to put in the shared fridge where all have easy access to their favorite food. I guess I want the end to be exciting for him. Or familiar.

Quickly, the new doctor agrees to give him more morphine than what he is on and I add song after song to the playlist. There is more time to talk here.

I watch him sleep or bop to music, smiling. And drugs transition him from pain to somewhere else where the music lives.

I text my brother.

"No pressure at all but if you want to speak to my dad before, you know, please let me know." He texts back, "I do, that would be great, Anna, thank you." Unable to share his information through a ton of phone calls, I text the people Dad has given me permission to tell. Many of his friends don't know this is even going on, because that's how he wants it. Except for the telemarketer whose call he picked up yesterday and who Dad fucked with while looking at me, telling the guy, "Well actually I'm DYING right now and so if you could FUCK OFF, that would be just peachy." And he said the word "peachy" like a woman.

I laughed a lot.

I don't want him to go.

The end is feeding your loved one ice from a spoon, combing their hair, brushing their teeth, moving their body parts so they stay comfortable or whatever version of comfortable is possible. It's lifting their head with a small rolled-up fleece blanket when their forehead falls forward during an uncomfortable sleep, neck bent like a straw. It's noticing when the catheter bag is full to tell a nurse, covering his feet with socks when you realize they are ice, taking off the blanket, putting on the blanket, relaying messages, holding the phone on speaker and pretending you aren't there as you hear others' final exchanges.

Or perhaps they won't be final, perhaps there will be time for one more, which is confusing. This is the dance.

You grieve the loss together as best you can and also sob in the closet so you don't expose them to your internal chaos. It's wishing sometimes I had a twin that cared about him as much as I do so we could have the same amount of worry and help each other carry it. My mother was the closest thing to that, and she keeps texting me: "No pressure, but you know I'd really like to see him." She is back at her house in Florida and brings me soup sometimes when I'm alone in my hotel.

Dad is in and out of sleep, and when he swims in peacefulness, I feel massive relief. Before this nap he told me that he didn't want to die alone. That was the only thing. He wanted me and Alex with him.

"I love Alex. My brother."

His brother.

And he loves George, our dog. And tells me, like the little boy with the soft hair in my dreams, that he named this white stuffed dog sitting on his belly Gracie because it was the female version of George. I laugh with him as I comb his hair, his lips barely able to move anymore, but then help him brush his teeth again because he wants me to.

Even now he wants to look in the mirror.

"Still good-looking," he says, and the nearest nurse laughs.

But he is.

He acts sick but doesn't look it, so much.

It's confusing.

And the doctor can't tell me if it'll be two days or two weeks, but with lung cancer, quicker is better. That's what they all keep saying.

And then Jamie calls. "Dad, Dad, it's Jamie," I say. Dad's awake, sort of—in a haze—a new haze that he's been sort of residing in recently. I hold the phone up on speaker.

"Do you want privacy for this?"

"Take it off speaker," he says, smiling, sort of tickled to finally have his stepson in reach.

Putting the phone to his ear, he looks amused and says, "Hey, Jamie." Sounding amused is code for deep satisfaction. Hearing a tinny voice through the atoms floating between me and Dad, Jamie says, "Hi, Peter," with the gentle singsong quality my brother has always spoken with. Careful, measured, and small.

"How are you?" Dad is still amused, tickled, but he can't say as many words as he could a week ago. Things are slower and simpler now.

I'm unable to hear Jamie's response, just my dad's, but he doesn't speak for a while and listens, swallowing a few times, and then says, "Thank you." He swallows again, eyes filling. "Well, you know, I love you. I'm sorry for my mistakes." There's a succinctness growing in my dad, maybe out of necessity. Something he's never really had. Also, taking responsibility is new. Hoping this is just as meaningful for Jamie as it is for my father, I look up to the sky and talk to Spirit. God. Whatever.

I note how four months ago, God wasn't really a thing for me—but now Spirit is present in whatever I did. I needed to talk to something bigger once every ounce of control had been taken.

"Please give them peace," I repeat.

And Dad says again, "I love you. Thanks for calling. Goodbye, Jamie." He looks to me, again, like a little kid.

"That was really special," I say. "Sounded that way at least."

"Jamie said after he became a stepfather himself, he realized how difficult it really is." He looks just below my eyes, like he's thinking deeply, and I've disappeared. "Means a lot," he says. "Forgiveness."

By the end of the day, when other people call, he says maybe just for himself, "People really do love me."

He had convinced himself that no one really did. "Of course they do, Dad. Even if you haven't seen someone in a while. They love you."

I ask him if he wants to see Mom because she keeps texting me for his answer.

I want to reveal how much she's been helping behind the scenes, how much she cares. I'd been asking him for weeks but ending each suggestion with "No pressure." And he'd either say no or that he'd think about it. This time I don't say "No pressure."

I just look at his face and wait.

Summer sun dances on his cheeks and eyes before turning emotional, facing angry winter. This was their pattern—summer, fall, winter, spring to summer again, the wetter, harsher the cold months, the flower-heavy spring and appreciation for the summer grew.

"No. Tell her no." Trying not to make this about me, about having our family back together just once more until the end of time, about my disappointment or the worry over my mom and how she will feel, I muster an "Okay."

I ask him one final time.

"Nope," he says hard, like he'd won the game, final chess piece moved. In the little-boy eyes of my dad, where his soul had always existed no matter his age, he'd been abandoned by her, and now, as the last thing he would ever do, he would abandon her back.

He spots the green knit blanket at the end of his bed.

"Is that from her?"

"Yes. It has prayers—"

"Get it off," he responds without lag. This pains me, but his anger about a blanket could almost be funny if it wasn't the end of their story.

It is his bed. It is his hospice room. It is his gown, his decision, his life. It is his water cup. It is his IV bag. His problems, his miracles, his gifts.

It is his death.

Dad grips his white stuffed dog, Gracie.

I'd always wondered if Mom and Dad would get back together, even if just for the last week of his life. To me, she was already here, always checking on him, supporting me with him—whether he liked it or not, Mom had been a part of his care because she was a part of me and I needed someone who knew him, really knew him. And really knew me. There weren't many others there, after all. And so I realize that we are together, as together as we can be.

They are together through me. Just like they'd always been.

Before bed, Dad says, "I'm not afraid to die, honey."

"Good, Dad. That makes me happy. Really happy."

"I love you," he says to me.

"I love you. Good night," I say to him.

His eyes close like maple syrup down a windowpane.

Lying in the pullout chair, I open my laptop for *Love Island* and I think to text Mom but she won't be up. I do it anyway.

Anna: He just said he's not afraid to die.

Mom: Wow. Passing people are profound.

Anna: You're up.

Mom: Can't sleep honey. You okay? u are so brave.

Anna: I wish you were here. Im sry to say this but he said no.

(. . .)

Anna: To you visiting.

Mom: To me visiting?

Mom: Oh yes. Yes. K. I figured. I came to understand that. And I do. I tried.

Anna: But you've been a part of helping this whole time. Helping me.

Thak you. I don't kow what I would have done without you. I'm so tired.

Mom: Do you think he has a while.

Anna: Yeah.

Anna: I dunno.

Mom: Mmm. Holding you in my heart and prayers and your dad too. You cannot do everything. You cannot be everything. Do your best it is enough.

(. . .)

She keeps typing and I know she may go on for a bit but I told her the news and now I just needed a minute of nothing. But I'm relieved she's not mad.

(. . .)

Anna: Sorry have to go to bed, love you mom. More soon. Night. Thank you.

(Texts on mute.)

I go back to *Love Island*, eyes wide open until they aren't.

I wake to the sound of him gasping for breath and coughing.

"I can't breathe—HMEEEGGHH"—that's his attempt at breathing—loud and broken.

"It's okay, Dad. It's okay. I'm getting your medicine," I say, as I run into the hallway like every morning at five and spot the nurse at the front desk. "He can't breathe—he can't breathe—" and when I know they've heard me and I see them moving, I jog back to the room, and someone trots next to me.

"Okay Peter—we are getting you the morphine, it's okay . . ."

"HMEEEGGHH!" But it's way more today—"I can't breathe—I can't breathe—I can't breathe—" His booming voice takes over the whole corridor and more nurses jog in.

"Dad, it's okay. Help is coming." But it's something different, he's holding his throat. "HELP! HELP HIM!"

A nurse with the morphine moves toward him. Dad's arms and legs jet off the bed—he hasn't been up on his feet for weeks—I've been moving his limbs myself—but here he is planting his two feet on the ground—towering over the nurses, ripping tubes as he stands and tries to pace—"HMEEEGGHHAA I can't fucking breathe! Help me. Help me. Help me."

This time I retreat away, now in a full panic. "Help him!! Help him!! Help him!!"

Someone catches me like a baseball. It's a nurse and all I can do is cry into her as she takes me into the next room.

"But I said I'd be there."

And across the hallway I still hear "Help me," but it's getting small now, his very voice smaller. I wonder if he's dying and I'm not with him. "Daddy," I hear myself say, "I'm sorry." But I feel like I'm falling. I wish my mom was here. Alex is at the hotel still. What am I doing? I've fucked everything up. "It's quiet," I say, because it is quiet.

We tiptoe into his room and he is comatose. Eyes blinking. An unbelievable number of drugs in him, that's clear. I hold his hand and look at him. I whisper to him, "I'm sorry, Dad. I'm sorry. This is what you didn't want to happen."

He stares at me and blinks.

"I love you so much. I'm not going anywhere, okay? I know you don't want to feel like that." He shakes his head. I look at him with unbroken eye contact and ask him, "Do you want this to be it? The end?" He doesn't say or do anything, so I keep going. "I know you didn't want to feel that. You don't want to drown. Do you want to . . . end it? Is that time now?" I hear myself say to him in a different way. He still doesn't respond. This is fucking awful. I shouldn't decide this for him.

The hospice doctor must have been called in at some point and stands behind me. I can feel his presence without looking and I want him to go away but I also don't want the drug to wear off and make my dad start yelling again and feel like he's drowning.

Should I put him somewhere even farther away? Dad won't confirm what I should do. He won't answer. Too many drugs. I'm very close, trying to see anything I can, a hand on his hand, the other on his arm. He suddenly squeezes my fingers, hard. A nurse gives him Gracie and he grips Gracie's paw. My nightmare is that he is hurting without being able to say. Paralyzed. His eyebrows knit together, trying to be one.

The doctor offers, "He's in pain still. I would say that's safe to say—the brows are a good indicator of that." I nod, face wet. I'm texting Alex.

"I don't want him to wake up and feel like he's drowning. I promised I wouldn't let that happen. Could that happen again?"

The doctor moves his head forward. It's a gentle yes.

"Like, any time?" I say, needing ultimate clarity.

Again, he nods yes.

"He could wake up right now and feel like he's drowning?"

He nods.

"And the answer to that?"

"Palliative sedation."

"Is that the end?"

"Sort of. Probably. The beginning." Wasn't hospice the beginning?

"Daddy, do you want that? To go?" I swear he moves his head like he doesn't, or maybe it's me that doesn't want him to. He made me promise to be with him when he dies and to not let him drown. I already failed at one. I can't fail at the other. I tell the doctor to give him more medicine. The medicine. The beginning of the end. What choice do I have? The ladies fly in like swans and inject new liquids from syringes into his IV bag. His eyes completely close and the brows move away from each other a little, though they stay looking unhappy.

I come up for air myself but I'm not here, really. "So this is the end?"

"It's been the end, this is the beginning of death. It could come in two hours or two weeks. Dying is still a mystery, even with us watching it all the time. A mystery still."

"See the button?" another nurse comes in and asks. No, I don't see a button, I'm trying to find my dad right now. Is he in the clouds? A soul, floating just above his body? Or fully in there, suffering while we've made him totally unable to express himself? Screaming for me to listen?

"Anna. This is important information, okay? This is a button." She says, "You have to press the button, see it? Press it to give him more medicine. The more you press it, the less pain he will be in." But it's like we are underwater and she's talking to me with bubbles shooting out of her mouth.

"The button?" I say, looking up. I'm trying to say goodbye to a version of my dad. The button.

"Look at me," she says firmly. "If you don't press this, he stays in pain. It's that simple."

And I see what she's talking about, another tube connected to a vein, with a button attached to distribute whatever is inside. I see it so I say, "Okay."

"His eyebrows are still like this," and she makes an angry face. "I can't tell you what to do, but you might want to press the button until they move apart again."

No one told me about the button when I said yes to the drugs. She watches me, so I stand, click it three times,

1

2

3

and sit down again. This has satisfied her enough to leave. She closes the door and I'm a mess. Turning up the music, I tell him everything.

"I'm not sure what I've just done, and I just really hope it was the right thing. Please know it's because I love you and I'm truly, truly trying to honor your wishes. I'll keep you clean and comb your hair while you sleep and hold your hand? Okay? Monkey is here."

I place him under my dad's head, which has moved to the side, and I think he looks uncomfortable again, but he is almost unrecognizable to me. I can barely see him.

"I'll try to keep you here in a way that you would still recognize, okay? The best I can at least."

I comb his hair again.

"I'm sorry I didn't do better."

I feel him squeeze my hand.

"I love you."

He squeezes my hand again.

"Can you hear me?" I say this over and over but he doesn't squeeze my hand another time.

I keep going. "I want to tell you all the ways you were a good dad, okay? Like an excellent dad. I mean, you were impossible also, so I guess I'll tell you the bad things too, then." This makes me laugh and I know he would be laughing too, but I can't stop looking at his eyebrows, which are still angrily woven together.

"You burned bridges, but maybe you were just going to your own drum. Maybe you were on the spectrum. Ha-ha. I dunno. Anything is fine. I hope you know I love you. No matter what. Are you gay? Bi? Free love?" I laugh at myself for giving options on his deathbed. Mainly because I don't know how he would have reacted. Maybe laughed. "You offend people, a lot of people, but you're so sharp and brilliant, Dad, and you shared the absolute best parts of yourself with me. You taught me to fish. You taught me to be funny, to be weird, to do woodwork. Your hugs, your performances, the way you made me laugh. To be myself. What actual funny is about."

I keep going like this, telling him how I feel, for over an hour. Alex pops his head in. Frank and Mary flew in to say goodbye. Deb takes twenty minutes to talk to Dad but comes out weeping and leaves abruptly after a quick hug. It's hard giving other people this time but nice to have community. He doesn't belong just to me.

When I go back in, I look at his eyebrows.

"This is you. It's entirely who you were, who you are and I know . . ." My voice catches in deep sadness as I go on, "I know I hadn't seen you for a long time, a really long time, I'm sorry. I hope you understand."

He squeezes my hand. This stops me in my tracks and I put my head to his belly and he holds me. In my mind, he holds me. "I love you so so much. You're my dad. You'll always be my dad. And your whole life was nine million times better than Italy. Italy is dumb. Not dumb but it's just another spot on Earth. You did

Earth, okay? The important beautiful parts. And even with the hard parts of our relationship, you made my life nine million times better. Because you are my dad dedicated to me, to my childhood joy. My dad. And I feel proud. I feel lucky. I'm sorry I didn't have the skills to work everything out earlier."

I finish crying into him and then I touch the wrinkles above his eyes to try to make them relax but it doesn't work. "Hey, you know how there is Little Italy? We did LA Italy, remember? And it's better because we did it together." Alex is sitting next to me. He's had his own private time to say goodbye somewhere in there. I kiss Dad's forehead. Alex hugs Dad too and calls him Brother, gently asking me the last time I pressed the button. I have no idea. I press it once more and wonder if I'm going to be sick. I can't do this.

We sit here, Dad, Alex, and me.

The nurse comes in. She looks worried with us.

"I've told you about my father, how he had lung cancer," she says.

"Yes," I say, not really wanting this but too empty to say anything like that.

"We were out in rural bumfuck, okay?" I stare into space, remembering how my dad would tap the cookie but this time I'm not looking for meaning, I'm just looking. "There were no hospitals, drugs were hard to get, and watching him die like that was torture. Lung cancer sucks. It sucks. That's why I became a palliative nurse. To make sure people go fast and painlessly."

She looks me in the eye so directly that it feels like she's talking to a child version of me.

"That's why the button exists. But you aren't pressing the button."

I look at her, helpless, like a fawn waiting for its mother to show it what to do next.

I fucking hate the button. I hate that it's my responsibility to press it.

"I know, sweetie," she says. "I know."

I guess I'm weeping. "I can't. I'm killing him."

"I know. I know." She nods small. "Do you want me to do it? I'm not supposed to, but—"

I nod small back.

She peeks out into the hallway to make sure no one is looking and clicks the button. I can see that even for this stranger, the simple task, the movement of her finger, robs her of something too. I look at her like I imagine I would have looked at a sibling.

Her thumb clicks again.

4

5

6

"Okay," I say. "Okay."

I don't want him to go. I don't want him to suffer. "Thank you, thank you." That's as many times as I'd pressed it all day.

Alex pets my hair and the nurse leaves the room. Our playlist for Dad rings out still.

Van Morrison, Cat Stevens, Beach Boys. Neil Young. Poets.

His guys. I think about how music is the most honest thing on Earth.

And I'm about to hyperventilate.

Alex offers to press it a couple more times. Okay.

7

8

I need air.

"Daddy, I will be back in ten minutes." I'd been in one room all day, since the drowning. I wouldn't let him go through that again. But I feel crazy.

"Is that okay? Is that okay?"

"Yes, take a walk," Alex says, holding my hand.

"See you in a minute, Peter."

"Dad, I love you." I put my forehead to his like a maniac, like a mother.

Outside, there is tea and crying.

Time doesn't feel like anything but I guess ten minutes must have passed.

My feet enter his room.

I think maybe I'm catching my father's last exhale.

I told him we would be right next to him when he left.

We're here, I say. It's okay.

Me and Brother.

On the speakers, *Harvest Moon* plays.

His hand with the Irish clatter ring lays in mine.

My father is not gone in a single moment, but in and out of many.

Which means he comes back too, sort of.

I lay down my head, nestled into him.

Alex holds his ankle and rubs my back.

We stay like this until it will be impossible to leave this time.

Until he is cold.

Epilogue

Wreck It Ralph plays on a TV that's too big, just like Ralph's arms. The other character, Vanellope, is a small girl and kind of looks like she could be Ralph's daughter. He lies on his back, effortlessly throwing a football up in the air and catching it.

Alex lies on our rug, an unintentional mirror of the guy. Our dog, George, is fat now and lies like a roll in his bed. Our four-year-old, Essie, sits on her dad's stomach.

Again, Ralph throws and catches the ball, still lying on his back.

"Can you do dat, Daddy?" Essie asks Alex.

"What do you think?" he says.

Ralph throws the football in the air and punches it, still lying down, until the ball flies past the end zone.

"Can you do *dat*, Daddy?"

"Yes, I can." Alex mimes really throwing a football with one hand and catching it with the same one over and over.

"No, no," I clarify. "We are wondering if you can do what the guy did next?

"Yeah, can you do *dat*?" Essie's emphatic too.

"What?"

"Ralph threw the football into the air and punched it into a touchdown," I say, not sure of the terminology.

Alex turns it back on our daughter, "What do you think, Essie? Can I?"

"Yes. You can do everyting."

"I thought Pop-pop could do everything too," I say but mostly to myself. "He kinda could."

And then the next things she says come out like a singsongy list:

"You can catch a owrange."

"Yes," Alex says.

"You can squeeze a owrange?" she genuinely asks.

"Yes."

"You can put a fingah in yo mouf?" she's not sure about this one.

"Yes!" And her daddy shows her. Fully satisfied that he's proven her original point, she dons a big-ass smile and says,

"Great!"

He can do anything, everything. He's her superhero. Mine too.

She catches my eye with a twinkle before she goes back to the TV.

It had driven me a little crazy when she was born, that her idea of me would be better than I actually was. But I'd do everything I could to live up to her impossible expectation. It took me months to figure out how close or not close my body should be to hers. Trying to sense her boundaries as best I could—what was too together?—until fully reckoning with the idea that she had just lived inside me. She wanted to be close. Probably as close as possible. And it would remain this way for many years. And when language was well grasped, she would tell me whether she wanted to snuggle or not. A kiss or not. My gut and my best would have to be good enough.

Now I put her to bed and we hold hands. It's easy to.

"Mommy. Cuddle me." I squeeze her.

"Harder." I squeeze harder.

"K, stop." I do.

I turn the lights off.

"Will you fawl asleep wit me?"

"I'll fall asleep with you, sure."

"PopPop."

"Yeah? What about him, babe?"

"He was yo dad."

"Mhm."

"Your daddy."

"My daddy, yup."

She snuggles in even more.

"What did PopPop sound like?"

She's always asking what people sound like. What does the teacher sound like, even when she knows them. But especially if she didn't, she wanted to know. And we'd always do their voices, to the best of our ability. But I don't really want to right now.

"He had a low voice, very low. He was funny."

"But what did he sound like?"

"I just told you, Es."

"Do his voice, dough."

"Do his voice, though?" And I breathe. Both soft and hard. "He kind of sounded like—" And I throw it low, deep, as deep as I can possibly go, even deeper actually, with bombastic charisma, like he's the star of his own show, here in the bedroom too, with Monkey, sitting by the side of the bed with both of us—*"THIS."*

"Hi, PopPop," Essie says. I wave as him and open the book we are about to read.

"Hi, PopPop." Another wave back but she wants more, "Hi."

I boom, low again, "Hi, Essie."

"Do you wish you got to meet me?"

A lot moves inside me. "OHHH *yes.*" Nodding as Anna and back to him. "I would have really loved to meet you."

"But you passed away!"

I swallow, picturing him smiling. "I passed away," I boom.

"But you watch us," Essie states, doesn't ask, and then I see she's holding Monkey in her other arm. Monkey had been driven from Tampa and delivered along with wooden furniture Dad had made, scattered around our home, like her cribside and now bedside table. Essie has twenty stuffed animals, but Monkey is a favorite.

"I do watch you." I go as low as I can.

"Have I met you before?"

I want to say yes, because I feel that they have, in the clouds, in some field, somewhere. But it feels unfair to make my hopes her reality. "I dunno, have you?" I say, still as Dad.

"I don't fink so." Then she thinks. "Maybe. You died. Do you wish you met me?" she asks again, needing to know more.

But it's easy to answer, because I know his answer. "Yes, I surely do, Essie." And it actually feels more like him speaking than me.

I keep thinking this moment is about to be over. It's so surreal, the channeling.

She's got more to ask: "Do you miss Mommy?"

The answer flows out of me again, low and smooth. "Yes, I miss your mommy so much."

"Mommy, do you miss yo daddy?"

Everything wells inside me. "Yes, I do." Now I am speaking in my own voice.

"Are you crying, Mommy?"

"A little, but Mommy is okay. Are you okay?"

She gets up out of bed and starts to do a silly dance.

Just another moment in her life, asking Mommy to do a voice. She's already on to something new but doubles back:

"I love you, PopPop."

I wipe my cheek like I'm moving a hair and hope she doesn't notice my soaked face. She waits.

I throw my voice down deep, chuckling a little like he would, without trying.

"I love you guys too."

She lets me hold her until she's sleeping.

The position will change, and when it does, I hope I don't wake her.

Acknowledgments

Saying *thank you* in this case feels like crafting hats out of tinfoil when I wished to give you steel buildings, or full caves of gold. *Sigh.*

Alex (Ralph), my love—you have been the ultimate partner through this marathon. Your belief in me was like repeat CPR. Es, you were in my belly when this began, my light. Mom, it cannot be an easy task reading a story that is also yours. Memory in print masquerading as fact. We are not fooled. And I see your unwavering faith in art and personal truth, despite the complexity of this. Jamie, you are the brother who I look up to. Ben Greenberg, ultimate editor and guide. Your brilliance, artistry, and patience are superhuman: Dumbledore × Batman × Falkor combined. To gift artists who are not squarely prose writers with your faith and lessons is gigantic. asidjj whoops. Just kidding. Steel building on the way. Daniel Greenberg (no relation), a rock and a gem. To my dearest friends and readers—Janna White, Courtney Lincoln, Jessy Hodges, Maya Erskine, Stephanie Sasser, Thomas Gibbons, Aaron Hartman, Alyse Kennedy, Emily Kochman, Kate Hopkins—love you. Mentors and readers: Brooke Pobjoy, Danielle Schoenberg, Gabrielle Hamilton, Marc Provissiero, Bates Wilder, Kevin Kuhlke, and Laura Levine—my teachers. To the Anfangers—for allowing me into your special family. To *Nick & Chris*, the McGowans, Erskines, and Dunmore crew—thank you for the same. To all the editors and RH team, namely Miriam Khanukaev and Leila Tejani, your insight has been invaluable.

Thank you to the editors and the rest of the RH team, namely Miriam Khanukaev and Leila Tejani. And to Diana Tay, for sharing your talents in a bind. George, my cattle dog—thank you for guarding me, rogue sheep that I am, through every single late night.

My pops—spiral of light—Dada, I miss you and there aren't words. Except there were a lot. But you told me to write it all. I kind of did; hope that's okay. I can't change our past and I would never change you. *Brother*, PopPop, Dad, we honor you.

ABOUT THE AUTHOR

Anna Konkle is the co-creator and co-star and a director of the critically acclaimed Hulu series *PEN15*. The series won the Gotham Award for Breakthrough Series and was nominated for four primetime Emmys, three WGA Awards, and three Critics Choice Awards. *Time* recognized *PEN15* as one of 12 Exciting New TV Shows created by women. Konkle has been named one of *Variety*'s 10 Comics to Watch, as well as one of Hollywood's 50 Most Powerful TV Showrunners by the *Hollywood Reporter*. Originally from the East Coast, Konkle is a graduate of NYU's Tisch School of the Arts.

@annaryankonkle
anna-konkle.com

ABOUT THE TYPE

This book was set in a Monotype face called Bell. The Englishman John Bell (1745–1831) was responsible for the original cutting of this design. The vocations of Bell were many—bookseller, printer, publisher, typefounder, and journalist, among others. His types were considerably influenced by the delicacy and beauty of the French copperplate engravers. Monotype Bell might also be classified as a delicate and refined rendering of Scotch Roman.